Prayer That Shapes the Future

How to Pray with Power and Authority

Brad Long & Doug McMurry

ZondervanPublishingHouse
Grand Rapids, Michigan

A Division of HarperCollinsPublishers

Requests for information should be addressed to:
⛪Zondervan Publishing House
Grand Rapids, Michigan 49530

Library of Congress Cataloging-in-Publication Data

Long, Zeb Bradford.
    Prayer that shapes the future : how to pray with power and authority /
  Brad Long and Doug McMurry.
       p.   cm.
    Includes bibliographical references.
    ISBN: 0–310–22540-X (softcover)
      1. Prayer—Christianity.   I. McMurry, Douglas.   II. Title.
  BV210.2.L6   1999
  248.3'2—dc21   99–18212

                                                    CIP

The quotation from *The Memoirs of Charles Finney,* ed. Garth M. Rosell and Richard A. G. Dupuis (Grand Rapids: Zondervan, 1989), on pages 208–9 is used by permission.

All Scripture quotations, unless otherwise indicated, are taken from the *Holy Bible: New International Version*®. NIV®. Copyright © 1973, 1978, 1984 by International Bible Society. Used by permission of Zondervan Publishing House. All rights reserved.

Interior Design by Melissa M. Elenbaas
Printed in the United States of America

99 00 01 02 03 /❖ DC/ 10 9 8 7 6 5 4 3 2

We dedicate this book to our mentor

and teacher, the Rev. Archer Torrey:

A visionary follower of Jesus Christ,

who demonstrated to us the power of

prayer to shape the future

Table of Contents

Preface

We have written this book for many reasons.

First, at the close of the twentieth century God is calling many people into prayer. Our book is intended to guide these people to respond to the call of God through practical instruction.

Second, prayer that shapes the future is the key to shaping one's own life and building a mature and stable household. We share principles to accomplish this based on our own engagement with Scripture and personal experience that this really works.

Third, only by dynamic prayer can we move against "the gates of hell"—the demonic, the occult, the false spiritualities that are gaining strength all around us. We teach out of long experience with spiritual opposition to prayer and the kingdom of God.

Fourth, winning cultural wars, doing evangelism, and undertaking world missions will only succeed through reality-shaping prayer. We call the church to rediscover that prayer is the most fundamental ingredient of renewal and true Christian revival in our society.

The purpose of this book is to lay solid biblical foundations for the discovery and faithful practice of prayer that shapes God's future. If you are desiring to take prayer more seriously, exploring the possibility of revival of our society, or seeking the renewal of the church, this book is for you.

Part One

LAYING THE FOUNDATIONS OF PRAYER

Chapter One

Prayer As a Creative Instrument

When Jesus came among us, he was in much prayer (Mark 1:35). The task he had been given by his Father was to preach the kingdom of God (1:14–15) and to build that kingdom. Jesus was the ultimate Creator, building a New Creation, which is to grow and grow until it fills heaven and earth for all eternity. His methods for building this new reality include prayer.

Often in the twentieth century, Christians have felt that they do not need to pray. Too many have abandoned prayer as a fruitless enterprise too passive or unproven for the active "builder and shaper" of things. Yet if anyone was ever a builder and shaper it was Jesus, and we imperil our efforts if we think we have a better way than his. Jesus gave his example to us so that we would follow in his steps (John 13:15)—and his steps led to prayer before they led anywhere else.

DYNAMIC PRAYER

The many ideas believers have about prayer have given rise to many types of prayer. This book is about a certain type of prayer, based on the conviction that prayer is for builders and shapers. If we want to build and shape the kingdom of God, we must learn this type of prayer.

This is not the sort of meditative prayer that New Agers recommend as a way of dealing with stress in the workplace. It is not the ritualistic prayer that Muslims pray five times a day as they face Mecca. It is not the flowery and poetic prayer of the pietistic movements of the past.

It is bold and gutsy stuff, a tool for creative people, like the rough hammer-and-nails materials used by framers of buildings. This prayer, which we are calling *dynamic prayer*, builds new realities—spiritual homes, safe neighborhoods, new churches, missions outreach—where before, none existed. By prayer, we are challenged to envision these realities in the midst of this world's devastation and emptiness. By sharing in this work of prayer we will shape God's future.

DYNAMIC PRAYER IS DIVERSE

Dynamic prayer takes different forms, depending on where we are in the process of building the projects of God's kingdom. By one kind of dynamic prayer—listening prayer—we receive from God his architectural plans. Through another sort of dynamic prayer—intercession—we can see the beginnings of a foundation in the middle of bare wilderness. In yet another kind of dynamic prayer—prayer of agreement—we draw other people onto the building site as we learn to pray and work together from the same architectural vision. And by another sort of prayer—warfare prayer—we see the new building rise to completion in the midst of enemies who always oppose God's building projects.

WHERE DOES DYNAMIC PRAYER APPLY?

This creative enterprise may have to do with any area of life where God wishes to build his kingdom—in our personal lives, our churches, our neighborhoods, our cities, or our country. God could even call us to build something in another country, say, a country on the other side of the globe where there is a people group who has never heard the Gospel.

But regardless of the area, the new enterprises to be built with prayer are always a continuation of the building begun by Jesus two thousand years ago:

> No one can lay any foundation other than the one that has been laid; that foundation is Jesus Christ. Now if anyone builds on the foundation with gold, silver, precious stones, wood, hay, straw—the work of each builder will become visible, for the Day will disclose it, because it will be revealed with fire, and the fire will test what sort of work each has done. (1 Corinthians 3:11–13, NRSV)

Paul advises us to take care how we build on this foundation. He probably means that we must be sure to build Jesus' way, not ours. That means prayer, if it means anything.

God is calling to Christians to pray as we have never prayed before. We begin by sharing with you our own discovery of dynamic prayer, as we stumbled into it ourselves. Perhaps God has done something similar in your life.

BRAD'S DISCOVERY OF DYNAMIC PRAYER

My (Brad's) journey into dynamic prayer began before I was born. My mother was told by her doctors that the baby she was carrying would probably not survive her cancer treatment. Faced with this terrible prospect, there was nowhere else to go except to God, so prayer became a dynamic reality in her life. She survived the cancer and I was born. Throughout my life, even when I have strayed far from the faith and was at times in physical danger, I have been aware of my mother's prayers. She prepared me for my own discovery of dynamic prayer.

My own prayer awakening came while living in Asia, during many visits to Jesus Abbey, a center for spiritual renewal in the mountains of northeast South Korea. The Director of Jesus Abbey, Archer Torrey, is the grandson of R. A. Torrey, the teacher whom God used so powerfully around the world during the great revival years of 1905–7.

Archer is a man of prayer, whose radical commitment to follow Jesus Christ has taken him into an outrageous adventure. Stepping out by faith in God's guidance and provision, he built Jesus Abbey as a laboratory where one could meet God and learn the life of prayer. Amid the wild-mountain terrain and rich fellowship I encountered there, God opened up to me a whole new world of Holy Spirit-guided prayer.

I learned four lessons concerning prayer at Jesus Abbey. ("Learned" is too mild. These were revelatory encounters with God that have become spiritual landmarks to me.)

Intimacy With God

The first lesson was how to come into intimacy with God. The structure of the life at the Abbey was that of the Order of Saint Benedict. The emphasis was intercessory prayer for the church and the world. Prayer took place at regular intervals, interspersed with hours of work, study, and fellowship.

Getting up at 5:00 A.M., wrapping myself in an Arctic parka against the cold of a Korean winter night, and huddling with others to pray through Scripture may not seem like an appealing or attractive lure into the life of prayer. But in the rigor of that discipline, I started to pray regularly, and the reality of God began to break in upon me. The Bible, which was our devotional guide to prayer, began to come alive as never before.

To be honest, I failed dismally as an early morning intercessor. After my first few days of this regimen, I recognized that I could not be an early morning person. (Most Koreans seem to have been born with a gift for early morning prayer, but not I.) I did learn to pray late at night. In the little chapel at the Abbey, I had many times of deep intimacy with God, where God began to direct my life, moving me along paths that I still walk today.

The Prayer of Faith

Second, I learned from Archer Torrey that the prayer of faith is the key to receiving God's provision for kingdom work. Archer founded the Abbey on the same faith principles that had guided George Müller in his orphanage work and that had guided R. A. Torrey in his ministries. Archer would share with his intercessors the vision of what God was wanting and state the need, but he would not go on fund-raising campaigns. Rather, the community would ask God for his provision. To my astonishment I saw it happen again and again: God provided for the needs entirely through prayer.

Once I accompanied Archer to a conference in Seoul at the Eighth Army Retreat Center. On the way, he told me that the Abbey had run out of money for daily operations. He asked me to join him in praying for provision. I was new to the whole idea of such prayer, but came along to see if God really did provide things exclusively through prayer. At the conference I made a real nuisance of myself, following Archer around, trying to learn everything I could. All the while, I waited to see how God would provide.

About midway through the conference I saw an American military man privately come up to Archer and hand him a stack of Korean money about a fourth of an inch think. I was amazed. Our prayer experiment had worked.

But this was just the beginning. The next day, a woman gave a report of some mission work that was being done in another part of Korea. She had urgent financial needs that, unless they were met immediately, would close down the work. After her plea for help, we all went into prayer for this situation. I watched Archer, who seemed to be struggling with some issue in his spirit. Then, during lunch, I watched him come up to this woman, pull out the stack of bills he had just received, and hand it over to her.

I could not believe it. He had just given away what I was sure was God's provision for the Abbey. I had touched another principle of prayer, but I did not understand it or like it: "the obedience of faith" (Romans 1:5, RSV). I continued my prayer for provision for the Abbey, but did not expect anything else to happen.

On the last day of the event, as we were leaving, a Korean woman came up to Archer and engaged him in a conversation in Korean, most of which I could not understand. I picked up enough to know that she was expressing thanks for some miracle that had taken place. She then pulled out of her purse a stack of won bills several times thicker than the first stack, and she handed it to Archer. She said, "This is for the Abbey in thanks for what God has done!"

As I watched this transaction take place, the Holy Spirit imparted to me the faith to believe that God does provide through prayer for his work in a way that brings him glory.

Dynamic Intercession

Third, God opened to me the world-changing work of intercessory prayer. Archer's vision was for the Abbey to be a prayer dynamo for world evangelization. The whole community would gather together in the main chapel each day at noon and in the evening to pray for the advancement of the Gospel throughout the world.

Often I joined in this intercessory prayer for the nations. Some days we would pray for persecuted Christians in China or for some new work in Korea. Sometimes we would follow a methodical plan by praying through a prayer list. Other times we would be led by the Holy Spirit to pray unplanned prayers. At still other times we received requests that came in from all over the world—and we would later learn of the miraculous answers to our prayers. More often, however, we had no idea what the effects of our prayers were.

Through this daily intercessory prayer for the nations, I learned by heart the point that Archer Torrey once made in an interview: "I think the Lord wants me to make the point that intercession is hard work, not always exciting, but desperately important and needs doing by faithful, regular intercessors."[1]

Prayer, the Foundation of All Other Ministry

Fourth, I learned that prayer is the first work of the Christian, the foundation for all other works. From those times of intercessory prayer, God spoke to me about my own work and calling. When I first started my mission work in Taiwan, I went to Jesus Abbey with Timothy Huang, my coworker. I was seeking guidance and direction for what I was to do in Taiwan. As I prayed for the church, alone up in the little chapel, I was caught up into a time of intimacy with Jesus. I felt him say to me, "Return to Taiwan. Do not be afraid. Be bold in teaching on the work of the Holy Spirit. Step out in faith and expect me to work in signs and wonders, bringing revival to the church."

When I brought this word down to Archer and Jane Torrey and the rest of the community, they confirmed that it was truly from the Lord. I returned to Taiwan and obeyed the word as best I could. Throughout the work in Taiwan I knew that I was sustained by the intercessory prayers of the community at the Abbey. My renewal ministry in Taiwan, and now as Executive Director of Presbyterian and Reformed Renewal Ministries International (PRRMI), has been envisioned and built with the prayers of the Abbey and other intercessors throughout the world. The dynamic prayer that I learned at Jesus Abbey has been the key to building many projects that God has given me.

A few years ago, after a long absence, I returned to Jesus Abbey. I set my eyes again on the main house on the side of the mountain, beside a stream. Above was a barn that had been converted into a dormitory for guests. I was struck with how small it all was, for it had seemed so vast to me when I first arrived at the Abbey. Perhaps it had seemed vast because it was there that I stepped out of the narrow world of my own thinking and into the vastness of the thoughts of God.

Jesus Abbey was established as a laboratory for exploring the life of prayer, a place to learn whether God really does answer prayer. Jesus Abbey is itself a prayer-built community, established in the remoteness of a Korean wilderness. There, through the work of prayer, a group of humble and powerless human beings joined their hearts and minds with the Holy Spirit and shared in God's work of shaping reality. It was here that I learned how to catch a vision from God, then build the vision into reality.

DOUG'S DISCOVERY OF DYNAMIC PRAYER

I (Doug) learned about dynamic prayer from Dick Simmons in 1983, during my years in Oregon. Dick had been an intercessor for many years, going back to the days when he and his wife Barbara studied in New York City with Pat Robertson and worked with David Wilkerson launching Teen Challenge. As Pat Robertson described in his biography, *Shout It From the Housetops*, Pat and his wife, Dede, and their four children moved in with Dick and Barbara to seek direction for their ministries in the early years. Also, Dick was the one who introduced David Wilkerson to John Sherrill, who authored David's biography, *The Cross and the Switchblade*. In those days, totally immersed in the needs of the Bedford-Stuyvesant district, Dick and Barbara were learning how to intercede, by doing it for many hours each day. Today, the two of them live in Washington, D.C., where they intercede for our nation's capitol.

Prior to 1983, I had always struggled to be faithful to a daily quiet time. But my struggles had not yielded much prayer. My prayer was impelled mostly by a sense of duty. The type of prayer that I had read about from the great saints of the past—Martin Luther, John Knox, Andrew Murray, and Jonathan Goforth, for example—was, for some reason, foreign to me. In fact, it seemed to be foreign to my generation.

Then I met Dick, who used Scripture and the writings of past church leaders to fire a vision for prayer in me. He invited me to commit myself to a daily regimen of two hours of prayer from 5 to 7 A.M.

Up until that time, a challenge like that would have gone in one ear, been met with fierce resistance, and exited my life without serious consideration. Pray two hours a day? Me? You've got to be kidding! I am a busy pastor.

But Dick had put fire in my soul. When I discussed the matter with my wife, who had been at my side to hear Dick's challenge too, she felt equally fired up about it. The result was that we decided to give his challenge a try. Could this perhaps be a leading from God—this sudden and simultaneous willingness to do the preposterous?

The next day, we found ourselves wide awake for prayer at 5 A.M. We woke up two minutes before our alarm went off and excitedly prayed for two hours.

The day following, we were astonished when the oven timer in the kitchen went off at precisely 4:59 A.M. It was as though an angel was using the oven timer as a trumpet call, gathering us into an army of two, to learn how to be prayer warriors. In fact, I know of no better explanation for what happened that day.

Encouraged by these quiet miracles, we began to experiment with a far greater commitment to prayer than we had ever tried before. We felt as though we had moved to an army camp for basic training, and Jesus was our commanding officer, as Paul had described: "No one serving as a soldier gets involved in civilian affairs—he wants to please his commanding officer" (2 Timothy 2:4).

We were being thrust into a whole new calling from God, on top of all the other callings that we had already received. And since this calling was requiring a two-hour commitment daily, we soon found that we had to reevaluate all our other priorities, like television, late night church meetings, "urgent" pastoral needs, phone conversations that kept us up late, and so on. We would kick each other out of bed as close as possible to 5 A.M. each morning and keep each other accountable to this new way of dynamic prayer.

Revival Prayer

On top of our daily schedule of prayer, Dick Simmons challenged me to be a part of a prayer team that would meet for three days the first week of each month. The goal was to pray for Christian revival in the state of Oregon.

At the time, Oregon was most known for being rainy, for being one of the least churched states in the country, and for being the environment where the infamous Rajneeshpuram cult took root in the United States. When we came together each month—a ragtag lot of a dozen or so intercessors (never the same group twice)—we were challenged to pray *for* revival and *against* the spiritual forces that had invaded Oregon through this neopagan Indian cult.

In neither of these two leadings did we have the least encouragement from the circumstances around us. As we prayed, we saw little evidence of revival, nor did the Rajneeshpuram cult seem to be weakening. We had to move forward by faith in the Word of God, which set forth God's heart and God's pattern for spiritual awakening. We continued in prayer, however, believing in what we could not see and clinging to the promises of God alone.

In Acts 1, for example, we saw how the apostles followed Jesus' command, "Ask the Lord of the harvest . . . to send out workers into his harvest field" (Matthew 9:37), gathering together in an upper room for intensive prayer. Then we saw in Acts 2–4 the result: "times of refreshing . . . from the Lord" (Acts 3:19).

The Rajneeshpuram Cult

Probably our most consistent leading for prayer had to do with the Rajneeshpuram cult that had sprung up in Wasco County. During those prayer times in Oregon, I kept sensing that I should pray for disunity among the leaders of that religious commune. This was a strong and consistent leading, and I kept praying this way month after month: "God, destroy the alliances that bind these people together. Cause leaders to turn against each other." For over a year, we kept praying this way whenever we would come together—with many other prayers mixed in, of course. Yet we saw no evidence that anything was happening at the commune. Armed with their bold neopagan message, they granted more and more television interviews and spoke on local talk shows, claiming, like the Gnostics of old, that they had a higher version of Christianity and that all the Christians should become Rajneeshies. If there were any cracks in their spiritual armor, they didn't show.

Our prayer team was often fractured—we had difficulty agreeing about our prayer style and could not always complete the fasting we had agreed to do when we came together. Discouraged, we stopped getting together, and I began to make preparations for my move to a new ministry in Virginia, as God was leading me to do early in 1985.

On the very day that I drove my family out of Oregon, we heard over the car radio that Anand Sheela, the second in command at the commune, had fled the community, taking millions of dollars of commune money and depositing them in a Swiss bank account. The community was in disarray because the leadership had suddenly lost all their unity. People were leaving the cult in droves. The Immigration and Naturalization Service was moving in, too, to prosecute their leader for immigration fraud. For the first time, deeds that had been kept secret for years were coming to light. Rajneesh fled to North Carolina, where he and several leaders were apprehended.

One of the prosecutors was a member of Saint Giles Presbyterian Church in Charlotte. This and other area churches continued the prayer battle, with frequent updates from the prosecutor. (I learned about this when I testified about the Oregon prayer battle at a conference in nearby Hickory, North Carolina, where the Saint Giles music team was leading worship.)

Finally, Rajneesh was expelled from the country. The entire effort to purge this cult from the country had been bathed in prayer from start to finish.

Sometimes, before we can build the kingdom of God, we have to tear out structures that others have built. But the goal is always to build for God. At the time of this writing, Young Life, the Christian evangelistic ministry, has received this property in Wasco County to use for Christian ministry. To quote a recent news article:

> The huge Rajneesh Ranch near this north central Oregon town was officially given to Young Life Jan. 15 as Montana business-man Dennis Washington signed over the title. Since then, Young Life has been busy raising funds and cleaning and landscaping the property, more recently known as the "Big Muddy Ranch...."[2]

Dynamic prayer was part of the process of building this new ministry by Young Life in Oregon, where once there had existed a neopagan cult.

Revival in Oregon

And what of the other focus of our prayers—revival in the church? Three years after that prayer effort, Joe Aldrich, president of Multnomah School of the Bible, began to draw pastors in various Oregon cities together across racial and denominational lines for four-day prayer retreats called Prayer Summits. These first Prayer Summits, as described in his book, *Prayer Summits*, were such powerful times of spiritual transformation that other cities in the Pacific Northwest began to request Dr. Aldrich to help them have similar pastors' Prayer Summits. At the time of this writing, Prayer Summits have spread to over three hundred communities.

In the midst of these retreats, pastors learn to trust each other, share their sorrows, pray for each other, strip themselves of pretense, worship God, and extend to each other the love of Jesus. They learn how to be unified, how to live and work as the body of Christ in a city. All this, I believe, is necessary preparation for spiritual awakening.

Prayer Is Hard Work

The initial efforts of my wife and myself to spend two hours a day in prayer, and to step up our prayer commitment through the monthly meet-ings, required great sacrifice. True, God gave us some wonderful initial signs to get us moving in that direction. Yet continuing month after month wasn't as easy as we thought it would be. We reasoned: Surely a husband and wife, both dedicated to Christian ministry, should be able to pray together with ease. Shouldn't every Christian couple do this as a matter of course?

Huh! We found it about as easy as shinnying up a fireman's pole together.

Just because God gave us a sign didn't mean that prayer would be easy. In my life, God seems to give signs when he wants to prepare me for something hard. The whole enterprise of dynamic prayer has proven to be difficult, in fact.

We recommend dynamic prayer not because it is easy, but because it is ultimately rewarding. In prayer, we cooperate with God to accomplish works that we could not do under our own power. God has called us into a type of prayer that creates things in the real world—not by human ingenuity or cleverness, but by his power. God allows us through prayer to connect with that power, and the result is that we can see new movements, initiatives, and works built with prayer.

EVIDENCE OF GOD'S CALLING TO PRAYER

God is calling Christians to pray creatively as we have never prayed before. In the United States alone, we see evidence of this calling all around us:

- A new emphasis on prayer walking, as described in Steve Hawthorne and Graham Kendrick's book, *Prayer-Walking: Praying On Site With Insight*
- An emphasis on revival prayer among men in the Promise Keepers movement
- Calls to prayer and fasting by such respected leaders as Dr. and Mrs. Bill Bright
- Prayer initiatives on behalf of the "hidden peoples"—those ethnic groups around the globe who have never heard the Gospel, as promoted by the U.S. Center for World Mission in its *Global Prayer Digest*
- Concerts of prayer—events that pull together the "city-wide" church, as promoted by David Bryant
- Prayer summits—extended prayer retreats that encourage pastors to pray together

- The World Prayer Center recently built in Colorado Springs under the visionary guidance of C. Peter Wagner and the United Prayer Track
- The influence of the Argentine Revival, which has been built with prayer during the last two decades

God is doing a new thing, which he was not doing twenty years ago. He is personally calling large numbers of Christians into serious prayer. Many testify to this invitation of God and have responded to the call. In this book about prayer, we are not interested in trying to get people to pray. God is already doing that. Our hope is that this book will be useful to those who already sense a calling from God and who are trying to understand it and get help to complete their call.

QUESTIONS FOR REFLECTION, DIALOGUE, AND JOURNALING

1. What evidence do you have that God might be calling you to grow in prayer? Look for these signs: a growing spiritual hunger, Scriptures that seem to come alive, people who are having an influence on you, and other intercessors who are praying for you.
2. Reflect on and trace the growth of prayer in your life thus far. Have there been periods in your life when you have been challenged in new dimensions of prayer? Try to identify a few special lessons that God taught you then that he does not want you to forget now.

Chapter Two

BUILDING WITH GOD

Of course, the type of dynamic prayer that we describe in these pages is not new. Others have discovered it before us, and we wish to showcase how they succeeded to build whole societies and launch great missionary endeavors through prayer.

MARTIN LUTHER

Martin Luther lived during one of the most corrupt and self-destructive eras of European history—the sixteenth century. The Germany of Luther's day was a spiritual wasteland. The church had corrupted itself with wealth. Sexual immorality was so widespread that it had entered even the monasteries—which, at the beginning, had invited people to live "unstained from the world." Political strife was so unsettling in the church that there were three popes at once vying for political control of the Roman Catholic Church.

Martin Luther, as a young man, sensed the desperation of his times, and God showed him an answer. He wrote:

> Open your eyes and look into your life and the life of all Christians, particularly the spiritual estate, and you will find that faith, hope, love, obedience, chasteness, and all virtues are languishing; that all sorts of terrible vices are reigning; that good preachers and prelates are lacking; only rogues . . . are ruling. Then you will

see that there is a need to pray throughout the world, every hour, without ceasing, with tears of blood, because of the terrible wrath of God over men.[1]

Most historians look back at the Protestant Reformation as a doctrinal debate, not as a spiritual awakening or prayer movement. But Luther, the father of Protestantism, saw prayer at the heart of everything—that without prayer, nothing enduring or good could happen. In a letter to Philip Melanchthon, his friend and fellow Reformer, he wrote:

Whatever aspect matters may assume, we can achieve all through prayer. This alone is the almighty queen of human destiny. Therewith we can accomplish everything, and thus maintain what already exists, amend what is defective, patiently put up with what is inevitable, overcome what is evil, and preserve all that is good.[2]

How did Martin Luther rise above the tainted Catholicism of his time and build Germany into a nation that followed the revelations of God's Word? Yes, in part it was due to the invention of the printing press, which provided Germany with Bibles. But there was a hidden force at work as well, a force that God had provided to the church and that Luther had rediscovered—the prayer of faith in God's power.

To political activists of our day and to pastors confident in church programs, professionalism, and good deeds, Luther would say this: "Where are the people who want to know and to do good works? Let them only undertake prayer and practice it in true faith, and they will find that what the holy fathers have said is true: there is no greater work than praying."[3]

Luther brought Christians back to the Word of God, the Bible, laying the foundations for the Great Reformation. The motto of the Reformation, *sola scriptura* ("the Scriptures alone"), is surely what we remember the Reformation for today. Yet for Luther, this motto was only half of the truth. The other half has been largely forgotten—the necessity of prayer accompanying the Word, or the discipline of praying God's Word into being. Luther wrote: "Now we have often spoken of prayer, both how necessary it is and what power it has. It is not enough for us to have the Word and to know and understand everything we should."[4]

Since Luther is such a shining example of prayer that shapes the future and because he wrote so much about prayer, we will quote him liberally in our book. The presence of the Protestant churches—whole denominations of churches—testifies to the validity of Luther's confidence in the prayer of faith. Yet most people in those denominations today do not possess anything like Luther's faith in prayer. We believe that the Protestant churches only need to rediscover the tools that Luther discovered at the beginning in order to build productive churches again.

PRAYING HYDE

Or let's look into the kind of prayer that God instigated through John Hyde, otherwise known as "Praying Hyde." A friend recently visited Assam State in North India. He came back with glowing descriptions of a healthy and vibrant church. In the United States Presbyterian churches are experiencing a decline. The best news that we have been able to come up with by 1998 is that the degree of decline has tapered off somewhat.

But in Assam State the Presbyterian churches are the soul of vibrancy. I asked my friend what had produced this extraordinary vibrancy—where the smallest churches are over one thousand members and where the people flock in excitement to "glorify God and enjoy him forever." I suggested that this great turning of events must have included some extraordinary prayer.

Challenged by my friend, who didn't think that prayer had much to do with it at all, I did some research. According to J. Edwin Orr's book *Evangelical Awakenings in India,* the turning of the tide in Assam State happened as a result of the great Welsh revival of 1905. Ever since then, the church has been growing relatively unhindered, with the Welsh Presbyterians at the center of the drama. Prior to this fantastic turnaround in northeast India, there was an extraordinary prayer movement. At the center of that movement was an American Presbyterian by the name of John Hyde.

Hyde was among those using prayer to reshape the future of Assam State and other areas in India. A friend described his prayer:

> Hyde and I have been having glorious times together. There were seasons of great conflict, and at times I thought Hyde would break down completely. But after all-nights of prayer and praise he would appear fresh and smiling in the morning. God has been teaching us wonderful lessons when He calls us to seasons of such wrestling.[5]

After reviewing the ministry of Praying Hyde, Dr. Orr described others whom God called into dynamic prayer:

At the turn of the century, a company of missionaries met together at a southern hill station, Kodaikanal, and decided that the time had come to pray definitely for a mighty awakening in the Indian Church. They issued a prayer circular, and sent it to Britain, America and Australia to mobilize intercession.

Orr goes on to mention the prayer resolutions that the Holy Spirit was inspiring around the world, including the prayer covenants among students and professors at Moody Bible Institute in Chicago, among Australian pastors in Melbourne, Australia, and at the Keswick convention in 1902, where "5000 Christians resolved to form home prayer circles for worldwide blessing, and praying bands all over India."[6]

What was the result of all this prayer? Orr describes how God began to move among Presbyterians in answer to fervent prayer:

The General Assembly of the Khasia Presbyterian Churches was held at Cherrapunjee, in 1905, and proved to be a remarkable one indeed. The delegates returned to their villages with an increased faith and intensified longing.

On the first Sunday in March, at Mawphlang, when their Bible lesson dealt with the baptism of the Holy Spirit, an unusual manifestation of fervor filled the congregation with prayer and weeping and praise.

A Presbytery meeting at Pariong broke the pattern of its usual procedure. When the chairman invited one or two by name to lead in prayer, others also stood up to lead the congregation in intercession. It became impossible to close the usual service the following Sunday, simultaneous prayer and praise and weeping, and even fainting affecting the congregation. These manifestations accompanied the extension of the awakening into other parts, and continued for eighteen months.

The Khasi tribe's people being headhunters, with human sacrifice persisting in obscure cults, it is therefore interesting to note how the impact of the Welsh Revival affected them.

The intense conviction of sin, which began in March, gave way in June to a wave of rejoicing. In a united presbytery meeting of fifteen hundred, singing overwhelmed the preaching, and many of the awakened people danced for joy, their arms outstretched, and their faces radiant. Missionaries were astounded to see principal men and leading elders jump for joy. At first some missionaries disapproved, changing their minds as the revival transformed Christians and won hundreds of non-Christians to the fellowship.[7]

These Presbyterians were discovering that prayer builds according to God's plans, not ours. When we learn to rely on prayer, we have to go where the prayer leads us, for that is where God's architectural plan would have us build new structures. When we pray, we must allow for new and startling works that may not be under our control, but which will produce results beyond our wildest dreams. Prayer is not an exercise by which we hope to curry God's favor on our plans—like the cartoon that shows a group of elders gathered around a conference table, with the pastor speaking the words, "Gentlemen, I'd like to close this meeting with a short prayer: Lord, let us get away with this little scheme just this once. Amen."

In prayer, we are confronted with the important difference between doing works *for* God and doing the works *of* God. In this sense, it is not like a building project as much as it is like a garden. God has designed flowers and vegetables to grow by a life that we cannot control. But we can learn how to cooperate with God by discerning how to create a productive garden. To do this, we have to learn how to grow things according to the plan of God, which he placed in the genetic structure of each seed.

By contrast, silk flowers have become the rage in recent years. It is entirely possible to make flowers of cloth that resemble real flowers. But their smell is different, and they do not show the delicacy or the life of real garden-grown, God-created flowers.

Many Christians have become manufacturers of silk flowers. When we want to start a church, we do it the manufacturing way. We do a scientific study of the population growth factors, resort to a plan of our own invention, build a building, start programs, and manufacture a church at will. Our churches have become silk roses; the life of God does not often course through our churches—or through our nation or our families.

Could it be that our churches, nation, and families lack life because we have not seen how to grow a garden? We are stuck in a manufacturing mode, and we cannot understand why everything we create seems to lack life. We have been making silk roses so long that we have forgotten how to grow real ones. The art of the gardener lies neglected.

JOHN WELCH

If you go back to the beginnings of most of our denominations and mission works today, you will find that they were founded on a base of dynamic prayer. This was true, for example, not only of the Lutheran Reformation, but of the Scottish Reformation as well. It was said of John Knox that Mary Queen of Scots "feared his prayers more than all the armies of Scotland." John Knox's nephew John Welch was also an intercessor. The books *Scots Worthies* described this man's ministry of intercession:

> Welch's custom was, when he went to bed at night, to lay a Scots plaid above his bed-clothes, that when he rose to his night prayers, he might cover himself therewith; for, from the beginning of his ministry till his death, he reckoned the day ill spent, if he stayed not seven or eight hours in prayer; and this the boy did not forget even to his old age.[8]

Thus, as we expose the roots of the Presbyterian movement in sixteenth-century Scotland, we find there evidence of dynamic prayer. Prayer planted the seeds of something fresh in the dark winters of the far north, which had known only the snows of paganism and the ice of medieval Catholicism. A fresh love of Jesus and his Word was scheduled in God's plan. But if it was God's plan, it could only come forth with prayer. The Presbyterian denominations, like so many others, have sprung up from prayer.

ZINZENDORF AND WESLEY

E. M. Bounds writes about John Wesley, the founder of the Methodist churches:

> John Wesley spent two hours daily in prayer. He began at four in the morning. Of him, one who knew him well wrote: "He thought prayer to be his business more than anything else, and I have seen him come out of his closet with a serenity of face next to shining."[9]

Wesley's conversion was itself the result of intensive prayer by the Moravians in Europe. In the 1720s, Count Nikolaus von Zinzendorf established a refuge for persecuted Christians on his estate in Moravia in southern Germany. He imagined a grand colony of nothing but Christian people. He called his refuge Herrnhut, meaning "The Watch of the Lord."

But Zinzendorf discovered, when he assembled these three hundred believers together, that they bickered endlessly with each other. In frustration, he instigated a twenty-four-hour prayer watch. Twenty-four men and twenty-four women covenanted themselves to pray one hour every day in scheduled prayer. Soon, all bickering vanished, the Spirit of God settled into the estate, and the Moravian church was built—on a foundation of prayer. It was Moravians who witnessed Christ to the Wesleys, George Whitefield, and other English leaders of the Great Awakening.

The kind of prayer we are calling dynamic prayer is not so much the rediscovery of personal piety or a strong devotional life. That is, leaders like Martin Luther, John Knox, John Welch, John Hyde, Count Zinzendorf, and the Wesleys were not rediscovering private meditation as a release from stress. They were discovering how to build with God by prayer something that God wanted to create.

DISCERNING OUR AREAS OF ACTIVITY

Not all of us, of course, are destined to build seasons of revival in our nation or to create new churches or denominations. But each of us is called to build something with our lives. God assigns to each of us a sphere of activity. We are "created in Christ Jesus for good works, which God prepared beforehand, that we should walk in them" (Ephesians 2:10, RSV). God has designed each of us for a limited scope of activity. In Christ, we can find out what it is. The apostle Paul wrote of his own area of calling:

> We, however, will not boast beyond *proper limits*, but will confine our boasting to the *field God has assigned* to us, a field that reaches even to you.... Neither do we go beyond our *limits* by boasting of work done by others. Our hope is that, as your faith continues to grow, our *area of activity* among you will greatly expand. (2 Corinthians 10:13–15, emphasis added)

As he did for Paul, God gives to each of us an "area of activity," a context within which we are called to work.[10] This usually begins humbly—with our personal life, our spouse and children, a few people we are discipling, or a few coworkers. The size of our calling is not the important thing. More important by far is whether we take up the tools God has given us—prayer being chief among them—and go to work.

The lessons we learn when our sphere is small and restricted often become the basis for an expanded area of activity as we grow older. Jesus said, "You have been faithful with a few things; I will put you in charge of many things" (Matthew 25:21). Therefore, we should not despise small beginnings. God is looking for faithfulness more than for grand schemes and a forceful personality. In the parable of the talents (Matthew 25:14–30), it did not matter that one servant received ten, another five, another one talent. The issue was what they did with what the master had given them.

As we are called into prayer, we will most likely be called to create something new in our present areas of activity. It is here, of course, that we discover the awesome choices we have been given, to shape reality for good or for evil. We can:

- Build *what God wants*
- Build *what we want*
- Build *what Satan wants*
- *Maintain* what others have built
- *Tear down* what others have built
- *Create nothing* at all

The outcome of our lives will depend on the choices we make.

Co-Creating in My Sphere of Activity

One day, after coming home from the office, my wife, Laura, told me (Brad) that our eight-year-old son had copied lines from a cartoon book, *Calvin and Hobbes*, illustrating them with his own pictures. The teacher had been impressed and had asked Stephen if he had written the material himself. He said that he had.

I went to Stephen and told him that lying did not please Jesus, and I advised him to ask forgiveness. As we talked, the reality of sin broke into his heart, and he realized that what he had done was wrong. At that moment, I realized that I was making momentous choices in my area of activity. God had given me authority to shape Stephen's life. His life would be deeply influenced by how I conducted myself with him. I could have let him learn to lie, I could have harshly punished him, and I could have excused the lie this time while teaching him not to lie in general.

What I did, instead, was to draw him into my arms, hug him, and assure him that, as he confessed his sin, Jesus and I both forgave him. We then prayed together that Stephen would always know how to tell the truth.

I believe that prayer was an important part of the building I did that day. I did not take authority into my own hands to shape Stephen's life as I saw fit. I trained him to speak to God about his problems. After all, I am not going to be his teacher forever. While I have the opportunity, I must put him in touch with his real Father in heaven. My role is to work with God in creating out of the raw material of Stephen's life a life of truth and goodness.

Through that experience, I awoke to the awesome choices that we have in our sphere of activity, whatever it may be. We can build with God; we can build on our own; we can build nothing; we can destroy what we have been given. These are the options.

They are the same options—whether we are talking about building a disciple out of a son or daughter, a Christian household, a strong nation, a healthy congregation, a denomination, or a godly place of business.

FIND YOUR AREA

If God wants to train us in prayer, it is likely that our prayer will grow out of our "areas of activity," which God has assigned to each of us. For some of us, prayer is the way we will find our area of activity. For most of us, the area of activity may look like the concentric circles of a target, expanding from ourselves to include our family, our place of work, our local church, and then other areas of authority and responsibility that God may give us.

Eventually, God is likely to stretch us, to expand our areas of activity. Many of us are discovering a burning passion to pray for a particular people group on the other side of the globe, or for some specific person we may not know. God is calling us into larger and larger spheres of influence, to see the height and length and breadth and depth of his love, stretching us beyond our natural human love.

SUMMARY

Dynamic prayer is a hidden but frequent, if not universal, ingredient in whatever God wishes to build on earth. Those who wish to do good works in God's kingdom must learn to distinguish between doing works *for* God and doing the works *of* God. To do the latter requires us to learn prayer, which produces ministries for God that have life. This hidden dynamic of prayer can be discerned behind virtually all revival movements of the past, which have produced most of the existing churches and denominations of the present.

QUESTIONS FOR REFLECTION, DIALOGUE, AND JOURNALING

1. Evaluate your life. Is it creative? How much of your life do you spend

   • creating nothing (being entertained)
   • tearing down what others build (with sarcasm or criticism)
   • building what you want (ambitions and hobbies)
   • building what God wants (faith working through love)?

2. Identify the "areas of activity" God has given you so far. Whose lives do you touch? How do you feel about the possibility that God has placed you in an arena so that you can cocreate something of his choosing (not yours or someone else's)?

3. Is God increasing your areas of activity right now? How might this affect your prayer life?

Chapter Three

Dynamic Prayer and Its Counterfeits

I (Doug) have discovered a pattern while investigating the lives of past men and women of prayer. I sensed among them an indignation toward the pale and false thing that some people classify as "prayer." For example, Jonathan Goforth, the missionary to China who brought the revival of 1905 into Manchuria, told of his frequent approach with Christians:

> I said to the people: "Please let's not have any of your ordinary kind of praying. If there are any prayers which you've got off by heart and which you've used for years, just lay them aside. We haven't any time for them. But if the Spirit of God so moves you that you feel you simply must give utterance to what is in your heart, then do not hesitate. We have time for that kind of praying."[1]

What Goforth had discovered was that false prayer hinders true Christian prayer. Prayer, in other words, that is not dynamic and creative but simply empty words addressed to God out of empty hearts, can drown out and discourage those eager to grow into dynamic prayer.

Martin Luther expressed this same contempt for false prayer when he wrote, "Let the monks despair of their praying; they have no knowledge of God and are altogether without faith. Their prayer is not a sincere request; it is arduous toil and actually an empty sound."[2] Of course, Luther was not condemning all monastic prayer, only the type of prayer that he had experienced as an Augustinian monk during one of the least fruitful periods of monastic history.

By contrast, hear this description of Luther's own prayers from an associate of his:

> Not a day passes in which he does not employ in prayer at least three of his very best hours. Once I happened to hear him at prayer. Gracious God! What spirit and what faith is there in his expressions! He petitions God with as much reverence as if he were in the divine presence, and yet with as firm a hope and confidence as he would address a father or a friend.[3]

E. M. Bounds, in *A Treasury of Prayer*, reflects a similar impatience with those whose very prayers reflect an unbelief in prayer:

> Prayer is humbling work. It abases intellect and pride, crucifies vain glory and signs our spiritual bankruptcy, and all these are hard for flesh and blood to bear. It is easier not to pray than to bear them. So we come to one of the crying evils of these times, maybe of all times—little or no praying. Of these two evils, perhaps little praying is worse than no praying. Little praying is a kind of make-believe, a salve for the conscience, a farce and a delusion.[4]

Some people, having only observed the "make-believe" prayer that Bounds (and Luther and Goforth) were describing, believe that all prayer is empty and unworthy of serious attention. They resist the calling of prayer because all they have seen is bad prayer, and they are not much impressed. As the antidote to bad prayer, we offer the model of Jesus, who shows us true dynamic prayer.

FOLLOW JESUS

Imagine that you are Simon Peter, getting to know Jesus for the first time. Most people have been attracted to him because of his miracles. But since Jesus is staying at your house, you become intimately acquainted with his habits and see into his life more deeply. What you observe bewilders you:

> Very early in the morning, while it was still dark, Jesus got up, left the house and went off to a solitary place, where he prayed. Simon and his companions went to look for him, and when they found him, they exclaimed: "Everyone is looking for you!"

Jesus replied, "Let us go somewhere else—to the nearby villages—so I can preach there also. That is why I have come." (Mark 1:35–38)

Simon Peter cannot understand why Jesus, or anyone, would get up so early and go off by himself into a deserted place. Would a physician go off like that, leaving his patients in the lurch in such an irresponsible way? Peter has not yet learned that Jesus is behaving as the true high priest of God.

Creative prayer, the kind of prayer that gains a vision from God and then births that vision into the world, is a foreign concept to Peter. What he thinks of as prayer comes from Jerusalem—from the priests at the temple and from the Pharisees, his spiritual leaders. Peter has never become a man of prayer because he cannot get excited about the Sadducees' and Pharisees' prayers.

Sadducees

Jesus wasn't very excited about those prayers either. Look at the Sadducees—the chief priests who had formed themselves into a political party of that name. They didn't believe in the power of God or in the biblical accounts of God's miracles. Yet they were in power at the temple, and they believed in maintaining their power through political influence with Rome. God had decreed long before that the descendants of Aaron should preside over the temple to make it a house of prayer for all nations (Isaiah 56:7; Mark 11:17). It is not hard to see why Jesus overturned the tables of the money changers in the temple. This was a visible demonstration of God's judgment against the chief priests at the temple, whose prayers were a pretense of piety to cover over political scheming and the accumulation of wealth.

Jesus came as the Good Shepherd and the true High Priest. One of his tasks in that office is to raise up a people of prayer. He came to offer prayer, to show us how to pray, and to build a house of prayer for all nations. That is where we Christians enter the picture—as the "royal priesthood" (1 Peter 2:9) who follows Jesus, the true High Priest. But the kind of prayer Jesus teaches is different from that of the Sadducees. It is dynamic prayer that builds the kingdom of God.

The Pharisees

Another religious party in Jerusalem was more conservative than the Sadducees. The Pharisees had a different belief system. They believed, like the Sadducees, that God no longer manifested his power today. But they insisted that he had once done so—in Bible times.

The Pharisees were self-appointed spiritual leaders who jumped into the spiritual vacuum left by the Sadducees. Prayer? They believed in it! They were willing to pray—and to show everyone how prayerful they were—in the marketplace, on the street corners, and so on.

Simon Peter, a practical man, must have seen through their religious hypocrisy. He was surely no more impressed by the prayer of the Pharisees, wailed piously on the street corners, than by the traditional prayers of the Sadducees, echoing hollowly in the temple. The Pharisees were sincere, yes. But sincerity did not necessarily make them better spiritual guides. Jesus comments: "Everything they do is done for men to see" (Matthew 23:5). Their prayers were little sermons preached to the people—self-conscious, flowery, impressive, and moralistic, intended for people, not for God.

Jesus' teaching on prayer was surely addressed to the likes of them: "And when you pray, do not be like the hypocrites, for they love to pray standing in the synagogues and on the street corners to be seen by men. I tell you the truth, they have received their reward in full" (Matthew 6:5). In order to help his disciples learn prayer, Jesus had first to address the bad prayer that was being modeled all around them. The same is true for us as well.

ABUSING PRAYER

To some, it may come as quite a shock that there can be bad prayer. Most of us try to be tolerant of everyone. No one likes to suggest that anyone's anything can be bad, especially prayer.

But God created prayer to be like a finely honed chisel designed as an instrument for building cabinetry. Prayer can be abused—just as a chisel can be used as a screwdriver. When that happens, because the user is unschooled in the use of carpentry tools, it hurts the chisel, and it can also hurt people who happen to be standing around.

The two of us have led many prayer meetings and prayer groups during the last fifteen or twenty years. In these situations, we have seen prayer abused in a great many ways. We have also known a great many people who are frustrated with prayer because they have seen its abuse but not the tool's potential. Therefore, we will list some of the common abuses.

"O God, Show Them What Fools They Are!"

The apostle Paul wrote: "And now these three remain: faith, hope and love" (1 Corinthians 13:13). Faith, hope, and love are our inheritance in Christ. They, more than anything else, characterize the eternal kingdom of God. They are the most important gifts that the King gave to his subjects before he went off, and he said, "Trade with these till I come" (Luke 19:13, RSV).

Prayer is one way of "trading" our Christian faith, hope, and love. Prayer is abused when we make it a vehicle of fear, despair, and bitterness. These ingredients defile us and grieve the Holy Spirit (see Ephesians 4:30–32; Hebrews 12:15). We abuse prayer when we simply use our prayer time to give vent to fear, despair, and bitterness. When we do this, we are burning trash, not incense, in the sanctuary of the Lord. For example:

- *Loveless prayer*: "Lord, show them what fools they are."
- *Faithless prayer*: "I've prayed and prayed and you never do anything and it just seems like that's par for the course."
- *Hopeless prayer*: "O God, my Jim is just getting sicker and sicker and the doctor says he's gonna die and he's in so much pain, and I just don't see what anyone can do and. . . ."

I do not mean that there is not a place in our prayer life to be truthful with God or to express our honest feelings. Prayer cannot be all "positive confession." In the Psalms, for example, David was often truthful, giving vent to his fears, doubts, and wounded spirit. He was just a man! Maybe that is why many people throughout the centuries have found the Psalms so meaningful. We can identify with how David felt as he was chased by the armies of Saul or was exiled among the Philistines.

But look closely at each of those psalms, and you will see that they almost always move into faith, hope, and love by the end. For example, desperation and abandonment are the themes of Psalm 22: "My God, my God, why have you forsaken me?" (v. 1). But the psalm finishes this way: "All the ends of the earth will remember and turn to the LORD; and all the families of the nations will bow down before him" (v. 27). When Jesus quoted this psalm from the cross, he spoke it out as a fulfillment of a messianic promise, not just as a cry of despair. He was surely aware of the entire psalm and had the whole psalm in mind when he quoted it. His cry, "My God, my God . . . " (Mark 15:34), was not just an existential cry of despair but also a total identification with the human condition and a statement of messianic promise in the midst of terrible suffering.

How can we make sure that we are not using prayer simply as an opportunity to rehearse old patterns of fear, despair, and bitterness? Try these three antidotes:

- Pray the Scriptures, especially the promises of God. These will help you to hold on to hope, even in troublesome situations. The Bible says, "Finally, brothers, whatever is true, whatever is noble, whatever is right, whatever is pure, whatever is lovely, whatever is admirable—if anything is excellent or praiseworthy—think about such things" (Philippians 4:8). One woman I remember contrasted the vulture and the hummingbird. The vulture and the hummingbird fly the same airspace. But one looks for bright and beautiful flowers and is attracted to such things to feed from. The other looks for the dead, the rotten, and the foul, and is attracted to those things for food. Strive to be a hummingbird.
- Confess negative and destructive speech as sin. It is always best to enter our prayer time asking the Lord to show us our sin, and confessing that before him. Confession of sin can prepare us for prayer by cleansing us of wrong attitudes that will otherwise have a subtle impact on our prayers. Without this, our prayers can be exercises of spiritual pride, as though it is only everyone else that needs prayer and not we ourselves.
- Receive all things with thanksgiving (Ephesians 5:20; 1 Timothy 4:4). Thanksgiving is another element to include at the front end of our prayer time because it cleanses out foul moods, which would otherwise pollute our prayers. Thanksgiving is a prelude that prepares us for what follows.

"O God, I Pray That You Would Remind Us That . . ."

Jesus told us to learn to "agree" in prayer (Matthew 18:19). He asks us to learn to pray together. But praying with other people can expose our bad habits of prayer. The other people may hear our prayers and grow weary of them.

The evangelist Charles Finney had often experienced the glory of true prayer during church meetings. He longed for such prayer:

Nothing tends more to cement the hearts of Christians than praying together. Never do they love one another so well as when they witness the outpouring of each other's hearts in prayer. Their spirituality begets a feeling of union and confidence, highly important to the prosperity of the church. It is doubtful whether Christians can ever be otherwise than united, if they are in the habit of really praying together. And where they have had hard feelings and differences among themselves, they are all done away, by uniting in prayer. The great object is gained, if you can bring them really to unite in prayer. If this can be done, the difficulties vanish....[5]

Yet we sense all the more Finney's frustration when Christians prevented this true prayer from taking place during prayer meetings. How did they do this? With counterfeit prayer that only wearied everyone who listened to it: "Some men will spin out a long prayer in telling God who and what He is.... Some pray out a whole system of divinity. Some preach, others exhort the people, till everybody wishes they would stop, and God wishes so too, undoubtedly."[6]

I (Doug) wince inside whenever I hear prayers that begin with the words, "O God, I pray that you would remind us that...." Some prayers are nothing but veiled speeches. And, of course, nothing will kill a husband-wife prayer partnership faster than one spouse using "prayer" to lecture their spouse while simultaneously lecturing God: "O God, I thank you that you have made wives (husbands) for the purpose of...."

"Gimme a Rolls Royce"

Witches pray. New Agers pray. Satanists pray. And what singles out these deceived people is not only the person they pray to but the style of their prayer. Satan encourages a manipulative type of prayer quite different from what God encourages.

I (Doug) remember a woman who had been invited to our city to minister to people in prayer. Yet there was something crass and hard about her. The more I heard her pray, the uneasier my wife and I felt, even though she was a Christian. In the end, it dawned on me: She was after our money. The woman was using this prayer gathering as a fund-raiser for her ministry. She prayed for miracles so that she could get money. God had to do miracles because she had to have that money. After that prayer meeting, the woman who had organized it said: "I felt a spirit of witchcraft there, not the presence of the Holy Spirit." To some people, prayer is a way of manipulating God, or the invisible powers of the spirit world, to get spiritual power and to harness it to one's own will.

By contrast, Jesus prayed, "Not as I will, but as you will" (Matthew 26:39). He was modeling creative prayer for us. In Christian prayer and in the Christian life generally, there is a self-surrender to the lordship of Jesus. Without that self-surrender, a counterfeit spirit can lead us further and further from God's will. Prayer that shapes the future is prayer that begins with a vision from God. This is the type of prayer that Jesus modeled and taught, and about which we will have much to say in future chapters.

New Christians often inadvertently think of God as their servant. They are learning the way of faith as reliance on God (and that is just what they should learn). But they have not yet learned to subject their will to his.

What is the antidote to self-serving and manipulative prayer? *Worship* moves us into God's presence so that we behold him truly before we ever ask him for anything. Worship moves us into the awareness of God's presence, and suddenly our needs appear much less important. From that time on, we make ourselves available to him rather than being full of our own need and of ourselves.

"O Lord, We Beseech Thee That Thou Shouldst Beseech the Very Angels of Heaven to . . . "

Early in my ministry, I used to spend a lot of time developing prayers for public worship. As an artist, I was intent on making the most beautiful prayers I could create. People would come up to me afterwards and tell me how beautiful my prayers were—they were poetic masterpieces. But this was not creative prayer in the sense that we are describing here. I did not believe that anything would be created from my prayers, except the "creative" prayers themselves.

I believe that there is a thing called a religious spirit, a spirit that helps people pray empty prayer because that is a clever way to keep them away from Christian prayer, which is creative and productive. It is a spiritual counterfeit that leads people to believe that they are doing the right thing while successfully preventing them from doing the right thing. Prayer like that ends up being like the prayers of the Sadducees—empty words, the form of religion without its power.

Jesus said that we should not heap up words, thinking that we will "be heard because of [our] many words" (Matthew 6:7). He must get tired of adult believers reading prayers meaninglessly from a book, or reciting rote prayers from empty hearts, or praying childish prayers they should have outgrown years before.

From his point of view a single prayer cried with fervency from a heart of trust is worth more than all the rote prayers recited religiously as a duty by people who are eager to get to the end of a service. In the words of John Bunyan, author of *Pilgrim's Progress*, "When thou prayest, rather let thy heart be without words than thy words be without heart."[7]

Outgrowing Bad Prayer Habits

Learning prayer is rather like taking a shop class. We are learning how to use a tool so that we can build something with it. In order for that to happen, we have to learn how to do it right and how to unlearn bad habits already learned. We can look at our bad habits, correct them, and replace them with good habits.

I (Doug) remember the time, early in my first pastorate, when a kindly old gentleman told me that he didn't think my prayers were prayers at all. I was shocked and a little hurt. But his word of correction caused me to look at my prayer life objectively and discern the difference between prayer and poetry. Though his confrontation nailed me between the eyes, it was good for me, and I learned from it.

Since my wife and I began to pray together fourteen years ago, we have had to be open and honest about each other's prayer style, speaking the truth in love when each other's prayers drive us up the wall. Sometimes we have told each other we thought the other one was trying to preach through prayer, or had stopped agreeing in prayer. By being submissive to each other out of reverence for Christ, we have learned to deal with our bad habits—a prerequisite for gaining the good habits of prayer.

Summary

False prayer hinders true Christian prayer. False prayer can arise from the bad habits of empty words, manipulation, spiritual pride, and vain repetition. Jesus is our supreme model for true dynamic prayer that leads to faith, hope, and love. Heartfelt prayer begins in worship. And in Christian prayer—as in the Christian life generally—there is a self-surrender to the lordship of Jesus.

QUESTIONS FOR REFLECTION, DIALOGUE, AND JOURNALING

1. Do you see any of the above "abusive prayer" habits in your own life?

2. Do you see any of them in your prayer partner(s)? How can you gently "speak the truth in love" (cf. Ephesians 4:15) without hurting their feelings?

3. What would keep you from humbly asking others, especially prayer partners, if they see any bad habits in your prayer life? Plan to do it the next opportunity you get.

Part Two

HOW A TRIUNE GOD
ENABLES PRAYER

Chapter Four

JESUS AND THE GREAT ABYSS

At a certain Buddhist temple in southern Taiwan, crowds of people offer incense before images of various deities. Once I (Brad) stood where I could see the worshipers' faces. I was struck with their sincerity and fervent belief in prayer. I stood apart, not sharing the hopes that had led them to pray so fervently to their gods.

After leaving the temple, my certainty that their prayers to pagan gods would do them no good was confronted with an uncomfortable surprise. By the door, piles of crutches and wheelchairs remained—evidence of many answered prayers. These Buddhist people had been healed—many of them!

So, what was I to conclude? Did God heal them? or Satan? How should I account for the answered prayers of Muslims, Buddhists, animists, or even New Agers? What distinguishes Christian prayer from other prayer?

PRAYER REACHES INTO THE SPIRIT REALM

In his book *The Fourth Dimension*, David Yonggi Cho, pastor of the Yoido Full Gospel Church in Seoul, Korea, wrote of similar experiences:

In America ministers do not have this kind of problem, but in the Orient I have real trouble in preaching about the miraculous power of God, for in Buddhism monks also have performed fantastic miracles.... In Korea many people involved in yoga are healing the sick by yoga meditation. When attending meetings of the Japanese Sokagakkai, many are healed—some of stomach ulcers, the deaf and dumb hearing and speaking, and the blind seeing. So naturally we Christians, especially Pentecostal Christians, have real difficulty in explaining these occurrences. You cannot put these things away simply as a manifestation of the devil....[1]

Cho goes on to describe what he calls the "fourth dimension," that is, the spirit realm, which can shape the material and human world. Here is how Cho interprets the power of non-Christian prayer:

So naturally these yoga people and Buddhist believers could explore and develop their human fourth dimension, their spiritual sphere; with clear-cut visions and mental pictures of health they could incubate over their bodies. By natural order the fourth dimension has power over the third dimension, and the human spirit, within limitations, has the power to give order and creation. God gave power to human beings to control the material world and to have dominion over material things, a responsibility they can carry out through the fourth dimension. Now unbelievers, by exploring and developing their inner spiritual being in such a way as to carry out dominion upon their third dimension, which includes their physical sicknesses and diseases....[2]

A powerfully held belief and an ardent hope, when expressed in prayer, can have actual consequences, as witnessed by the crutches left at the door of the Buddhist temple. All prayer that takes place along certain principles for engaging the spiritual realm (or what Pastor Cho calls the "fourth dimension") will shape the future. These principles have been discovered and taught by the world's religious systems and have brought results. If there had been no results, people would have stopped praying long ago.

How Much of This Is Satanic?

Sometimes prayer opens the door into the demonic. This is certainly the case with witchcraft, satanic rituals, and much prayer in Hindu or Buddhist temples, crowded with false deities, behind which exist real spirit powers and principalities. In many cases, these people are praying not to

God but to demonic powers ("gods" and "goddesses"), while the Creator God remains a mysterious being they believe to be beyond reach.

There is a New Age meditation center in the mountains where I (Brad) live. Once when I had just returned from Taiwan, my eight-year-old daughter, Elizabeth, and I stopped by for a visit. About a dozen people were in meditation and prayer at the center. I felt the same sincerity in these people that I had often seen in the temples in Taiwan.

As Elizabeth and I walked from room to room, I became aware that my spirit was unsettled. The people themselves were kind and receptive to me. Yet the spirit in me was out of sync with the spirit of this place. Suddenly, Elizabeth looked up at me and in Chinese whispered, "Daddy, let's get out of this place! This has the same kind of bad spirits as the temples in Taiwan. They don't like Jesus." I thanked the people for their hospitality and we left. The prayer in that place was opening a door to spirits who were real and powerful, but who were opposed to Jesus.

In the same way, I (Doug) became aware of the hostile presence of spiritual forces in the Rajneeshpuram community, even though the leadership of that community was professing it as a "new and better version of Christianity." Many of the people attending that community were disenchanted Christians, mostly intellectuals from mainline churches of "the secular city" era, who had never found God and had never learned to pray. Now, their eyes were opened to see the spirit realm, and they felt that what they were getting in touch with was far more real, engaging. and exciting than anything they had ever experienced in the Christian churches.

However, just because this was real and exciting did not mean that it was of God. Our job, as Christian intercessors, was not to say, "Oh, all roads lead to the same God; these Indian people have their way and we have ours. Let's all just do our thing." Our job was to pray that Jesus would triumph over these beings, whose presence in Oregon had been strengthened by countless prayers. We prayed that the power of Christ would be manifested over this religious community and that Christ would put all his enemies under his feet.

SOME PEOPLE ARE EARNESTLY SEARCHING FOR CHRIST

Christians, however, must not too quickly assume that all non-Christian prayer is a doorway into the demonic. Sometimes the prayers of non-Christian people are neither good nor bad. Sometimes they are ways of feeling for God, ways that God honors because they are offering to him the best they know. The Bible calls such people "God-fearers"—a technical term in the Bible for pagans who have converted to monotheism without becoming Jewish converts (cf. Acts 17:17).

Cornelius, for example, was "devout and God-fearing" (Acts 10:2). An angel said to Cornelius, "Your prayers and gifts to the poor have come up as a memorial offering before God" (v. 4). Cornelius at that time was not a Christian, nor was he a Jew, yet God heard his prayers, and he was chosen to be among the first of the Romans to receive the Gospel.

I (Doug) have intimately studied the early years of white-Indian relations in the American West. What I discovered there astonished me, as I have opened my heart to native believers who have told their cultural and spiritual history. For example, while I was in Spokane recently, I read the story of the Coeur d'Alene people. Back in the eighteenth century, they had a great prophet and shaman by the name of Circling Raven. According to the Coeur d'Alene historian Joseph Seltice, Circling Raven received a prophecy that long ago a savior had been born, and he should lead his tribe to begin celebrating the birth of that savior each winter. In this way, the Coeur d'Alenes began to celebrate Christmas long before any missionaries actually preached to them about Jesus. They worshiped God as far as they knew.

Some Christians today believe that all Native American shamans are and have always been satanic—or at least pagan. To hear some Christians talk, Native Americans were all pagans before the coming of the white people in the nineteenth century.

Most natives I have talked to find this judgment by white Christians just one more example of misunderstanding and arrogance, by people who have never been known to be good listeners. I must confess that I am inclined to agree with them. In my study of tribal history on the Columbia Plateau (eastern Washington and northern Idaho), religious leaders were far more likely to be God-fearers than Satanists. Without knowing the history of Judaism or the Christian Gospel, they recognized and worshiped God, whom they called "Creator" (or the word for *Creator* in their own language) and whom they worshiped as best they knew.

When George Simpson, head of the Northern Department of the Hudson's Bay Company, took his first trip up the Columbia River, he was besieged by a dozen native chiefs from every tribe, asking him to send people who could tell them about "the Master of Life." Simpson had no idea what they were talking about, of course. He considered himself a Christian just because "all Englishmen are Christians." He hardly ever prayed unless he had to, to keep up appearances. But the chiefs who came to him with earnest inquiries after the Master of Life (they called Jesus by this term, because they did not know his name yet) were men of devout prayer, who really did want to know God better.

Brad and I are uncomfortable with painting all non-Christians as pagans—and equally uncomfortable suggesting that all religions are basically roads to the same God. We believe that reality is more complex than either of these extreme views allows.

Most people are somewhere on a road to discovery of the spirit realm. In that discovery, some are moving toward God and others are moving toward demonic deception, believing it to be also from God. Christians need discernment to figure out how to help people move in God's direction from wherever they are. In some cases this will involve having them renounce alliances with demonic powers, but in many cases it will not. In such cases, people simply need to pull from their culture the unique ways that God has already been preparing them to "feel after God" in prayer. Consider these three ways of looking at the spirit realm:

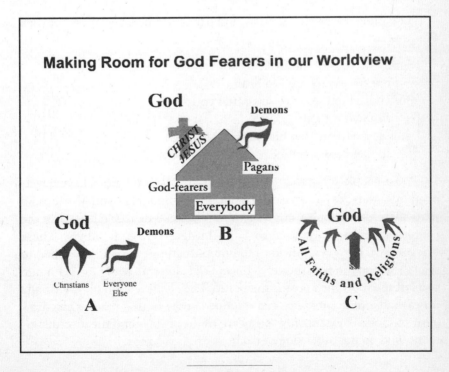

- According to the model on the left, people are either Christians or pagans. This simplistic view offers only the two alternatives "Christian" and "heathen."
- According to the model on the right, everyone is in a journey toward God, and there is no awareness of spiritual deception. This view usually comes from an aversion to arrogance, but it is not well informed. It does not recognize that many of the people of non-Christian faiths would say of God that he is unknowable. Many of these religions are ardent in their devotion to spirits other than God, because they do not believe that God can be known. This view, in other words, is as naïve as the first one.
- The middle model acknowledges that most people are seeking after God in some way, but demonic spirits sidetrack many. Others are earnestly seeking after God, and when they hear about Jesus, they become overjoyed. For many of these Corneliuses, God has already been moving to teach them about himself and to draw them to Jesus.

THE ABYSS

The Bible reveals that there is, and has always been, an abyss between God and us:

> Surely the arm of the LORD is not too short to save,
>   nor his ear too dull to hear.
> But your iniquities have separated you
>   from your God;
> your sins have hidden his face from you,
>   so that he will not hear. (Isaiah 59:1–2)

Most people sense that God is far away. Many religions have developed this awareness into a cardinal doctrine—Buddhists and Muslims, in particular. Most people cannot seem to relate closely to God. So over the centuries, people have tried to build bridges across the abyss. These bridges have been magnificent religious structures, but all have failed to span the chasm. In fact, the very concept of fellowship with God is foreign to all of them—which proves the point. They believe God to be virtually unreachable, and some are even offended at the notion that we can draw close to God. They are only too aware of the abyss—and the inscrutability of God on the other side of it.

But from that other side of the abyss, God himself built a bridge. He sent Jesus to die for us and draw us back to himself.

> Therefore, if anyone is in Christ, he is a new creation; the old has gone, the new has come! All this is from God, who reconciled us to himself through Christ and gave us the ministry of reconciliation; that God was reconciling the world to himself in Christ, not counting men's sins against them. And he has committed to us the message of reconciliation. (2 Corinthians 5:17–19)

Jesus is the way across the abyss. When he died, the curtain in the temple in Jerusalem was torn in two; through that event God was inviting people to follow Jesus into a place of intimacy and fellowship with him. This is what makes Christian prayer unique, and it becomes the foundational principle for prayer that shapes the future.

According to apostolic teaching, the key to this amazing invitation is the shed blood of Jesus. In the mind of God (who makes the rules), there had to be a perfect sacrifice, the Sinless One sacrificed for the sinful ones. In the end, all other faiths must come to recognize this fact: Jesus is the only bridge to God. Through him alone we can enter into fellowship with God.

For example, even the Vedas, the oldest Hindu scriptures, written between 2000 and 1000 B.C., prophesied: "The one who rules the world in order to atone for the sins of many allowed His body to be crushed and offered as a sacrifice."[3] God has planted in the heart of Hinduism the first direction-markers toward the bridge.

Mme. Bilquis Sheikh, a Pakistani woman, described in her book, *I Dared to Call Him Father*, the difference between a Pakistani Muslim, who remains on this side of the abyss, and one who crosses to the other side. Mme. Sheikh described the moment she first took notice of the bridge as a result of a conversation with a Christian friend, Dr. Pia Santiago:

> Finally she leaned forward and in a confidential tone asked, "Madame Sheikh, what are you doing with a Bible?"
>
> "I am earnestly in search of God," I answered. . . . "Whatever happens," I emphasized, "I must find God, but I'm confused about your faith," I said finally, realizing that even as I spoke I was putting my finger on something important. "You seem to make God so . . . I don't know . . . *personal*."

The little nun's eyes filled with compassion as she leaned forward. "Madame Sheikh," she said, her voice full of emotion, "there is only one way to find out why we feel this way. And that is to find out for yourself, strange as that may seem. Why don't you pray *to* the God you are searching for? Ask Him to show you His way. Talk to Him as if He were your friend."

I smiled. She might as well suggest that I talk to the Taj Mahal. But then Dr. Santiago said something that shot through my being like electricity. She leaned closer and took my hand in hers, tears streaming down her cheeks. "Talk to Him," she said very quietly, "as if He were your father."[4]

This startling concept was new to her, as it must be new to everyone who has never known Christ—because it is Christ alone who introduces us to God the Father. He alone is the bridge across the abyss. And those who have never walked across the bridge to the other side of the abyss cannot know what it is like to talk to God "as if He were our father."

We invite you to walk with Jesus and learn from him about prayer as he prepares you for life on the other side of the abyss. For as he guides us across the bridge, he instructs us about how it is with God, how we can come close to him—how, in short, we can truly pray. And with him as our mediator, we will learn things about prayer that we could not have learned before we had stepped onto the bridge with him.

SUMMARY

Only Jesus provides a bridge across the abyss that separates us from God. Therefore, only Jesus opens the way for us to know God. Other religions have developed prayer as a form of spiritual power but remain closed to the personal knowledge of God. Jesus Christ shows us that true prayer is birthed out of a relationship with God, which is made possible by his death on the cross. All Christian prayer, therefore, grows out of a personal encounter with God—Father, Son, and Holy Spirit.

QUESTIONS FOR REFLECTION, DIALOGUE, AND JOURNALING

1. Have you believed that Christians have opportunities for fellowship with God that unbelievers do not have? How do you feel and respond to this idea?

2. Do you make use of this bridge across the abyss as a great privilege
    God has bestowed on you? When you do, do you sense the "fel-
    lowship . . . with the Father and with his Son" that the apostle John
    described in 1 John 1:3?

Chapter Five

HOW THE HEAVENLY
FATHER ENCOURAGES PRAYER

hen the disciples came to Jesus asking for instructions about prayer, he taught: "When you pray, say: 'Our Father in heaven . . .'" (Luke 11:2, NKJV).

Jesus often prayed intimately with God as his Father. When, for example, he stood at the tomb of Lazarus, he prayed, "Father, I thank you that you have heard me" (John 11:41). When he was in the Garden of Gethsemane, he prayed, "*Abba*, Father!" (Mark 14:36). (*Abba* is the Aramaic word for "Daddy.")

JESUS INTRODUCES US TO THE FATHER

Other people pray to God in general, or to the Creator, or to the Great Spirit, or to "the Ground of all being." But Jesus called God "Father." He makes it possible for us to enter the kingdom as little children learning how to trust their daddy. This is the heart and uniqueness of Christian prayer. It becomes intimate with God.

> By [the Spirit] we cry, "*Abba*, Father." The Spirit himself testifies with our spirit that we are God's children. Now if we are children, then we are heirs—heirs of God and co-heirs with Christ, if indeed we share in his sufferings in order that we may also share in his glory. (Romans 8:15–17)

When "Father" Is a Curse Word

Some people are uncomfortable with this idea. They do not like to speak of God as their Father because the word "father" brings up a host of bad memories. Their earthly fathers wounded them. Their fathers were adulterers, or drunkards, or crack addicts. Their fathers violated them, abandoned them, or cursed them. How, then, can they think of God as a "father"? How can they enter into this intimate prayer with *Abba?*

If you are such a person, the answer to this problem is to let Jesus reconstruct your image of what a father is. This is an important way that Jesus introduces us to God the Father. Isaiah called Jesus "Everlasting Father" (Isaiah 9:6). When I (Doug) first read this little verse, I thought that Isaiah had become confused about Jesus. Jesus was not the Father; he was *the Son* of God. How could Isaiah call Jesus the "Everlasting Father"?

Of course, within the Trinity Jesus is the Son, not the Father. But in relation *to us*, he is a father. Jesus came to us to reflect the Father's nature perfectly into our lives, to show us in human terms how God is. He who has seen Jesus has seen the Father (John 14:9). Jesus came to this earth so that all the lies about God that the evil one has been whispering can be cleared up, and we can gain a true picture of how God the Father is. The result is that Jesus becomes a "replacement" father for us.

But what is often happening today instead is that women (and some men, too) are saying, "Reject the Fatherhood of God. We need to reimagine God in female form, because maleness and fatherhood are evil. Now we will follow female deities or female 'versions of God' because we cannot tolerate God being a father." These people are letting the darkness that was in their earthly fathers dictate how they think of God.

What God wants (what Jesus wants) is to heal the terrible memories connected with our fathers. He does not want that bitterness to become a permanent feature of our lives, much less to dictate how we will think of God. He wants to separate us from our earthly fathers and replace those images in the "divine imagination" of our hearts. Jesus said, "Anyone who loves his father or mother more than me is not worthy of me" (Matthew 10:37).

It seems that Jesus actually wants us to cut a spiritual tie (or bondage) with our parents. He wants to become a father and show us what a true father's heart is like, especially if we did not get that picture from our earthly fathers. Jesus will teach us about the fatherly heart of God. Jesus will become our avenue, our bridge across the abyss of human sin (including the sins of our earthly fathers), to God. When he becomes our everlasting Father, he can even heal our relationship with our earthly fathers.

Forgive Your Dad and Get in Touch With Your *Abba*

I (Brad) had to go through this healing and forgiveness of my own father before I was truly free to grow in relationship with God the Father. My dad and I are of entirely different personality types. I never quite conformed to his image of how I was supposed to be. He always seemed so busy trying to change me that, deep down, I wondered whether he really loved me.

But through prayer and confession, I was healed of these hurts, most of which he had no idea he had inflicted on me. I was able to forgive him from the heart. Now I can tell him that I love him, and he can express his love toward me. This improvement in my relationship with my father ran parallel to a deepening in my prayer life with *Abba*, Father.

My situation, of course, is no match for the deep agony that a woman feels who has been sexually abused by her father or cursed with angry words during the entire course of childhood. But the need for forgiveness and healing is just as necessary if she is to move forward in a relationship with God the Father and develop a healthy prayer life.

The possibility of inner healing is beyond the scope of this book. But problems in identifying God as "*Abba*, Father" can almost always be traced back to childhood abuse, neglect, or belittling by a father in the early years. To pursue this type of inner healing, we recommend the books of Leanne Payne: *The Healing Presence*, *Restoring the Christian Soul*, and *The Broken Image* (for people whose early childhood wounding has led to sexual identity problems).

Jesus is the bridge to the Father. This is important for prayer because Christian prayer is different from all other prayer. It grows from a personal love relationship with God. If prayer does not grow out of such a relationship with God, it is not *Christian* prayer.

If God's Gonna Do What God's Gonna Do, Why Pray?

The possibility of shaping the future through prayer brings up all kinds of other questions about God the Father, questions that can torment us and hinder prayer until we get some answers. For example:

- "If God has predestined all things from the beginning, what difference does prayer make?"

- "How could a high and sovereign God entrust the power to change the world to such childish imbeciles as us? Wouldn't this be terribly foolish and irresponsible of God? I get a great deal of assurance from knowing that God is in charge—and not people."
- "In prayer, you're just getting close to God and letting him change your own heart, right? Prayer doesn't actually change anything but yourself, does it?"

The Sovereign Authority of God

All these questions gnaw at the edges of the great theological debate that has fired the minds and hearts of Christians for generations: the question of the sovereignty of God. "Let God be God, and let us not try to be God. Those who understand God's greatness and our smallness will not presume to pray at all, except perhaps, 'Thy will be done, O Lord,' whatever that may be."

And, of course, there is little point in praying even that prayer if you really believe that God's will completely bypasses us humans. Why pray about anything if everything is predestined in a sort of completed story, like a dime novel in God's back pocket?

What these people do not understand is the Father heart of God. Like a good father, our Father in heaven invites us into his projects and says to us, "Here, let's do this together." It is this very dimension of God's love that we learn in prayer. God reveals his projects, and he wants us to cooperate with him in getting them done. Prayer is cooperation with the Father.

"God is in control," you say? Yes, that is true. But how are we to fight against evil and build something good in our world?

"Go to college," you say? "Learn sociology, political science, medicine, ecology, biology, anthropology, and all the other -ologies"? That is all very well. But has God himself given us no tools, outside of our own rational minds, with which to battle evil and produce good? Haven't we learned by now that this ardent faith in science can only take us so far? Is a Christian just the same thing as a humanist or altruist—but with the name of Jesus attached? Is there no power in the cross of Christ to produce change? Or in the Holy Spirit? Or the Word of God? How are these powers, so prominent in the Bible, to be appropriated for us today? Is there no strategy by which we can learn to work in cooperation with God?

"Young Man, If God Had Wanted . . ."

Whenever I (Doug) think about predestination and the sovereignty of God, I think of the story of William Carey. In his day few Christians had the least interest in proclaiming the Gospel of Jesus to unreached peoples. Yet Carey was fired up with a vision to preach the Gospel to those in India who had not yet dreamed of Jesus. In 1792 he founded the first Baptist Missionary Society. But the pastors he went to for support upbraided him with these words: "Young man, if God had wanted to save the heathen in India, he could certainly do it without the likes of you or us."

These pastors had a view of the sovereignty of God that excluded human involvement. Their view of predestination amounted to an unbiblical fatalism. That attitude, wherever it exists, can also affect prayer. People end up saying, "If God's gonna do what God's gonna do, why pray?"

Calvin Versus the Calvinists

No one had a more secure grip on the sovereignty of God than John Calvin, the great Swiss Reformer. By his careful reasoning from Scripture, he reinserted the doctrine of predestination into historic Christianity (with much help from other Reformers like Martin Luther). People with a firm belief in predestination and the sovereignty of God are still called "Calvinists" today.

Surely, you would think, someone like John Calvin would recognize that "God's gonna do what God's gonna do" regardless of human efforts and prayers. Yet John Calvin had a surprisingly vibrant prayer life. In his *Institutes of the Christian Religion*, his chapter on prayer stands adjacent to his chapter on predestination. In his mind, the sovereignty of God did not cancel out prayer, but incorporated prayer into itself.

It was the later Calvinists (and less biblical thinkers) who used the doctrine of predestination as an excuse to avoid human responsibility. This is what Calvin said about them: "They act with excessive foolishness who, to call men's minds away from prayer, babble that God's providence, standing guard over all things, is vainly importuned with our entreaties. . . ."[1] Calvin goes on:

> Words fail to explain how necessary prayer is, and in how many ways the exercise of prayer is profitable. Surely, with good reason the Heavenly Father affirms that the only stronghold of safety is in calling upon his name [cf. Joel 2:32]. By so doing we invoke the presence both of his providence, through which he

watches over and guards our affairs, and of his power, through which he sustains us, weak as we are and well-nigh overcome, and of his goodness, through which he receives us, miserably burdened with sins, unto grace; and, in short, it is by prayer that we call him to reveal himself as wholly present to us.[2]

God has ordained prayer as a means by which his grace, love, and power are birthed into our lives. The Reformer Martin Luther agreed:

Let us learn that prayer is highly necessary, and let us not allow ourselves to be deceived by this evil temptation, that we think that even without our prayer God will give us what we need, and that since He knows what benefits us most, there is no need of prayer. Augustine is right when he says: "He who made you without you does not want to save you without you."[3]

In another of his works, *The Bondage of the Will*, Luther's credentials as a believer in God's sovereignty are proven impeccable. Yet Luther prayed. Three hours a day, he prayed!

Prayer, in other words, *is* the sovereign will of God. It is how God himself has chosen to accomplish his will. Whatever projects he has envisioned for our world, he does not like to do them by himself. He wants us to pray them into existence.

"God'll Do It!—Or No, Maybe We Should!"

Without prayer, we get confused about whether God is supposed to minister to people or whether we are. A prayerless person tends to do all sorts of good works. When bad things happen to people and the good works prove powerless to change things, such people then blame God. They are forever confused about who is supposed to do what. The concept of cooperation with God is hard for them to grasp. They do not understand the heart of God, who longs to do his projects with us.

Prayer guides us in a middle way between two extremes—complete irresponsibility on the one hand ("Oh well, God's will be done"), and taking matters into our own hands on the other ("Modern man has come of age, so don't expect God to do anything for you. God helps those who help themselves"). Prayer is the middle way of doing things together with God. In this, we fulfill the longings of his fatherly heart.

A CHINESE PARABLE

Years ago a Chinese pastor told the following parable. A man built a house for his children. When he had completed the house, it came time for him to sign over the deed to those for whom he built it. From the moment the house was deeded over to them, he limited himself. He could no longer enter the house whenever he wanted to. Instead of barging in and out at will, he would come to the door and ring the doorbell. Only if they opened the door and invited him in would he come into the house— even though he had built the house himself.

So it is with God. He stands at the door and knocks (Revelation 3:20–21). But we need to open the door from within, because God respects our space. He will not come into our house, our "areas of activity," unless we ask him to, even though he created those areas and appointed us to them. He respects our space, for which he made this world of space and time. Prayer is the invitation we give to God, without which God rarely meddles in our affairs.

This surely is the reason God so often says, "I looked for a man among them who would build up the wall and stand before me in the gap on behalf of the land so I would not have to destroy it, but I found none" (Ezekiel 22:30). Again and again, we see God's astonishment about our prayerlessness—we don't want God involved in our areas of activity. We think we can do everything by ourselves, and God expresses his disappointment:

I revealed myself to those who did not ask for me;
    I was found by those who did not seek me.
To a nation that did not call on my name,
    I said, "Here am I, here am I."
All day long I have held out my hands
    to an obstinate people,
who walk in ways not good,
    pursuing their own imaginations.... (Isaiah 65:1–2)

We seem to blow hot and cold with God. One moment we want to do everything ourselves—so full of our own ideas and ambitions and imaginations. The next moment, we are blaming God because he "allowed" such and such an evil to happen, and "How could God have allowed this, when he is sovereign Lord of the universe?"

What God is looking for is our invitation for him to come into our areas of activity, which we submit to him daily in prayer. As we do this, God begins to give a surprising authority to our prayers.

SUMMARY

If Jesus reconciled us with the Father in heaven, it is because our Father has plans for us. He has projects for us to accomplish. He comes to us to tell us what those projects are and show us how to pray them into being. To understand this concept, many of us need to be healed from the wounds inflicted by earthly fathers who did not treat us this way. We also must gain a healthy understanding of our cooperative relationship with the sovereign Lord of the universe, which is neither self-sufficient nor fatalistic.

QUESTIONS FOR REFLECTION, DIALOGUE, AND JOURNALING

1. Does your picture of God the Father match the thoughts of this chapter? Do you see God as wanting to have you join him in a project because he loves you? Where does your picture of God the Father come from?
2. What would it take to believe that God loves you enough to draw you into his projects together with him? Why not ask him to let you create something with him? What thoughts and feelings does this possibility generate in you?

Chapter Six

THE ROLE OF THE HOLY SPIRIT IN PRAYER

We have seen how Jesus introduces us to the Father so that we may have fellowship with both Jesus and the Father. We have seen how the Father draws us into projects of his own design and sets us to cooperating with him through prayer.

Now we are ready to look into the Holy Spirit, the third person of the Trinity, who helps us shape the future through prayer. Each of these persons of the Godhead (three persons, one God) takes a different role in producing prayer. But each reflects in his own way one perfect will—the will of God, who is one. How does the Holy Spirit get involved in the prayers of Christians? Here again, we find promises about prayer that make Christian prayer different from other prayer:

> Likewise the Spirit helps us in our weakness; for we do not know how to pray as we ought, but the Spirit himself intercedes for us with sighs too deep for words. And he who searches the hearts of men knows what is the mind of the Spirit because the Spirit intercedes for the saints according to the will of God. (Romans 8:26–27, RSV)

SEVEN EYES AND SEVEN HORNS

The Holy Spirit is the perfect discernment and power of God. He sees perfectly and can speak to us God's wisdom and discernment; wherever

God's power is manifested on earth, it is through the Holy Spirit. This, at least, is the picture that the apostle John gave in the book of Revelation when he pictured the Holy Spirit as the "seven eyes" and "seven horns" of the Lamb of God (Revelation 5:6). The Holy Spirit is the perfect (seven = perfect) power and discernment of Jesus, who sits "at the right hand" (the authority-wielding hand) of the Father.

This Spirit of perfect discernment and power roams throughout the earth and works through the prayers of Christians to bring about God's will on the earth. In this way, Christians are "a kingdom and priests to serve our God, and they will reign on the earth" (Revelation 5:10). The Holy Spirit, in other words, is the presence of God the Father and God the Son, and he carries out God's will among us through prayer.

The prophet Zechariah, a visionary like John, described this phenomenon as a "spirit of grace and supplication" (Zechariah 12:10) that would be poured out in the last days. Prayer, in other words, is more to a Christian than religious ritual or personal devotions. It becomes an encounter with God, infused with power and discernment. It is a ministry birthed by the Spirit of God, a way of yielding ourselves to divine power flowing through us. In this way, we not only do works *for* God; we can do the works *of* God. We can pray the prayers of God that birth those works.

The working of the Holy Spirit in prayer can take two forms. (1) The Holy Spirit gives guidance to our rational mind so that we can pray according to God's will. (2) He actually enters into us and prays prayers in us— prayers that we may not even understand.

HOLY SPIRIT GUIDANCE FOR PRAYER

Let's look at the first of these concepts: the Holy Spirit's guidance or intelligence for our prayers. In 1994, at the Wichita General Assembly of the Presbyterian Church (USA), a group of intercessors gathered together to pray for the Assembly. On Monday of that week, into the middle of the prayers for this denomination there came to me (Brad) a word to pray for unity between North and South Korea—a subject that none of the intercessors had come together to pray for. Yet one member of the team after another began to sense an urgency to pray for this, and with each fresh prayer, there came a growing awareness that God wanted to do something in Korea.

As the intercession intensified, Alan Leach began to "see" cracks forming in the wall that divides North and South Korea. Other team members "saw" people from South Korea streaming into North Korea, after decades of separation. Alan encouraged us to stand together and place our hands on an imaginary wall and speak its destruction. After about an hour of vociferous prayer by the entire team of twenty-five or thirty, the prayer intensity lifted.

That Friday, we were surprised to read in the newspaper that former President Jimmy Carter had been in North Korea and had just that week achieved a diplomatic breakthrough, reducing tensions and easing the threat of nuclear war. At the present time, four years later, talks have started in Geneva to open up diplomatic relations between North and South Korea. Of course, the Christians of South Korea have been praying for this for decades. But in our little team of Presbyterian intercessors, God allowed us a glimpse of how the Holy Spirit can guide us to pray for whatever is on the heart of the Father, so that we, too, could help him build something new and fresh—a united Korea.

Prayers for a Friend

The example of praying for North Korea is a dramatic one. Most of the time, the Holy Spirit's work of giving intelligence is more ordinary than this. The Spirit of God also can guide us in any "sphere of activity."

For instance, I (Brad) awoke one morning with the strong impression that I needed to intercede for a close friend and coworker in Taiwan named Howard Chaw. I had not heard from him for eight months and had no idea of how he was doing. But this morning I felt a strong impression that I was called to pray for him because his life was in grave danger. So I prayed not really knowing how to pray, but prayer led by the Holy Spirit with urgency, that God heal him of some fatal illness. After two weeks came the command: *Call him in Taiwan. Call him now!*

This guidance was clear, but I was afraid to follow through and make the call. What if this whole thing had been wrong or misguided? What if there was nothing wrong and I would look like a fool? After wrestling with this guidance all day, finally at 10 P.M. I direct-dialed his number in Taiwan. When his wife answered the phone I asked, "How is Howard? I have been praying urgently for him for two weeks. Is everything okay?"

"No!" she answered. "Everything is not okay! For the last two weeks Howard has been in the hospital with cancer. It has been very serious, and we were afraid that we were going to lose him. He has just gone through surgery." When I called the hospital and Howard heard my voice on the other end, he was astonished. When I told him that for two weeks God had me interceding for him, he wept. He told me that he had been through a terrible time feeling abandoned by God. My call, literally from the other side of the world, was like Jesus speaking to him to say that he knew his pain and that he was loved.

This was an astonishing experience for me. My prayers had apparently made a difference in the life of a brother. Would Howard have died of cancer if I had not been obedient and prayed? I do not know. What I do know is that the Holy Spirit gave the right intelligence to know how and when to pray. God invited me to take part in what he was doing in the life of this brother on the other side of the world.

Prophetic Hearing

There are many other ways in which intercessors receive vision and guidance for prayer from the Holy Spirit. One of these has been called "prophetic hearing." By this method, the Holy Spirit brings a Scripture alive to us and applies it in a particular way, to birth vision for a particular situation.

For example, at the 1998 General Assembly prayer vigil of the Presbyterian Church (USA), God began to give me (Doug) words of Scripture about our task, which was to pray for the General Assembly from the opening gavel to the closing prayer—fifteen hours per day of prayer for a week. First, the Holy Spirit gave me John 10:3: "The watchman opens the gate for [the Shepherd], and the sheep listen to his voice." I simply opened my Bible to this verse, and it leapt out at me. I sensed immediately that this little verse was an encouragement to the team from the Holy Spirit about our role as intercessors. Whatever the original passage may have meant, the Holy Spirit wanted us to see that our role was to open the gate for the "sheep" who were gathering in the Charlotte Convention Center, so that they could better hear the voice of Jesus.

But I also sensed that the Holy Spirit was not finished instructing us about our role as watchmen. He had another passage for me about this. So I opened my Bible again at random and looked at Isaiah 21. It said:

Day after day, my lord, I stand on the watchtower;
    every night I stay at my post.
Look, here comes a man in a chariot
    with a team of horses.
And he gives back the answer:
    "Babylon has fallen, has fallen!

All the images of its gods
    lie shattered on the ground!" (Isaiah 21:8b–9)

This passage goes on to actually use the word "watchman"—so that it was clear that God was using John 10:3 as an introduction to this word in Isaiah. He was putting these two words together as guidance for our prayer team. We were supposed to learn something about how he wanted us to pray as watchmen on the wall of the Presbyterian Church (USA). He wanted us to be alert to the first signs of a turnaround that he was starting to bring in this denomination.

This denomination has come under the influence of all sorts of wrong doctrine and of morals contrary to God's will. We should keep our eyes peeled for the first signs of this, coming at us like "a man in a chariot." As we meditated on this word in Isaiah, God used it to teach our prayer team all sorts of lessons about our work and to encourage us in prayer. We knew that the Holy Spirit was guiding us—first, because the two passages fit so perfectly into each other; second, because what was revealed in Scripture actually started happening, in the votes and decisions of the General Assembly. God has consistently given us unexpected victories not only at this Assembly, but at each one, to bring the denomination back to biblical standards.

Prayer Pictures

Often, the most powerful indicators of God's guidance for prayer are given in picture form. The Holy Spirit began to expand the picture of the watchman on the wall opening the gate for the Shepherd so the sheep could hear his voice. Our prayer team began to "see" that the sheep of the Presbyterian Church (USA) had piled rocks on the inside of the gate, rocks that were keeping Jesus out of the church. We asked the Lord, "What are these rocks?" We began to get words like "intellectual pride," "hatred and bitterness," "sexual immorality," and so on.

We began to confess these as corporate sins, then as personal sins; then we asked the Lord to forgive these sins both in us and in the church corporately. In this way, we were removing the stones from before the gate of the sheepfold. Then Tim, one of our intercessors, "saw" Jesus coming into the gate with a healing vial, full of oil for the healing of the sheep. He also saw that the sheep were full of infections, draining sores, bleeding wounds, and diseases. That new addition to the vision led the team into an entire evening of prayer for wounded women in the church, then for men who also needed inner healing.

Later, another of the intercessors "saw" the church covered over with a gelatinous dome that had mirrors attached to it on the inside. The people, in looking up, could not see God, but only the mirrors reflecting back on themselves. The Holy Spirit began to interpret this picture: The church was not worshiping Jesus but itself. People were testifying not to the power of Jesus but to their love of "the church." The church had become an idol, actually replacing Jesus at the center of our life together. We were to pray that the gelatinous dome would come tumbling down so that the people could see Jesus more clearly. One intercessor, Shirley, also saw rays of light coming down through the dome "like a stun gun, bringing judgment for some, blessing to others." We sensed that Jesus was starting to penetrate through this dome of resistance and was beginning to soften the hearts of the Presbyterians gathered there.

Prophetic Confirmation

That was not all, however. Sometimes the Holy Spirit brings intelligence for prayer through objective means, from people who know nothing about what we are praying for. This confirmation is intended to encourage us to keep praying, because much prayer is needed before the thing God is creating can actually be birthed into reality.

After we had been praying for the mirrors of the dome to come tumbling down, one of the intercessors produced a yellow sheet of paper that had been given to her by a friend on the floor of the General Assembly. On this paper had been scribbled a prophetic word, which the Holy Spirit had given to this friend for us:

> Hear my voice. You will marvel at the days ahead. I will move in might and power. My glory will be seen by my people. Those who have ears to hear, let them hear. Those who have eyes to see let them see. I am the Lord; in its time I will do this swiftly.

What an encouragement this was—confirming so wonderfully the very prayers we had been praying! It enabled us to lay hold more firmly to the vision God had given us, so that we could pray it into being. It was an important "marker" that we were on the right track, praying according to God's will for this denomination.

Team Confirmation

When Christians pray together, the Holy Spirit can speak the same thing to two or more intercessors as they pray. This, too, is a way of guiding the intercessors to pray according to God's will.

At this same prayer vigil, I (Doug) sensed the Lord telling me to open my Bible up to Malachi 3. As I began to read this passage quietly to myself, Shirley, to my left, began to read it out loud to the group! Since I was looking at the very same passage and even had the same translation, we ended up reading it to the team in unison. The Holy Spirit was again giving intelligence about our denomination:

> You have wearied the LORD with your words.
> "How have we wearied him?" you ask.
> By saying, "All who do evil are good in the eyes of the LORD, and he is pleased with them" or "Where is the God of justice?"
> "See, I will send my messenger, who will prepare the way before me. Then suddenly the Lord you are seeking will come to his temple; the messenger of the covenant, whom you desire, will come," says the LORD Almighty.
> But who can endure the day of his coming? Who can stand when he appears? For he will be like a refiner's fire or a launderer's soap. (Malachi 2:17–3:2)

This passage, like the other leadings the Holy Spirit had given us, encouraged us to pray for a visitation of God among Presbyterians. It encouraged us to believe that God wanted to bring a refining and purifying of this denomination, and we prayed more fervently for this, because the Holy Spirit had confirmed his guidance through two intercessors simultaneously.

This type of guidance is important, because most of the time it is hard to see the answers to our prayers right away. God has to encourage us in our prayers, for he expects us to pray according to faith, not according to what we can already see. Prayer shapes the future, not just the present. It is a way of birthing the new while the old is still all about us. So we have to learn how to walk by faith for a season, while everything around us ridicules and scorns our faith. That is a hard thing to do. But it is necessary if we are to shape the future through prayer.

God knows that it is hard for us to walk by faith. So he gives us these gifts of the Spirit to guide and encourage us while the vision is still being formed—a hidden thing in the womb of God, which no one else can see.

THE HOLY SPIRIT PRAYS IN AND THROUGH US

The other way the Holy Spirit helps us pray according to the will of God is by entering into us and praying in us prayers that we may not even understand. One way this happens is through the gift of tongues, given as a prayer language.

In this gift, God apparently grants the ability to speak languages we have never learned. This, at least, is how Paul clearly defines this gift in 1 Corinthians 14:15. Seldom, in our experience, does ecstasy, a trance, or anything of that sort accompany this phenomenon. Tongues, 99 percent of the time, is simply a form of prayer, like any other form of prayer. It requires us to open our mouths and to speak out words that are welling up within us, not from our minds but from our spirits. With tongues, the words are not understandable to the mind.

Most westerners believe this to be foolish because we cannot get our minds around it. For a season, westerners actually accused tongues-speakers of being mentally ill. Tongues was considered a form of dissociation— divorce from reality. Today, most people realize that these were prejudicial statements, which did not spring from a familiarity with God's Word.

A great deal of controversy still surrounds this gift. We have tried to deal with some of these issues in our book *Receiving the Power*. Those who have been hurt by the gift of tongues or who have received negative teaching about it might profit from that book. [1]

Pray in the Holy Spirit

In a small number of cases, tongues is used as a form of prophecy in church and is accompanied by interpretation. But in all other cases—at least 95 percent of the time (in our experience)—tongues is given to help us do what the Bible calls "praying in the Spirit." We believe that God wishes to empower Christians with the ability to "pray in the Spirit on all occasions with all kinds of prayers and requests" (Ephesians 6:18a). We interpret this to mean, at least in part, that we can pray in tongues and we can pray our prayers in our learned language—both have a place in spiritual warfare and intercessory prayer.

It may be that some people are to be excluded from the practice of praying in tongues; at least, this is how people sometimes interpret 1 Corinthians 12:30: "Do all have gifts of healing? Do all speak in tongues? Do all interpret?" But if that is the case, Paul gives no hint of it in Ephesians, nor does Jude give any hint of such limits in Jude 20, which says simply, "Pray in the Holy Spirit." These commands assume that Christians are capable of praying in the Spirit.

How, then, does one deal with the other passage in 1 Corinthians 12, which implies that not all people were intended to use the gift of tongues? There are at least two options. It could mean that in the context of worship services, where the gift was to be used prophetically with interpretation, not everyone will speak in a tongue (even though everyone could pray in a tongue in private). Or it could mean that not everyone is supposed to have the gift of tongues even for private prayer. Nobody really knows what Paul meant, and most people seem to read into the passage what they want it to mean.

While many people have used tongues as a badge of spiritual superiority, we see it as a childlike gift that God gives to shame the wise—just because it is so simple and foolish to the worldly wise. It is a form of prayer and a way of shaping the future.

How Doug Opened Up to Pray in the Spirit

Opening up to the gift of tongues can be, for many people, astonishingly simple, as long as we don't expect too much. For me (Doug), tongues began to emerge after I had done a thorough and completely rational study of every Scripture about praying in the Spirit and had decided that God wanted it for me because he had given it as a simple command. I asked him to help me learn how to pray in the Holy Spirit, as Jude 20 instructed me.

When I mentally began to "hear" syllables in my mind, even though it seemed childish, I spoke them out loud, as an experiment of faith. It would have been easy for me to convince myself that this was nothing but gibberish. Nevertheless, I was ready to cling to God's Word long enough to see what would come of this experiment—at least to try it for a few weeks. Back in those years, I was so spiritually starved that I was ready to try anything!

After a while, I felt that this little experiment was growing into something good and important. It did indeed "edify" me, as Paul said it would do (1 Corinthians 14:4). That is, I began to have more faith for prayer when I yielded my tongue to this mystery of sounds. When I did not, it seemed as though my prayer life was more pedestrian.

Some people may think that this was all just human contrivance and self-deception, and that for tongues to be real, it needs to come with a great onrush of emotion (which is how it happened to Brad). But even people who have the onrush of emotion still have to learn to pray in the Spirit when the onrush of emotion isn't there, or the gift will die within them like a fading flower. I insist that the gift of tongues as a prayer language must be learned and practiced, just like any other form of prayer. It isn't something that "happens to you" so much as something that you do, by the inspiration of the Holy Spirit.

The Wonder of Spiritual Language

In the years since that gateway in 1972, the gift of tongues has become a many-faceted wonder for me, just as my prayers in the English language are also many-faceted and can be used in many different ways.

- At times I feel, when I am praying in tongues, that I am coming incredibly close to God, as though he is just two inches from the front of my face.
- At other times, I find myself caught up in a powerful expression that sounds like a Jewish mama scolding her children. I believe that, at these times, the Holy Spirit is using my voice to rebuke demons.
- There are times when my spirit is lifted up in worship of Jesus, and the Holy Spirit is inspiring me to chant in an unknown language.
- At other times, my prayer in tongues leads directly into prayers in English, as though I am interpreting my own tongue.

These facets of praying in tongues are but a few dimensions of this mysterious prayer language that started so simply in my life a quarter of a century ago.

Most people who are unable to be open to this reality are hindered by a lack of understanding (and we refuse to believe in anything we don't understand), or by a hurtful experience. I could be wrong about this, but I believe that God wants to give this gift broadly, perhaps to all Christians. Brad and I covet this gift for all Christians because it is a great boost to our own prayer life. There are times when I am tired and mentally not very alert. What a wonderful thing that God makes it possible to "pray in the Spirit" while "the mind is unfruitful."

Other Ways of Praying in the Spirit

Tongues is not the only form of praying in the Spirit; in fact, in the past it has not even been regarded as the main one. To Reformers like Martin Luther, "praying in the Spirit" meant praying with greater and greater fervency until the Holy Spirit actually births something through prayer.

It is regular and customary for the Holy Spirit not always to touch our hearts with ineffable groaning (Romans 8:26). But when He does touch them, then it is definitely decided that the prayer has penetrated the clouds and has obtained what is sought in heaven and on earth. Otherwise heaven and earth would have to go to ruin.[2]

For Quakers like Isaac Penington, praying in the Spirit meant waiting on the Lord until the Spirit definitely gives you God's will:

True prayer is not in the time, in the will, or in the power of the person praying. Rather, it is a gift of God that resides in his Spirit. It is not ours, but it is given to us. Therefore, it is ours to wait upon the Spirit, to wait for the Spirit to move and breathe in us, and to give us the ability to call upon the Father and give us the power of prevailing with the Father, in the name and through the life of the Son.[3]

Clearly, praying in the Spirit has meant different things to different Christians, and it should probably have a broad, not a narrow, meaning, because the Scriptures permit a breadth of interpretation.

Tongues and Travail

My wife and I have provided leadership for our annual Presbyterian Church (USA) General Assembly prayer team for the last six years. Each year, God has brought our prayer to a crescendo at some point during the week.

At these times, our prayer takes on a very fervent tone. Everyone in the room breaks out praying together for a specific prayer burden, such as the ReImagining[4] controversy of 1993 that threatened to split our denomination wide open, or the issue of ordaining homosexuals in 1996. On those occasions, my wife would break out in a desperate and uncontrollable weeping, which would last from ten minutes to half an hour. Simultaneously, I would break out in a powerful rebuking tongue, while the whole room would burst into loud prayer of many kinds. Her weeping in prayer sounds and feels like a woman giving birth and is usually called "travailing prayer"—another type of praying in the Spirit (Romans 8:26). We had the strong sense that God was birthing something in the realm of the spirit that would actually start to take shape in the denomination before we went home.

In most cases (but not all), the results would be astonishing and almost immediate. A powerful change would happen on the floor of the General Assembly within the next few hours or days. In the case of the ReImagining controversy, the denomination moved through the controversy almost overnight, coming into complete harmony, so that the Assembly was able to fire the appropriate staff persons who had promoted that conference and reaffirm the basic boundaries of historic Christianity.

In the case of the homosexual ordination issue, the church reaffirmed scriptural sexual standards for all ordained people in our denomination, above and beyond anything we could have hoped for, while also reaffirming that God loves homosexual people. He loves the sinner but not the sin. In almost every case where we have been led by the Holy Spirit into such a crescendo, we have found that confusion was dispersed, and God's Word came powerfully to guide our General Assembly in direct response to the prayers uttered in the prayer room.

We believe that God provided us with the ability to "pray in the Holy Spirit" because the prayers of the Holy Spirit spoken through our voices were somehow important in the protection and creation of a newborn work that he has for Presbyterians to do.

This vision has not yet been completed at the time of this writing. But we have seen the Presbyterian Church (USA) turn a corner, aligning itself more and more with God's Word and naming the name of Jesus more frequently than before. God has encouraged us greatly, and this encouragement comes from the Holy Spirit.

The prayer battles at our General Assembly have provided an important context for us to learn the dynamics of how the Holy Spirit enables us to work with God in prayer. Of course, the same lessons can be learned in any "sphere of activity."

SUMMARY

Because prayer is difficult for us, God sends the Holy Spirit to help us in our weakness. The Holy Spirit guides us and empowers us so that prayer can reach its full potential. He gives us visual pictures, prophetic confirmation, simultaneous prayer leadings, and a spiritual prayer language among his tools for building with prayer. Many times, the Holy Spirit fills us with fervency or with groanings for some prayer objective that God has on his heart.

QUESTIONS FOR REFLECTION, DIALOGUE, AND JOURNALING

1. How do you honestly feel about praying in tongues and travailing prayer? Do your feelings about these forms of prayer come from specific experiences you have had (either in your own prayer, or from other people)? What does God want you to do with those past experiences?
2. Have you ever had an experience of prayer clearly guided by the Holy Spirit? How can you attune yourself to the Holy Spirit to have such experiences more frequently? Do you ask the Holy Spirit to guide you in prayer and believe that he can do so?

Part Three

HOW TO GAIN GOD'S VISION AND BRING IT TO BIRTH

Chapter Seven

THE POWER OF VISION

In a famous Norman Rockwell painting crowds of Americans are pictured passing to and fro in front of a great cathedral. They are all looking at the ground with sour expressions on their faces, intent on getting where they are going. The priest of the cathedral stands a dozen steps higher, looking down on them and wondering which of them might take just one moment to look up to God. But no one does. They just keep walking the sidewalks in front of the cathedral, traipsing one direction in the morning and back again at night. It is as though their feet are held by iron grips on a two-way treadmill that will take them back and forth in front of this cathedral for the rest of their lives.

The Holy Spirit's work is to enable us to look up from the sidewalk, to see the big picture of what God is doing and how we can help. The Holy Spirit's passion is to lead us into the marvelous discovery of the potentials of our new birth in Christ: "For we are God's workmanship, created in Christ Jesus to do good works, which God prepared in advance for us to do" (Ephesians 2:10). Jesus has a work for us to do. The Holy Spirit conveys that to us as a vision for our lives. We believe the capacity for vision is given to every single Christian who is in touch with the Holy Spirit. This surely is the meaning of Peter's quotation of Joel:

In the last days, God says,
> "I will pour out my Spirit on all people.
Your sons and daughters will prophesy,
> your young men will see visions,
> your old men will dream dreams.
Even on my servants, both men and women,
> I will pour out my Spirit in those days,
> and they will prophesy." (Acts 2:17–18)

The gift of prophecy promised to all of God's children is primarily that of vision. Prophets were called *seers*. Today all Christians are invited to *see* what God is doing and participate with him in it. This capacity for receiving vision from God is what enables us to shape the future with God.

LETTING GOD GIVE US HIS VISION

If we want to prepare ourselves to receive God's vision for our lives, we must cross the abyss via the bridge of Jesus and begin to listen to God. In recent years Richard Foster has been calling Western Christians to learn how to do this:

> Right now people are desperate and distracted. They are trying programs. I say: "Wait, shut up, be quiet and listen to God."
> I entered a time about 12 years ago where I felt God told me to be quiet. I stopped all speaking and writing, and for 18 months I just listened. Out of that has arisen a God-given vision of great streams of life following a kind of mission.[1]

If only we could learn how to listen to God, to gain his vision and learn to cooperate with him in building his projects, we could move forward with confidence and joy. But without that vision, we may shape nothing of ultimate worth for the kingdom of God; our talents and time are wasted.

Gaining God's vision normally happens in prayer—prayer that shapes *our* future. In prayer, God comes to us and says, "Here, I have a project for you. Let's work on it together." How can we enter into that kind of prayer so that we can gain God's vision? Also, how can we keep from losing God's vision along the way so that we hang onto it until it has been birthed into reality? Then it will no longer be a vision; it will be an accomplishment.

That's what has happened to both of us. We each gained a vision for our lives and saw them birthed into reality.

DOUG GAINS A VISION

Back in the 1960s I (Doug) entered seminary. But I did not know what my life was for. I was definitely one of those people treading the sidewalk in the Norman Rockwell picture. I was spiritually hungry. I lacked vision and my life had no clear direction. I wanted to look up but did not know how. Though I had entered seminary, I did not have a personal relationship with Jesus.

My quest for purpose and direction was typical of that era. I had taken an aptitude test to determine what I should do "when I grow up." I believed in the answer of my culture: "Get an education. Then get a job that fits your aptitudes." That was the way we were taught to solve the problem of visionlessness—scientifically. Take a psychological test!

Following the aptitude test, I had gone into art education, but I had not enjoyed teaching art, so I tried seminary. I entered seminary out of an altruistic impulse, wanting to be "a man for others." Yet after graduating from seminary and entering the ministry, I still had a sense of emptiness, a lack of vision that gnawed at me. I had conceived of the Christian ministry as "one of the helping professions," not as a personal calling from God. I had been taught to serve and love the church, not Jesus. I sensed that something was wrong with this approach, but I did not know what.

God did not begin to build a vision in me until I surrendered my life to Jesus in 1972, during the second year of my ministry. All God's promises came rushing into my life, and I gained a personal relationship with God. I began to understand Ephesians 2:10—that I am created in Christ Jesus for good works, which he prepared beforehand for me to walk in. From this vital relationship with Jesus I started to receive clear vision directing my life and work. Also, when I asked Jesus to baptize me with the Holy Spirit, the Holy Spirit started giving me gifts and guidance for my ministry.

Staying Before Jesus As He Winnows Us

It took me quite a while to sort through all the options available to me for a life calling. Soon after I surrendered my life to the Lord, I began to get excited about the Bible. This was no ordinary interest or curiosity, but a consuming passion. The Holy Spirit was giving me an appreciation for the Bible I had never had even as a student of Hebrew. This was a devotion of the heart, not only of the mind. I read the Scriptures every day as though they were a love letter straight from God—I could not get enough of these writings.

81

What was God doing? I see it now: He was preparing me to be a teacher of God's Word. He was equipping me with the practical tools I would need to fulfill the vision that he was giving me as an architectural plan for my future. Part of the process of receiving vision is being given the tools to fulfill that vision. Receiving vision without receiving the tools is like a sculptor receiving inspiration for a statue but having no chisel.

The Bread Group Vision

Soon I got it into my head to try to get down on paper the foundations of the Christian life as I was discovering them for myself, so fresh and new. I withdrew to a place away from the telephone and began to write. In that place of solitude, with pen in hand, the vision of discipling others through small groups began to emerge. Like Paul on the Damascus Road, this vision defined the direction of my life calling.

The more I wrote and the more time I spent with the Lord, the more I felt that someone should try to publish a book that would help new Christians learn the basics of Christianity. It seemed to me that most Christians were not well equipped to lay the foundations of Christian faith in the lives of new believers. Compelled by the vision, I wrote a booklet called *Bread: An Introduction to the Christian Life*. God encouraged me by leading the owner of a printing business to my church at the right time, who offered to print this booklet free of charge. Encouraged by this provision, I used the five hundred copies in my work of disciple-making, and I sent some to other pastors, who used them as well.

In this way I began to build according to the architectural plan I had received from God—discipling people in small groups. The vision has birthed a number of expressions in which God has used me as a teacher. I helped to create the PRRMI *Dunamis Project*, which trains leaders to rely on the Holy Spirit for their ministries. I also wrote a new version of *Bread*, published five thousand copies (through miraculous provision again), and trained people how to lead Bread Groups throughout the United States.

I have continued to listen to God in prayer and have walked in obedience to the vision. However, I recently felt that the Bread Group vision should be abandoned. Almost all my Bread books had been used up, and the ones that remained were falling apart at the binding. Besides, the book was fifteen years old and seemed out of date.

Just then, while conducting a *Dunamis Project* at Williamsburg, Virginia, a pastor named Frank Drake, who had received my training in Bread Group leadership, read the following testimony of Hauke D. Powers in Chesapeake, Virginia (I include only parts here):

> In the fall of 1992, at a church called Willowood Presbyterian Church, a small band of young men, none of us very sure of how to relate to God, met for the first Bread Group meeting. It was a very diverse gathering: a retired Navy Chief, a carpenter, an outside machinist, a computer programmer, a psychologist, two painters, and a minister.
>
> This humble beginning in a Bread Group would change me forever. In this group, God came alive to me. He became as real as I am real in the flesh.
>
> After the Bread Group ended, nearly all the members of the group wanted to go deeper with God in the *Food Groups* book. This book took me to a level of such intimate contact with God that, to this day, I still remember the feeling of total love He gave me every time I truly opened up my heart and soul to God. How great it felt to have someone to really lean on when the road gets rough. I learned for the first time in my life that it's OK to cry—go ahead and cry! God knows just what you are feeling. Whether the tears are of joy or crushing pain, God knows.
>
> After having gone through such a wonderful experience, I felt that God wanted me to spread this type of good news somewhere outside the church. The place was a European-owned shop that produces machines that make machine parts.
>
> It was also filled with people who really needed God. *Playboy*, *Hustler*, and *Penthouse* centerfolds graced locker doors and machine tool cabinets. Alcohol was consumed in the company parking lot during lunch. Drugs were sold and used on company premises. Yes, indeed, this was gonna be challenging. But being a recovering alcoholic, I knew the benefits of living with God, rather than Budweiser, as my leader. I wanted others to know those benefits.
>
> Taking a copy of *Bread* in hand, I went to see the plant manager for approval. One look at the book, a minor warning against doing it on company time, and a handshake was all it took. God makes things easy when we do things for Him!
>
> The first company Bread Group met in the fall of 1993. One of the members was an African-American follower of Islam. By the end

of Bread Group #1, he became a Christian. There was no hard sell, no pushing, and no harassing. Just the truth of the Word. Too bad his mullah was miffed at me.

The summer of 1994 rolled around and we started Food Groups. By the spring of 1995, others in the plant wanted some of that "church stuff," as it was sometimes referred to. Through the ensuing years, God has produced four more Bread Groups and two Food Groups at the shop. Members of my first group lead newly formed Bread Groups and Food Groups. I have been blessed with a group of strong, committed Christian friends at the company. They help organize the study groups at homes, churches, and, of course, in the shop.

The porn pictures are down now at work, replaced with family pictures or calendars relating to that mechanic's hobby, like NASCAR races. Out of Bread and Food Groups came Bible study and prayer groups. I now have three a day.

God has moved my life 180 degrees—from a hard-drinking idiot to a crazy God-loving man. I've come a long way since my DUI in 1989. From losing our apartment for non-payment of rent, to buying our first house in May of 1998. From being totally uncaring about God, to being a living example of God's fantastic grace at work. Yes! This is how life ought to be. Praise God!

Of course, this was an encouragement to me. But as I came to the Lord in prayer, quite unexpectedly he began to give me a fresh vision about this disciple-making vision. It was as though he had used this testimony as a way of saying, "Don't give up on the Bread Group vision. It is my vision for you." I began to sense that I should rewrite *Bread* and call it *Fresh Bread*. Then I should pursue the vision of discipling people in small groups wherever God would lead me. The vision continues into the twenty-first century!

Most of the leadings of the Spirit of God that have shaped my future have come to me during seasons of prayer and retreat into the presence of God. I need to keep scheduling these seasons if those visions are to remain strong and fine-tuned with the fresh nuances God brings to them periodically.

Without such vision-inspiring prayer, I am afraid that my life would have been a pastiche of different visions from different people—all forcing on me their priorities and their opinions of what I should do. This is often how it is for pastors, who end up torn by a hundred different demands on them, only a few of which really come from God. If we allow this process to rule us, the pastoral ministry is too often captivated by worldly, but well-meaning, job descriptions devised by elders who themselves do not have God's vision. I can look back on my life and see how God gave me his vision, and I have spent my life working with God bringing it into reality.

BRAD'S VISION FOR RENEWAL MINISTRY

Vision may be given not only for a life calling, but also for a specific project. For example, Paul received a vision of a man from Macedonia begging him, "Come over to Macedonia and help us" (Acts 16:9). Then he set out for Macedonia.

I (Brad) discovered this form of vision while serving in Taiwan as a missionary. In 1980, after arriving in Taiwan, my wife, Laura, and I visited the Presbyterian Bible College, where we were to be assigned after language school. This visit was a devastating experience that would have sent us on the next airplane out of Taiwan—if we had been able to leave. Founded in 1952 by missionaries to train church workers, the school was so out of touch with Taiwanese society that it needed to be closed. From the buildings that were in disrepair to the dwindling number of students, the place was in an advanced state of decay.

After looking at what was supposed to be our future ministry in Taiwan, Laura and I spent two years of enforced withdrawal from ministry in language school. During this wilderness time we struggled against God and did not want to go to the Bible College. We seriously considered invitations to work in other flourishing institutions in Taiwan. But during prayer, I was drawn deeper and deeper into an encounter with Jesus Christ. Then God started to draw up for us a new vision for a school—a center for spiritual renewal, where people would be equipped in the gifts and power of the Holy Spirit to witness to Jesus Christ. To that end, we envisioned building a major conference facility on an abandoned, run-down part of the campus. After completing language school in 1982 we moved to the Bible College in Hsinchu.

Our first act of obedience after receiving the vision for the Lay Training Center was to write it down. The second was to share it with others. The third was to form a prayer group to pray for the fulfillment of the vision. Our prayer team of several faculty and students prayed faithfully for months. Amid weeds, old rusted cars, and piles of trash, we met several times a week to pray for the Center.

As we prayed, I again and again saw the vision of Presbyterians gathered in prayer, consumed with the love of Jesus Christ and empowered with the Holy Spirit to be his witnesses. This vision guided our prayer. We were often called into travailing prayer, in which the Holy Spirit prayed through us. We knew that the Lay Training Center was being formed *within us*, so that it could be shaped in reality.

Month after month we prayed, but nothing visible resulted. In fact, as we started to share the vision, we began to see how impossible the whole idea of a Lay Training Center was. We had no money and no resources. Except for the few people gathered in prayer, everyone from missionaries to top church leaders told us that our Lay Training Center vision was impossible, that the Bible College was useless to the church and needed to be closed.

The Beginning

Then I received the leading of the Holy Spirit to take Timothy Huang, my Taiwanese coworker, to Korea to look at lay training centers there. Our purpose was to observe some models and refine the vision of what God might wish to create in Taiwan.

This was our plan, but God had other ideas. From the moment we arrived in Korea, everyone we visited talked to Timothy about the need for him to open his life to the Holy Spirit. We ended up at Jesus Abbey, where Timothy was powerfully baptized with the Holy Spirit. He returned to Taiwan, filled with new power to minister in Jesus' name.

What I did not realize at the time was that, by baptizing Timothy with the Holy Spirit, God was making *us* his vision for the Lay Training Center. We were becoming living examples of what we were to produce—a Spirit-empowered community through whom God would equip Christians to witness to Jesus. Here is an important principle for receiving vision: God not only gives us the tools to fulfill the vision, but also shapes us so that we begin to embody the vision. Then we are better able to enlist others in building that vision.

When we returned from Korea, everyone saw a profound change in Timothy, and they all wanted to know what had happened there. As we started sharing our testimonies to the power of God, the vision was being birthed, even though we hardly noticed it at the time.

Stepping Out In Obedience to the Vision

One day as we were praying, we felt the Holy Spirit say, "Now is the time to start! Go, found the Lay Training Center." I argued with the Lord, reminding him that there was nothing there but some rusting cars in an overgrown parking lot. But the guidance was clear. So, though I felt rather foolish, Timothy and I went out to the abandoned parking lot that doubled as a junk pile and conducted a little ceremony, establishing the Presbyterian Lay Training Center. Principal Wang, who fully supported the vision, came with a shovel, and we each turned over a clod of dirt.

A few weeks later while in prayer, God said, "Now offer your first training conference on the work of the Holy Spirit!" "Lord," I answered in astonishment, "we don't have any facilities!" But the Lord said, "The Lay Training Center is not a building, but a movement of my Holy Spirit to equip people to be my witnesses. You can do that anywhere." So we negotiated for some rooms with a Catholic Convent across the street from the Bible College.

My next objection was, "Lord, what if nobody comes?" The Lord said, "Trust me, I'll bring those whom I choose!" So Timothy and I offered our first Holy Spirit conference to the students at the Bible College. Only four students showed up. Timothy shared with them how he had been baptized in the Holy Spirit in Korea, and I taught on the work of the Holy Spirit. After three days of teaching, they were baptized with the Holy Spirit. Those students became the core prayer ministry team for the work of the Holy Spirit at the college.

Next, Laura and I were led to take another outrageous step of faith. We offered a retreat for missionaries on the person and work of the Holy Spirit. To our astonishment—and not a little consternation—practically all the Presbyterian missionaries from around Taiwan registered for the conference. We had never done anything like this and felt insecure because we were the youngest of all the missionaries. But after sharing the teaching on the Holy Spirit, the Holy Spirit came in power, and the missionaries entered into dimensions of spiritual power that they had not known before.

To receive and fulfill a vision, we must take the risk of acting in obedience and begin! Unless we start, nothing will happen. The Holy Spirit has his own timing and process for fulfilling the vision. When the Holy Spirit says, "Now!" if we hesitate, we may miss the moment of opportunity that has been arranged by him to clothe the vision in reality.

Many a vision has been aborted because we waited until everyone agreed or the money was provided and there was no risk of failure. It is not people but God who fulfills the vision, so we must move and act on his timetable.

Our small acts of obedience were being used by the Holy Spirit to shape a new reality. In this early stage it was fragile and perceived mostly with the eyes of faith made keen by God's vision burning within us.

God Brings a Breakthrough

About a year after these small acts of obedience, Howard Chadwick, from the Presbyterian Outreach Foundation, dropped by to visit the Presbyterian Bible College. While walking around the campus observing the outward signs of decay he asked me, "What is your vision for this place? Does it have a future?" I took him to the abandoned parking lot and said, "For the last two years we have been praying for a Lay Training Center where people would be equipped by the Holy Spirit to spread the Gospel to the 95 percent of people in Taiwan who do not know Jesus." I shared with him how in faith we had already started the Lay Training Center and how we were already offering training events with good results. I handed Howard a vision statement that we had crafted in prayer.

His excitement was immediate. He said, "Yes, this vision is from the Lord! It connects with our heart for evangelism. I'll see what I can do!" He left and returned to the United States. Several weeks later we received a check in the mail for $10,000 with a note that said, "A first step toward the vision! Keep praying!" Over the months that followed we prayed urgently with renewed commitment, expecting that something tremendous was about to happen.

Several months later there came a remarkable gift of $200,000 from First Presbyterian Church in Dallas, Texas. The president of the college then traveled all over Taiwan, sharing the vision of the Lay Training Center and telling the Taiwanese that a church in America had given this huge gift. This inspired a flood of gifts from the Christians in Taiwan.

Today, as a visible testimony to the power of a God-given vision, there now stands in that old abandoned parking lot a million-dollar conference facility. More important than the building, however, are the hundreds of Taiwanese Christians who have been strengthened in their faith in Jesus Christ and filled with the Holy Spirit to empower them for Christian witness. None of this would have happened if it had not been for the vision that God gave in prayer. In this vision he let us see the reality that he wanted to create for the work of Jesus Christ. Our role was obedience and prayer.

There is a principle here that I believe applies to every Christian. Vision does not come through the church, through parents, or through well-meaning people. Vision comes through Jesus. Apart from him we are blind to the plans and projects of God. We are created *in Christ Jesus* for good works that he has prepared beforehand. Christian vision is above all a vision of Jesus Christ. While Doug and my callings are very different, for both of us the turning point in receiving vision was an encounter with Jesus.

EVEN THE GREAT SAINTS START SMALL

It is common for people to believe that God especially selected the prominent Christians of earlier generations because of their talents, spirituality, theological training, or "charismatic" personalities. We look at the great saints of old and conclude that they had been born great servants of God with extraordinary vision and destiny. They seem so great, and we seem so insignificant—and God seems so unfair!

But those great saints of old started small, and most were unknown when they began to pray that vision into reality. Consider Jonathan Goforth, for example, who became one of the greatest revivalists of the twentieth century. Beginning in 1907, everywhere he went in China he brought Holy Spirit revival. But this is how he described his beginnings:

> Upon returning to China in the fall of 1901, after having recuperated from the harrowing effects of the Boxer ordeal, I began to experience a growing dissatisfaction with the results of my work. In the early pioneer years I had buoyed myself with the assurance that a seedtime must always precede a harvest, and had, therefore, been content to persist in the apparently futile struggle. But now thirteen years had passed, and the harvest seemed, if anything, farther away than ever. I felt sure that there was something larger ahead of me, *if I only had the vision to see what it was and the faith to grasp it.* Constantly there would come back to me the words of the Master: *"Verily, verily, I say unto you, he that believeth on Me, the works that I do shall he do also; and greater works than these shall he do. . . ."* And always there would sink deep the painful realization of how little right I had to make out that what I was doing from year to year was equivalent to the "greater works."

Restless, discontented, I was led to a more intensive study of the Scriptures. Every passage that had any bearing upon the price of, or the road to, the accession of power became life and breath to me. There were a number of books on Revival in my library. These I read over repeatedly. So much did it become an obsession with me that my wife began to fear that my mind would not stand it. Of great inspiration to me were the reports of the Welsh Revival of 1904 and 1905. Plainly, Revival was not a thing of the past. Slowly the realization began to dawn upon me that I had tapped a mine of infinite possibility.[2]

Eventually Goforth found himself in Korea among people in whom God had birthed a similar vision for revival—the Methodist and Presbyterian missionaries around Pyongyang. Of them Goforth writes, "As I remember, those missionaries at Pyongyang were just ordinary, everyday people. I did not notice any outstanding figure among them. They seemed to live and work and act like other missionaries. It was in prayer that they were different."[3]

Through prayer, God had already been birthing a vision for revival in Korea. While Goforth was in Korea, God poured out revival among the Koreans, a move of the Spirit that has deeply affected Korean society to this day and birthed a vibrant Christian church in that nation.

Yet after returning to Manchuria, Goforth felt to the core his inadequacy to be a revivalist:

When I started on the long journey to Manchuria in February, 1908, I went with the conviction in my heart that I had a message from God to deliver to His people. But I had no method. I did not know how to conduct a revival. I could deliver an address and let the people pray, but that was all.[4]

This is how all vision seems to start. God uses ordinary people who have nothing more to offer God than a willing heart. When a vision is truly from God, it appears to be impossible. We become aware of our inadequacy, our human failings. But God assures us that, if we put our confidence in Jesus, he will work cooperatively with us to create something impossible, and it will become possible by his power. Jesus purposely picked ordinary people, choosing as disciples men and women of doubtful ability, so that they would not think that it was by their own strength and ingenuity that the kingdom of God was built.

With this conviction sealed in our hearts, we will look in the next few chapters at some principles for gaining and achieving God's vision for our lives.

SUMMARY

If God wants to have us helping him on a project in some sphere of influence, how can we find out what that project is? We can do this by crossing the "bridge" of Jesus and entering into dynamic prayer, which grows out of a personal relationship with God. Such prayer is true Christian prayer, and it is found only among Christians. In the midst of an intimate relationship with God, we can begin to sense his calling and his projects. God's vision is birthed in our hearts.

QUESTIONS FOR REFLECTION, DIALOGUE, AND JOURNALING

1. Was there any point in your life when you believed God gave you a vision or a calling that was uniquely suited to you? How did it happen?
2. Do you believe that you are "created in Christ Jesus to do good works, which God prepared in advance"? What evidence do you have of this?
3. If visions normally start small, is there anything that has come into your life that could be a vision from God, which you did not recognize as such at the time?

Chapter Eight

How to Receive Vision From God

How, then, are we to receive vision from God? We are looking for something that has God's life in it—something conceived by the Holy Spirit, not manufactured by human methods and good intentions.

Everything that has life begins small. If we are looking for something grandiose at the beginning, it is because we are used to human ways. When we plan and manufacture our own lives, we can make them as big or as small as we want. But God's visions, like babies, always start small—like mustard seeds or yeast. This is the way with things that have life. If we are then willing to nurture the vision with prayer, it will grow and be born outward in its proper time.

A living, breathing vision is not produced by techniques. God births it in a Christian. There are no surefire methods for gaining vision. Vision comes from God, and we have to learn to listen to God. This is a way of life that most of us find alien to our busy and noisy culture.

Separation

If we are to gain a vision from God, we must first separate ourselves from all that prevents us from gaining a vision. Surrounding us are all sorts of people who have their own plans for us, or who want to fix the world, or who "need" us to fit their need. The countless gods of this age and their instruments of vision—computers, television sets, movie theaters, and videos—also surround us. Moreover, we cannot help but see human need that clamors and lays hold of us for help and comfort—even when we have nothing to give. We can sometimes let ourselves be shaped by the need of the world rather than by God.

Remember the time when Peter sought Jesus in the desert, demanding that he come back to Capernaum to heal the sick (Mark 1:36–39)? Jesus did not comply. Instead he replied, "Let us go somewhere else—to the nearby villages—so I can preach there also. That is why I have come" (Mark 1:38). Jesus did not fall into the well-meaning trap Peter laid for him. He had gained the Father's vision by going to the wilderness for prayer, and that vision was not leading him back to Capernaum.

Many faithful Christians are trying to minister love to broken people out of Peter's well-meaning altruism rather than out of the true vision of Christ. If we are to gain God's vision, we must separate ourselves from the sound and fury of human need and from human plans and agendas. This requires a decisive act of separating ourselves from people to unite ourselves with God. He may lead us back to these people, but when he does, it will be with clear vision that will release his power for them.

François Fénelon writes of the result, from his perspective in eighteenth-century France:

> So let us scorn earthly things, to be wholly God's. I am not saying that we should leave them absolutely, because when we are already living an honest and regulated life, we only need to change our heart's depth in loving, and we shall do nearly the same thing that we were doing. For God does not reverse the conditions of his people, nor the responsibilities which he himself has given them, but we, to serve God, do what we were doing to serve and please the world and to satisfy ourselves.
>
> There would be only this difference, that instead of being devoured by our pride, by our overbearing passions, and by the malicious criticism of the world, we shall act instead with liberty, courage, and hope in God.[1]

A Rhythm of Withdrawal and Return

Evelyn Underhill, reviewing the lives of Christians who have been most active in changing the world with a God-given vision, summarized this process of separation:

It is true that in nearly every case such "great actives" have first left the world, as a necessary condition of establishing communion with that Absolute Life which reinforced their own: for a mind distracted by the many cannot apprehend the One.[2]

Arnold Toynbee confirmed this observation in a review of the lives of the greatest shapers of world history. He observed the following pattern: They withdrew from the world for a season, then returned to it on a higher plane and with a higher vision.

The withdrawal makes it possible for the personality to realize powers within him that might have remained dormant if he had not been released for the time being from his social toils and trammels. Such a withdrawal may be a voluntary action on his part or it may be forced upon him by circumstances beyond his control.[3]

During this time of withdrawal the shaper of reality encounters God. Having received vision, the next necessary phase is a return to daily life, where the work begins:

The soul of the great mystic does not come to a halt at the [mystical] ecstasy as though that were the goal of a journey. The ecstasy may indeed be called a state of repose, but it is the repose of a locomotive standing in a station under steam pressure, with its movement continuing as a stationary throbbing while it waits for the moment to make a new leap forward. . . . The great mystic has felt the truth flow into him from its source like a force in action. . . . His desire is with God's help to complete the creation of the human species. . . .[4]

This describes perfectly the role of men and women of God who, through the Holy Spirit, receive a vision. They then return and, with God's help and guidance, bring the vision to fruition.

Moses' Withdrawal and Return

Several cycles of withdrawal and return occurred in Moses' life. First, *he withdrew* from Egypt and spent forty years in the desert tending sheep. After meeting God in the burning bush, *he returned* to Egypt with the mission of setting the Hebrews free. After liberating them from bondage, *he withdrew* again to the desert of Mount Sinai to meet with God. There he received from God the vision of a people who would be to God "a kingdom of priests and a holy nation" (Exodus 19:6). After being on the mountain for forty days and nights, *he returned* to the people, where he saw the impossible challenge of building the vision God had given him: The people were worshiping idols. Moses spent the rest of his life building on the vision of a nation who would worship only the Creator and would put away all other gods. This vision, received on the mountain during a time of withdrawal, has shaped a people's destiny for over three thousand years and has helped shape the entire world.

Jesus' Withdrawal and Return

In the life of Jesus we see this pattern of withdrawal and return repeated. After being baptized with the Holy Spirit in the Jordan River, Jesus was driven into the desert. There, in the refining fire of Satan's temptations, he clarified his mission and his intention of radical obedience to the Father. He returned full of the power of the Holy Spirit to heal the sick, cast out demons, and preach the Gospel of the kingdom.

In the midst of his intensive and demanding ministry with people, Jesus often withdrew to a lonely place for prayer. "Very early in the morning, while it was still dark, Jesus got up, left the house and went off to a solitary place, where he prayed" (Mark 1:35).[5] Jesus practiced this discipline of regular withdrawal to maintain intimacy with the Father and to remain clear about his Father's wishes. After the season of withdrawal, he always returned to in-depth engagement with the world and to the hard work of shaping reality. His last and greatest withdrawal from the world was his ascent into heaven, and from that withdrawal he will also return in glory at the end of the age.

This dynamic of withdrawal and return was so vital for kingdom work that Jesus trained his disciples in it. He taught the necessity of prayer and modeled the dynamic of withdrawal and return by occasionally taking his disciples with him. He wanted them to cultivate the means of discovering God's vision for their lives.

We are called to gain vision in the same way. As we share in God's purposes and do the work of prayer that shapes the future, his Spirit will invite us or even drive us to follow Jesus in this same pattern of withdrawing into the heart of God and then returning to shape the world.

Involuntary and Voluntary Withdrawal

Sometimes withdrawal is forced on us, either by the Holy Spirit's strong compulsion or by a change of circumstances—losing our job, falling ill, or entering midlife crisis. These enforced times of withdrawal can be God's invitation to die to ourselves, to grow in intimacy with him, and to receive vision from him. Such seasons of spiritual wilderness often become turning points in our lives.[6]

Most of the time, however, the Spirit will call us to withdrawal as a voluntary spiritual discipline. This is a regular and willing entry into the desert, where we may meet God. Frankly, if we are to cultivate friendship with God and become his coworkers in building his kingdom, we must learn how to do this.

Catherine de Hueck Doherty, a Russian Christian who has lived much of her life in the West, recommends the Russian tradition of the *poustinia* as a way of withdrawing from the demands of the world for a season and then returning to the world, empowered by God's vision:

> The word "poustinia" is Russian meaning "desert." It is an ordinary word. If I was a little Russian girl, and a teacher during a geography lesson asked me to name a desert, I might say, "Saharaskaya Poustinia"—the Sahara Desert. . . .
>
> The word to the Russian means much more than a geographical place. It means a quiet, lonely place that people wish to enter, to find the God who dwells within them. . . .
>
> However, a poustinia was not necessarily completely away from the haunts of men. Some people had reserved, in their homes, a small room to which they went to pray and meditate, which some might call a poustinia.[7]

A person who makes a *poustinia* or wilderness retreat takes nothing but a Bible, a prayer journal, a loaf or two of bread, and something to wash it down with, such as tea. He or she specifically does not take a television set, radio, video player, romance novel, friends, golf bags, or anything else, because the purpose of the *poustinia* is to regain intimacy with God. These other things, the tools of an idolatrous culture, interfere with our ability to listen to God, so that we cannot gain God's vision. Thus, if we wish to gain God's vision for ourselves, we must leave these things behind.

Each of us needs to establish our own pattern for withdrawal from the world. I (Brad) try to go up into the mountains of Montreat weekly. Often I go alone, accompanied only by my dog. I take my Bible, a pen, and paper. At other times I have been accompanied by a close friend who is also making a wilderness journey.

My (Doug's) wilderness is usually a chair in my living room. There in the early morning hours I place myself in a desert place of the soul. From time to time, I have also taken a *poustinia*-type retreat for three days.

SELF-SURRENDER AND RECEPTIVENESS

Such seasons of withdrawal will be a waste of time if we are not really interested in hearing from God. Many people believe that God should help them in their ambitions and passions. "What is God for, if not to help me achieve my dreams?" they ask indignantly.

Such people are not ready for God's vision. They have not yet reached spiritual puberty. Spiritual puberty is a state of readiness to let God make us fruitful so that *his* vision—not ours—can prosper in us. It is the state of being receptive to ideas from God that may be different from our own and that will carry us beyond where our ideas have already carried us. This receptiveness implies *surrender*, a willingness to listen to whatever God may say and to try whatever God may ask of us. Not everyone is ready for this. Without this self-surrender and receptiveness, we are unlikely to gain a vision from God, even if we do retreat from the world into the desert.

For both of us, self-surrender has been a process of dying. We grew frustrated with our own all-too-human efforts to serve God, of the endless church programs, boring worship services, altruistic ministries, codependent relationships—and the unhealed wounds that drive all this human machinery. We were finally reduced to despair and helplessness and driven to God, ready for anything. We sought him like the prodigal son, deeply aware of our human weakness and unworthiness. Having despaired of our own abilities, by God's grace we discovered that God had created us in Christ Jesus for good works that he prepared beforehand. Brought to such a point of futility, we started to receive vision from God. We believe that God will take all Christians who seek vision into a similar process of self-surrender.

Those who see that they bring nothing to God on their own merits have arrived at spiritual puberty. They have grown out of the self-deception of the child and have arrived at a more accurate assessment of their potential, based on the words of Jesus: "Apart from me you can do nothing" (John 15:5). This humble attitude is what invites a vision from God. And though it is as small as a pea, a genuine God-given vision is worth more than truckloads of good intentions birthed from mere altruism.

A Willingness to Listen

The fruit of surrender is a willingness to really listen to God. Ah, but now we face another perplexity: God's unpredictable ways! Our attitude of surrender will be tested immediately, because God may speak to us about unexpected things that have nothing to do with what we want him to say. What we must be willing to do in our wilderness retreat is to start where he wants to start, not where we want to start.

Christian vision begins with a person, Jesus Christ, who cannot be predicted or controlled. He may speak about a character issue we have hidden away, a past memory that has dogged our steps, or some relationship that is out of whack. We may have escaped to a desert place for a vision to change the world, only to be confronted with our own need for healing or repentance.

This dynamic of hearing unexpected and unwelcome things from God is usually deeply personal—too personal to put in a book of this nature. But I (Brad) will risk one illustration. For the first three months of 1998 I was driven almost daily up the mountain to pray for guidance about how to ignite a movement of evangelism in the Presbyterian Church. I had been deeply humbled when another evangelism program had failed, and I had died to illusions that I could do anything at all. I was ready to listen, but God did not speak to me about evangelism. Rather, the Holy Spirit nailed me to the cross with some areas of my life that had not yet been surrendered to Jesus. I found in myself a deep fear that I would fail again, and with this fear an unwillingness to risk obedience.

As I struggled with God about all this, the Lord brought to me the recognition that deep down I had not forgiven a coworker who had hurt me badly. All it took was a mention of his name and the anger and hurt would start seething in me. I knew that until we were reconciled, I would not be able to move forward with any new vision for evangelism that God might speak to me about, for this coworker had been connected to the last one. I struggled and prayed. I fought with myself and was able finally to forgive this brother. I also was able to recognize all the mistakes that I had made in the relationship. Working through this took many nights of prayer. Finally I reached a point of peace, and I knew that the inner work was done.

A few days later, I received a surprise e-mail from this person asking forgiveness and taking responsibility for his part of what had happened. This led to a face-to-face meeting that reconciled us completely. Now I was ready to truly listen and obey the new vision for evangelism that Jesus was speaking into my heart.

True Listening Begins with the Bible

How shall we listen? The Holy Spirit may speak to us in many ways: Through words whispered in our hearts, through pictures and images that grasp our minds and fire our imaginations, or through life-transforming mystical encounters with the Triune God. Yet the starting point and the measuring stick to evaluate these ways is the Bible. God's inspired Word must be our grounding in our quest for vision.

As we surrender and start to listen, the Holy Spirit will lead us into the Bible we have brought with us to our wilderness retreat. Prayer that receives vision takes deep draughts from God's written Word. If we are to receive the blessings that God places in his Word in the vision-inspiring way he intends, we must slow down and let the Word touch our hearts. The Bible is an inexhaustible source of vision when ministered to us by the Holy Spirit. If we have cleared away those things that grieve the Spirit, we are ready to receive whatever vision God may give us.

Lectio Divina—"Divine Reading"

If the Scriptures are to have this sort of impact on us, as they have for so many generations before us, we must approach them differently than most Western Christians do. For the most part, seminarians are trained to approach them *scientifically*. We stu dy the biblical text with all the scientific tools that human intelligence has devised. We tear them apart, analyze them, explain them as mere products of ancient Near Eastern culture, archaeologize them to death—and end with a handful of ancient manuscripts that cannot possibly have any relevance to us. Such an approach is an informational approach. I suppose this is inevitable, because we live in an informational age.

This approach, however, bears no resemblance to the one that ministered to earlier generations and pumped vision and purpose into their hearts. They discovered secrets that have eluded the supposedly "higher" and "critical" scientific approach of the last hundred years. The older approach is summed up in the phrase *lectio divina*—"divine reading."[8] Here is Richard Foster's definition of that ancient approach to Scripture:

> This is a kind of reading in which the mind descends into the heart, and both are drawn into the love and goodness of God. We are doing more than reading words; we are seeking "the Word exposed in the words," to use the phrase of Karl Barth. We are endeavoring to go beyond information to formation—to being formed and molded by what we read. We are listening with the heart to the Holy within. This prayerful reading, as we might call it, transforms us and strengthens us.[9]

Traditionally *lectio divina* has been seen to have a flow or a process of growing in intimacy with Jesus Christ. Thomas Keating offers this summary: "*Lectio divina* is the most traditional way of cultivating friendship with Christ. It is a way of listening to the texts of scripture as if we were in conversation with Christ and he was suggesting the topics of conversation."[10]

This conversation with Christ through the Word directed by the Holy Spirit is often experienced in clearly defined stages. They are distinct but form part of an organic whole. The phases in the process have their classic expression in the words of Dom Marmion[11] and are given the following Latin names:

We read	(*lectio*)
under the eye of God	(*meditatio*)
until the heart is touched	(*oratio*)
and leaps to flame	(*contemplatio*)[12]

A rural Southern minister used down-home lingo to say essentially the same thing:

> I read myself full,
> I think myself clear,
> I pray myself hot,
> and I let myself go.[13]

Below is a fuller description of each phrase.

We Read (Lectio)

We ask God to speak to us by his Word. In this form of reading we put away our commentaries and our expositions by famous preachers. We now cease to ask questions of the text, such as, "What did the author mean?" Now we just let the Holy Spirit speak to us through the text. "This is a special and unique way of reading. It is a slow, reflective reading, reading with a longing to be touched, healed, and transformed by the Word. It is not at all, then, a hurried reading. It is quality reading rather than quantity."[14]

Under the Eye of God (Meditatio)

At some point in the process of reading, the Holy Spirit may lift out a verse, a word, or an image and give it a special sweetness and intensity. When this happens we cease reading forward and linger at that place of sweetness.

This is what it means to read under the eye of God. We are open to seeing the text and our life as God sees it at that particular moment in our lives. When this happens, we begin to enter the stage of meditation. This marks the transition from "*logos* word" to "*rhema* word," which is God's word spoken specifically to us.

As we linger with this word and dwell on it, we may be given an image. For instance, we may compose in our minds a particular biblical scene, such as Jesus on the cross. We may hear him speak the words, "*My God, my God, why have you forsaken me?*" Sometimes there are no images at all, just the word leaping like fire into our hearts.

Until the Heart Is Touched (Oratio)

We now begin to enter the phase when the Holy Spirit speaks to the heart. This *oratio*, or prayer of the heart, is a moving of the Holy Spirit, who melts us; and we begin to respond in awe, joy, and peace. We may respond with petitions of needs, intercessions, or just silent yearning. We may respond with a surrender and new willingness to obey.

It is often at this phase that God speaks a vision into our whole being. When he speaks, it is not just a picture or a word but the reality of the thing on God's mind that is breathed into us. The vision may be for a lifelong calling, or it may be specific guidance for the moment.

And Leaps to Flame (Contemplatio)

Here we enter into the intimate presence of God for which there are no images and no words. It is a silence that is the music of God's words and presence. It is pure, sweet communion in which we know ourselves loved and known by our Creator. In the words of St. John of the Cross,

"Contemplation is nothing else than a secret and peaceful and loving inflow of God, which, if not hampered, fires the soul in the spirit of love."[15] Or, in the words of Thomas Merton, "Contemplation is the light of God shining directly on the soul. . . . The soul of the contemplative is an instrument played by the Holy Spirit."[16]

Doug and I can point to only a few times in our lives when we have been caught up into this depth of intimacy. When it has happened, it has been an unexpected gift from God that has sealed a vision in our hearts through a fiery encounter with God himself.

To give you a glimpse of what such a prayer experience may be like, I (Brad) was surprised with such a contemplation of God while receiving the vision and call to lead our ministry into a new evangelistic endeavor, the Philip Endeavor. My seeking vision had started with meditation on Scripture, especially Acts 1:8 and Revelation 22:1–2. Soon I was caught up into a vision of Jesus, in which he spoke to my whole being, calling me to go forward with his agenda of bringing people into the river of life. But then the vision kept going and took me into the heart of God. From my spiritual journal:

> Then something incredible started to happen. Like a deeper vision within a vision, or a dream within a dream, it was moving into even deeper reality from what was already real. Jesus was saying, "Come further in! Come further up!"[17] I felt myself drawn into a deep wordless silence into depth upon depth! It went deeper and deeper. All words and all images fell away. I knew myself simply in the heart of God, loved beyond love. It was like sinking into a vast still ocean, there was an infinite peacefulness and a depth unfathomable. I knew myself simply loved, forgiven, and blessed beyond all words and all thoughts. Above me I could still feel the rushing river of the Holy Spirit upon me, but I knew I had sunk beneath the current and had entered into the depth of God's heart.

This contemplative experience seared my soul with the holiness of God and birthed in me a conviction deeper than anything I had ever experienced of Jesus Christ. I know without doubt that I am called to move forward with this evangelistic initiative. But the essence of what happened to me is not the confirmation of a program, but the reality of a person, Jesus Christ.

Write the Vision

As we conclude our wilderness retreat, we must make preparations for transition into the world. The first step in moving out of the wilderness is careful reflection on what has taken place. The best way to do this is by keeping a prayer journal in which to record such encounters with God. It is good to write the vision for several reasons:

- Writing the vision forces us to clarify to ourselves what God has actually done and said.
- When a vision is put on paper, we may carefully evaluate and discern the experience against the witness of Scripture. It thus helps to protect us from self-created delusions and deception.
- Until we have written the vision down, we will have great difficulty communicating the vision to others. Some visions from God do not need to be communicated to others (for example, a calling to pray for a particular people group around the world). But most do, and therefore the writing of the vision gets that process started.

"God Wants You to Do What!?"

A vision from God may not appear glamorous to others; but to the one who receives it, it is a great treasure. Like much fine gold, it puts joy in one's heart and a spring to one's step. Others may think that we have been assigned a prison sentence. They cannot understand why we are so excited about this thing God has given us to accomplish.

Can you imagine how Mother Teresa's friends might have reacted when she told them that her calling from God was to minister to the poorest of the poor in Calcutta's slums? Or when Francis of Assisi told his merchant father that God was leading him to rebuild a ruined sanctuary in the middle of nowhere? These visions of God were sweet to the people who received them because they were full of life for them. But at the beginning, only the one who has seen the vision can feel excited about building it.

QUESTIONS FOR REFLECTION, DIALOGUE, AND JOURNALING

1. Have you ever gone off by yourself, just to be with God? What was the result, what lessons did you learn, and would you do it any differently if you were to do it today?

2.   Do any of the ideas in this chapter strike you as new? Can you visualize yourself trying them?

3.   Does the thought of taking away the "props" of our culture appeal to you or terrify you? How would you feel about being in an empty room with just you and God present?

4.   What vision is God birthing in you? Write it down.

Chapter Nine

HOW TO BIRTH VISION IN PRAYER

We have said that to gain God's vision, we must enter into a pattern of withdrawal and return. In the withdrawal phase we enter into intimacy with God through prayer and meditation in order to know his heart. Our return into the world also involves us in prayer, but it is a different type of prayer than the listening, contemplative prayer that conceives God's vision. It is intercessory prayer—prayer that births God's vision and destroys the works of the evil one that would oppose it. For just as King Herod searched to kill the baby Jesus after he was born, so does Satan lie in wait for God's projects to be born so that he can destroy them.

Prayer is not, after all, merely a building project that we get an idea about, and then we plan how we are going to get it done. There is more to the kingdom of God than simple methods, projects, and building materials. There is something vibrant that happens, a fiery passion, a glowing love for God, and a deep conviction about a particular project, which are transmitted together from God's heart into ours. Those who are familiar with prayer recognize that there are direct parallels with the biological world. There is a conception, then a birth, and then the nurturing of a small "child" during its helpless years.

The second part of this process—intercessory prayer—is prayer that gives birth to the works of God. This type of prayer is often as active, laborious, engaging, and exhausting as a woman giving birth to a baby. We have seen people anointed for this type of dynamic prayer who literally look and sound as though they are giving birth. They cry out, they moan, they shout, they even scream as though in labor. While not all intercessors pray this violently, still, intercessory prayer is never contemplative. What was conceived in a moment of intimate communion with God must be birthed in the work of intercessory prayer mingled with our obedience. We now must make the move from withdrawal to return.

We Need Both Love and Labor

As we walk this path from withdrawal to return, let us make a few observations about these two destinations in prayer. Both prayer places are worthy places to visit frequently, and we do well to develop a rhythm between the intimacy of contemplative prayer and the burdensome labor of intercession. Just as God has designed a rhythm of intimate love and violent labor in the conception and birth of a child, so there is a rhythm between contemplative and intercessory prayer to conceive, birth, and fulfill the enterprises of God.

I (Doug) recently became burnt out in prayer, because my prayer times had become overburdened with heavy intercessory prayer needs; I was neglecting the more upbuilding times of being strengthened by sitting in Jesus' presence. Recently I have been learning to retain balance in my prayer life.

As we move from the conception of vision to the birthing and fulfillment of vision, it is important that we still go back to those love-rendezvous with Jesus and that we not neglect listening prayer. This will be important for the fine-tuning of God's vision, the maintenance of relationships, and the maturing of perspective in our intercessory battles. Yes, God gives us projects to do with him, but we should not get so involved in the projects that we forget to enjoy the relationship that is at the heart of everything. Besides, why forego the joy and invite only hard labor when God offers both?

Is the Vision Conceived Really From the Lord?

One nagging question may gnaw at us as we begin to face the challenges of the return: Is the vision burning within us really from the Lord? Or is it merely from our own imagination or even from Satan? A friend of a friend recently received a vision in which the voice of "God" was telling him that the stars were all space-ships and that they were going to come to earth on a great mission. He was to be the one these aliens would be using to spread the message. More and more people are reporting such encounters with spiritual beings claiming to be God. To those people, the experience is very real, but we believe them to be deceived.

Many Old Testament prophets offered a vision of everlasting peace for Jerusalem as opposed to Jeremiah's vision of impending judgment. These prophets may have prophesied sincerely, and they even spoke with good precedent. In 701 B.C., Sennacherib of Syria invaded Judea and besieged Jerusalem. The prophet Isaiah received a prophetic word that God would protect the city and Sennacherib would depart. That the words received by Isaiah were truly from the Lord was proved by historical events. An angel of death passed through the invading army's camp and slew 185,000 soldiers. The city was saved and, according to the prophecy, Sennacherib, upon returning home, was murdered (2 Kings 18:26–19:37).

A century later, however, Jeremiah discerned that visions similar to these were not from God.

> Then the LORD said to me, "The prophets are prophesying lies in my name. I have not sent them or appointed them or spoken to them. They are prophesying to you false visions, divinations, idolatries and the delusions of their own minds. (Jeremiah 14:14)

It is easy for us to look back and affirm that history proved that Jeremiah had the vision from the Lord and those who envisioned peace were deceived. But at the time, discerning the vision was difficult. So too it is sometimes difficult, but always necessary, to discern the source of the vision conceived in us. We have found the following characteristics in God-given visions.

A Vision From God Will Pull Us to God

While a true vision sends a person into work, it is never primarily about work, but rather about God. This preeminent focus on God, however, may yield colossal works. Oswald Chambers offered profound insight on this dimension of vision:

> A man with a vision of God is not devoted to a cause or to any particular issue; he is devoted to God Himself. You always know when a vision is of God because of the inspiration that comes with it; things come with largeness and tonic to the life because God energizes everything.[1]

Visions that come from God will draw the visionary back to God. They will inexorably draw one into deeper and deeper intimacy with the Father, Son, and Holy Spirit, because when God gives us vision he is really giving us himself, through the indwelling of the Holy Spirit.

A Vision From God Will Be Consistent With Scripture

The practical way that we affirm whether a vision is from God is to measure it against Scripture. It is in his Word, the Bible, that God has revealed his mind and intentions. Because a vision is God's words spoken to a particular person in a particular time and place, it will be unique to that setting. This may be a setting that Scripture does not speak to at all. For instance, there is no mention of China in the Bible. But God wants to bring the people of China into salvation. While the details of a vision may be unique to that time, they must be consistent with God's nature and intentions as revealed in the Bible.

A Vision From God Will Start Small But Then Grow Bigger Than We Can Manage

A vision from God will have God's heart in it. It will be God's project, starting small, like a mustard seed, but it will grow to the point that it stretches us beyond our abilities. Such a vision will be humanly impossible to fulfill without God. Oswald Chambers once again describes well this characteristic of vision: "The proof that we have the vision is that we are reaching out for more than we have grasped. It is a bad thing to be satisfied spiritually.... Our reach must exceed our grasp."[2] This means that the fulfillment of the vision will require both our abiding in Christ and our receiving the gifts and power of the Holy Spirit.

God's vision and calling will be consistent with our "sphere of activity" and the gifts given to us. But vision from God will relentlessly draw us into God's heart and drive us beyond ourselves into the role of creating that which is impossible without God's own infusion of grace and power. When we follow God's vision, it becomes an incredible adventure of stepping further and further out into faithful dependence on him. We may start by praying for our own family and job. But that is not likely where God will leave us, if we are really listening to him.

A Vision From the Lord Will Eventually Be Confirmed by Circumstances

How do we know if a vision is really from the Lord? It will begin to be borne out. There will be hints and confirmations coming from unexpected places. Finally it will actually create the reality that is contained within it. This reality will no longer be in the realm of ideas but concrete observable actualities.

Soon after I (Brad) arrived at seminary years ago, I noticed a lovely student named Laura. Actually, she accidentally poured hot coffee down my back at the school cafeteria, so I was abruptly awakened to her presence. From the moment I saw her, I was attracted to her. I resonated with her sweet, warm personality. I was uplifted by her vibrant faith. As I would be in prayer, there started to be conceived in me an outrageous vision. It was of us being in love, married, and serving Jesus together. (Surely I am not the only Christian man who has had a vision of serving Jesus with a beautiful Christian woman.)

I struggled to sort this vision out. I knew my own needs for someone to love were strong. I also knew that her physical beauty was something that excited me. The chemistry was just right; all my switches flipped on whenever I was around her. Was this vision from the Lord? Or was this just natural physical attraction with a spiritual-sounding rationale? I prayed desperately that it was truly from the Lord, but then again I forced myself to admit that it might not be. I waited for the Lord to speak to me through circumstances.

In the meantime, the vision seemed to have a life of its own and went on being birthed within me despite my efforts to squash it. Over the five months that followed, in a series of what felt like divine appointments, we kept meeting and fell passionately in love and were married. The divine confirmation of this vision was that Laura saw the same vision and agreed to it. Many Christians have had visions of this sort but did not check to see if they were confirmed by circumstances. That vision was from the Lord. It has happened, and we are now serving the Lord together in our marriage, family, and ministries, and the vision is still shaping our future.

A Vision From God Has His Timing

Another complication in the discernment of a vision is the timing of its fulfillment. Visions brought forth by God have their own inner timing that fits into the big picture of what God is doing worldwide. At conception we may have some idea that this will take a long time, but we never know whether it really is from the Lord until we get the timing right and see the vision emerge. This means that a vision may remain in us for years as something conceived but not yet born.

In 1975, while Laura and I were serving in Korea, there was conceived in me a vision of building a prayer center for world evangelization. I could see this place in the eyes of my spirit. While in Korea I wrote down the vision. I was sure it was from the Holy Spirit and expected it to come to fruition immediately. Every day I prayed a birthing prayer, and the vision became real within me. On several occasions Laura and I took bold steps in obedience, but the timing was not right and nothing happened. The vision waits its own time. Is it from the Lord? I believe so, but I cannot be positive until the timing is right and we start to see things beginning to happen.

BIRTHING MEANS LABOR AND PAIN

Be sure of this: The birthing of a vision does involve hardship and pain. Many people who want to avoid hardship and pain would like to stay on the mountain in contemplative prayer and stay there for the rest of their lives (see Mark 9:5–6). On the mountain they can get God's vision and meditate on God's love and goodness. Though this type of contemplative prayer is sweet and uplifting, little is actually created by it. The birthing of something divine into this world of ours can never be sweet, easy, and painless because the world is under the dominion of death. Our job is to birth life into that place of death.

We have seen many people come under an intercessory burden. What happens to them? They begin to weep. Suddenly for them, prayer is not an easy walk with Jesus in the garden. Something awful, yet wonderful is happening to them. They are experiencing the pain of God over a fallen world. They are entering into the alienation of people from God and the unhappiness that sin brings to both God and people. They are experiencing the struggle of God's vision being birthed first in their own spirit and then into the world. Many of God's visions are aborted at this stage because the visionary does not want to face the pain or thinks that conception is all that is needed.

This pain and these tears are not a rational idea grasped with the mind. They are birthed in the spirit and felt in the heart. They are a consuming passion of divine love. God wants to create some new act of goodness. Suddenly those having received a vision realize that there is no place for this act of goodness to be birthed. Many people don't even want this goodness and will oppose it if it comes to them. The grief of the situation suddenly dawns on the spirit of those having the vision. This is, in fact, part of the vision God gives—a picture of what the world is like *without* the new thing that he wants to birth into it.

THE PHILIP ENDEAVOR

In January 1998, there was conceived in me (Brad) a vision of a process of doing evangelism in the Presbyterian and Reformed churches. I had been spending time in prayer asking for guidance about the future ministry of PRRMI, especially how we were to do evangelism. This was the withdrawal stage that began to birth vision. The conception took place when the Holy Spirit fell on me at Montreat Church. This started in a prayer meeting in the pastor's office before the worship service. Within myself I felt the Holy Spirit giving the gift of faith. This came as a deep, peaceful, joyful knowing that God was going to act that day. I had the inarticulate awareness that somehow he was going to speak about evangelism.

At the worship service, the Stephen Ministers were to be commissioned. Our pastor explained that the Stephen Ministers were there to assist him and the elders with the pastoral care ministry of the church. After the sermon the elders gathered around the Stephen Ministers and laid hands on them. Just at that moment God spoke to me as clearly as someone speaking audibly behind me. The import of the words echoed through my whole being, though no audible words were spoken. I "felt" God say, "Yes, Stephen Ministers are good! But what I also want in my churches are Philip Ministers, who will assist the pastor and elders in Holy Spirit-empowered evangelism."

Immediately I was caught up in the glory and majesty of God. Jesus was showing me his broken heart for the lost and a way to bring them into the river of life. I left the church with the giddy feeling that I was spiritually pregnant! I even made a fool out of myself trying to tell the pastor's wife and my wife's prayer partner what I had just experienced. At this stage the vision was just an incoherent jumble of words and disconnected thoughts wrapped in intense excitement that God had just spoken. This was the conception! There followed the process of spiritual birthing through travailing prayer.

From January to the end of March 1998, I entered a time of intensive inwardly focused prayers. Each night I would be driven up the mountain to seek God for the details of the vision. I could feel the program beginning to take shape within me, not just as a set of plans but as an actual thing that I could see happening. I could see and experience the training events. I could see the materials being written and in a glimpse saw not just the outline of their contents, but saw people doing what was being taught. I saw Philip Ministers being raised up across the country and then teaching others how to do evangelism the way Philip did with the Ethiopian eunuch (see Acts 8:26–40).

Obeying the Holy Spirit, Philip went to the Jerusalem-Gaza road, where he met an Ethiopian as he was returning home after worship in Jerusalem. As he talked with the eunuch, Philip listened carefully for open doors into what God was doing in the man's life. Then he acted in obedience to the Holy Spirit's guidance and effectively witnessed to Jesus Christ. I realized that the dynamic of cooperating with the Holy Spirit continues today and that we, like Philip, are called to participate. This is the key to doing evangelism.

More than any of these program details was the awareness of the presence of Jesus Christ. He was wonderfully present, showing me his heart. On and on it went, night after night, this birthing in the realm of the Spirit through travailing prayer, tongues, and tears.

This strange work of birthing prayer went on for about three months. Then one evening when I went up the mountain to pray, I found that I could no longer pray travailing prayers, and I knew this phase was over. The creative work in the realm of the Spirit was done; the Philip Endeavor had been created! Yet there was still nothing at all to see except a new name for what God wanted us to do and a vision statement I had written on a prayer card. In the next chapter we will examine the next steps of praying a vision to fruition. But before we do, Doug will share his experience receiving an intercessor burden for Native Americans.

A Prayer Burden for Native Americans

In 1992, I (Doug) was receiving prayer for back pain. During the course of that prayer, one brother suggested that I begin praying for Native American people; he sensed some sort of curse, and he thought that I should pray for them. I had been studying these people, especially the history of the tribes of the Pacific Northwest, but this prayer request made no sense to me. It still makes no sense to me—yet when I obeyed this suggestion, I broke out weeping uncontrollably. Suddenly, God gave me a heart of prayer for native people.

After that, these tears would break out without warning from time to time. It took little to bring them on. I have known very few Native Americans, yet they became an "unreached people group" whom God assigned to me for prayer. Through the years, I would weep for them at the drop of a hat. Tragedy and sorrow have welled up in my heart at the mere mention of these people, especially those of the Pacific Northwest.

These times of weeping in prayer have been at once sweet and painful. They have been an experience of love, but of broken, scorned love. I was entering into God's heart over the pain of dishonor that we white people have inflicted on Native Americans, and this pain was birthing something new God wanted to do among native people. I was sensing that they have been treated as if they were the last people on earth. But God wanted to take the last and make them first.

What was the result of this pain and travail of soul? Was anything objectively real being birthed? I recently visited Spokane, Washington, and got acquainted with some of the very people for whom I have been praying. These circumstances were divinely arranged—I had no friends in Spokane. You cannot imagine the joy in my heart when I heard a local pastor, John Knight, report that revival had broken out among the Spokanes! Teenage boys and gang members have been turning to Jesus in large numbers through the ministry of a local church that is adjacent to the Spokane reservation. I believe that God arranged for me to know John Knight just so that I could hear this bit of information and see the result of my travailing prayers.

I believe that God is bringing into being something new among Native Americans and indigenous people worldwide. He has been raising up many people to intercede for them in the 1990s, because he has something in mind for them. Many Christians are being asked to join the Father in this intercessory project. But that can be painful, and for some it is leading to painful confession of sin and involvement in direct ministry to native peoples.

WHY PAIN?

Where does this pain in birthing God's vision come from? Is it necessary? Why can't we just move blissfully into the creation of something good and wonderful without the painful travail? Why can't the kingdom of God be a fun project, like painting a beautiful watercolor or creating a lovely garden in the backyard?

Jesus came down from the Mount of Transfiguration with Peter, James, and John. It had been a beautiful time of receiving vision—astonishing, heavenly vision. Immediately they were confronted with a demonized boy from whom the disciples were unable to cast out the demon. After that Jesus went to Jerusalem to be rejected by the chief priests and the elders and to be crucified. Jesus could not just build the kingdom after being on the mountain. The world was hostile to his presence and to the heavenly vision embodied in his life. There had to be pain.

Often a double whammy greets us when we come down from the mountain: the sin of us weak humans and demonic power that exploits it. Anything that is going to be birthed in cooperation with God is going to have to confront this double whammy. Before the birthing there will be opposition, conflict, suffering, and pain. Intercessory prayer is confrontive prayer. It sets its face against those who oppose God, and it works its way through invisible, demonic principalities and powers that are trying to bat it down.

THE BIG PICTURE

The whole world is in pain. It is "groaning in travail," as Paul observed (Romans 8:22, RSV). Jesus said of the international conflicts, wars, famines, and persecutions of this age that they are "the beginning of birth pains" (Matthew 24:8).

The remainder of the birth pains is described in the vision of the seven trumpets in the book of Revelation (Revelation 8–11). In this vision (which is really the third vision in a series of seven) the apostle John makes it clear that the suffering of this earth is actually brought on by the intercessory prayers of the saints (8:3–5). We all want world peace and harmony, but the Bible tells us that it cannot come without terrible sifting and wrenching. The pain of the Great Tribulation at the end of the age is a necessary pain, a pain that will bring to birth, at last, the new creation and the New Jerusalem. The book of Revelation is a reminder of these uncomfortable realities, and prayer is right at the heart of all that God is bringing to pass. Our prayers actually bring God's judgments, pain, and struggle, and it is all, unfortunately, necessary.

BORN, NOT MANUFACTURED

What is true in the vision of the ultimate kingdom of God also applies to all preliminary struggles and birthings. We are to pray, "Your kingdom come, your will be done on earth as it is in heaven" (Matthew 6:10). Every time this prayer is answered it will be by birth, not by any technical manufacturing process. When something is truly of God, it must be birthed, and prayer is part of the travail of that birthing.

Most Christians hope that when something is really of God, it will emerge with the greatest of ease, prosper immediately, and bring wonderful blessings everywhere. If we run into difficulties, then maybe that is a sign that the thing was not of God. But the reality is quite different. What I read recently in my *Global Prayer Digest* about the Surma people of Ethiopia seems to be far more normal: "One pastor prayed for over 20 years for the Surma people to come to Christ. Last November the Ethiopian Surma church was born with 98 people being baptized."[3] Twenty years of conceiving a vision, then birthing it in the missionary, and then finally fulfillment in the life of the people.

Prayer is like the blood that flows into the womb that nurtures the baby. Without it the fetus does not survive. Perhaps this is why Jesus encouraged us to keep on praying fervently, even when we don't see the results right away (Luke 18:1–8). He did not apparently believe the teaching that was popular twenty years ago—that we should pray for something once and then stop. Some held if we pray for that same thing a second time, it is a sign that we did not believe that God heard our prayer the first time.

Elijah apparently prayed for the resumption of rain seven times with his face between his knees before he saw the first rain cloud on the horizon (1 Kings 18:41–46). This little cloud he then saw was the beginning answer to the birthing prayer, and he knew that what was started in the womb of God would come to completion soon.

Intercessory prayer is not a cakewalk. Birthing the works of God is rarely done in a day, and it is rarely easy and quick. Once it is accomplished, there is still another sort of dynamic prayer that nurtures the vision while it is small and helpless. To this third season of prayer we will turn in the next chapter.

SUMMARY

True Christian prayer is aimed to bring about the kingdom of God. Contemplative prayer leads into intercessory prayer, as God gives us his heart for some project, person, community, or corner of the world. At this point, the call to prayer does not end but changes into intercession, a bearing up of a prayer burden over a period of time. Intercessory prayer is heavy, often filled with struggle, and it usually requires us to labor for a long time until we see God bringing to pass the thing in the vision. This can often feel like a birth to the one who interceded for it.

Questions for Reflection, Dialogue, and Journaling

1. Have you ever experienced a prayer burden or felt grief in prayer? How do you feel about the whole idea of bearing burdens in prayer or sharing God's grief?

2. Between contemplative prayer and intercessory prayer, do you spend more time in one than the other? If so, what could you do to gain balance between the two?

3. Where are you in this birthing process in visions you have received from God? What pain and struggle have you endured as you have pursued a vision?

Chapter Ten

HOW TO FULFILL VISION

Vision starts in the heart of God, is conceived in the heart of the visionary, and then is birthed in his or her soul. Then the vision must make the transition from inward certainty to outward reality. The primary way for this transition to occur is still the hard work of intercessory prayer, but the nature of the prayer changes. Now the direction is intentionally outward as one is called to pray with and for others, who will become a part of the vision's birth into the world.

Added to this birthing work of intercession God may require some steps of obedience to the leading of the Holy Spirit. Prayer and our obedience work together to fulfill the vision.

A FIRST STEP: SHARING THE VISION

There comes a point when one must take the risk of sharing with others the vision that has been birthed within one's soul. This is often the first act of obedience. There are four important reasons why one must share.

1. Other people help to test the vision, to discern whether it is really of God. Just about every time God has given me (Brad) a vision, my initial response has been, "This is crazy and impossible! Is this really from you, Lord?" As the vision starts to take shape within me during the birthing process, I have found it extremely helpful to bring a trusted Spirit-filled friend in on the process.[1] I submit the forming vision to this

person for observation and discernment. Such a person can often help sort out what is my own imagination and what is truly from the Lord. He or she may also actually become part of the vision-birthing process by getting God's Word to speak into the vision, just as Ananias did for Paul during his three days of blindness.

2. A trusted Christian friend can hold us accountable to the vision once it is formed and we begin to endure the struggles and discouragements of bringing it to fulfillment. For example, after getting the vision of how PRRMI was to work toward renewal, nothing seemed to happen. God had not started providing financially, so we were eating up our savings just to live. There were few people and almost no program. I seemed to spend my time not building anything new, but fighting battles with the past. After half a year of this I grew discouraged and was ready to quit. In despair I said to my wife, "Sweetsum, please tell me why we are here. Please tell me why we left Taiwan and have moved to Oklahoma. Please tell me what working with PRRMI is all about. I don't know any more." She looked at me in amazement and I think started to make some wisecrack, but then she realized that I had really lost my way. I had lost the vision.

She sat me down and told me again about the call I had experienced in Korea to an international ministry of renewal. She quoted to me in my own words the vision of the work of PRRMI. As she loved me, the vision returned and with it the hope and purpose for which I was doing the work. She held me accountable to the past revelations of God and helped me regain my bearings.

3. A third reason for bringing people in on the vision is prayer support. This is what Paul did. Again and again in Acts and in his letters we find Paul sharing the vision of the Gospel going to the Gentiles. He was constantly asking the churches to pray for him and his work. He asked that they pray for his protection and for the Gospel to go forth.[2] Often at this stage it is helpful to build prayer teams or triads, or even to lead whole congregations to pray for the fulfillment of the vision. We will share strategies for this in later chapters.

4. A final reason for bringing others into the vision is that they may become the practical means God uses to fulfill the vision. Most visions from God require the participation of the body of Christ for their fulfillment. This is true whether it is as personal as raising a Christian family or as vast as evangelizing China. The fulfillment of God's vision and the

creation of his future will usually be a community enterprise requiring the prayers, gifts, and participation of many people.

The apostle Paul certainly recognized this. His vision on the Damascus Road was a profoundly personal experience, but before long he made the fulfillment of the vision a community enterprise. Thus, in addition to raising up a host of intercessors, we see him traveling with a mission team and doing God's work with others who had come to share his vision.[3]

PREPARE FOR LONELINESS

To conceive and birth vision takes time. During this time, the visionary does not always see immediate results and may actually be ridiculed for the vision God has given. Visionaries must be prepared at first for loneliness. They are seeing what no one else can see. They may be met with rejection, scorn, misunderstanding, apathy, and opposition. While a few kindred spirits may from the start share the vision and join in its fulfillment, most other people will be unable to share in its fulfillment until the vision is clothed with actions. Then after the hard, risky work of birthing is done and there is something to see, they are eager to join in work and share in the blessing.

I think of a pastor I recently prayed with who has a vision of the church he serves moving more intentionally in witnessing to Jesus Christ as led by the Holy Spirit. But he is lonely because only a few others can see the vision yet.

The visionary must prepare for this loneliness and not let it turn to anger, bitterness, or judgmentalism. These contrary emotions will stymie the vision's fulfillment. Love is the best medium for communicating God's visions. If the vision is from the Holy Spirit and one perseveres despite the loneliness, then as the vision is fulfilled, one often finds that loneliness replaced by deep fellowship with those in Christ who also share the vision and join in committing their minds and hearts toward its fulfillment.

BEWARE THE VISION QUENCHERS

As you start to share the vision, be aware that you will run across vision quenchers. They come in many different forms but the result will be the same: They try to kill vision and block God's work in the world.

Eagle-Eyed Perfectionist

One kind of vision quencher is the eagle-eyed perfectionist, who criticizes first steps because they are not perfect. A vision that is struggling toward fruition is like a child learning to walk. If the child does not make those first tentative steps, she will never learn to walk.

So it is with vision. Vision must at first be clothed with reality through small acts of obedience. These require a nurturing, trusting atmosphere that allows for risk-taking and discernment. Many churches and Christian ministries have been robbed of vision because of a flock of eagle-eyed perfectionists who relentlessly criticized anything that was not perfect. Nothing can grow in this kind of atmosphere.

You will inevitably run into this type of person, especially as the vision becomes more public, but you do not have to invite them into your trust during the birthing and fulfilling process. You need people who will help you discern. But don't ask perfectionists to help you. They will block you from action because they expect little babies to walk perfectly.

Many individuals have lost a true vision from God that could have profoundly shaped their lives for God, but an overly critical person quenched it. This nearly happened to me (Brad). After two years of preparation a vision born in Korea of doing prayer mountains took a giant step toward fulfillment. We conducted our first Prayer Mountain, in which 140 people gathered for three days in Montreat, North Carolina, to pray and fast for an outpouring of the Holy Spirit on the Presbyterian Church. It was an incredible event in which we experienced the Holy Spirit's guiding us in prayer.

The wonder was that the event had happened at all. What had been conceived in my heart as a vision from God had actually been clothed with reality. Most amazing to me, a number of people had caught the vision and were committed to seeing more Prayer Mountains take place. But then as the leadership team reviewed what we could do to improve the next Prayer Mountain, a pastor handed me a four-page critique of everything he felt was wrong. This first attempt had not measured up to his standards of perfection and was deemed a failure. The new baby had taken some missteps. I was devastated. It required a great deal of prayer and the encouragement of those who had caught a glimpse of the vision before I was able to take the risk of obedience again.

Fearful Advisors

The second type of vision quencher is the worldly-wise but fearful advisor who sees clearly the human impossibilities but does not see God's possibilities. Too often visionaries in the church have been met by those placed in authority who are well experienced in the ways of the world and see with great clarity all the reasons why doing something is impossible. Wise advice must be sought and discernment is important, but it must be wisdom that is acquainted not only with the world but also with the ways of God.

If you are going to pray prayers that shape the future, get used to hearing the phrase, "That's impossible!" Or, "We have never done it that way before!" But this sort of thinking is thinking without God. You will need to find people who are wise and have no illusions of the cost, but who are people of faith filled with the Holy Spirit. They will be able to see with God's eyes and help discern his will. For them nothing is impossible if it is what God wants.

Amalekites

Another type of vision quencher is the person who, with no desire to please or know God, resists change. Such people put stumbling blocks in God's way. In the Old Testament when Moses, leading the newly liberated slaves, was marching toward the fulfillment of his vision, the Amalekites refused to let them pass through their land. Armed with weapons, these people devoted themselves to blocking the vision of the Promised Land (Exodus 17:8–16). A famous battle ensued in which the people of Israel defeated the Amalekites. The story ends with this warning: "The LORD will be at war against the Amalekites from generation to generation" (Exodus 17:16).

The opposition of the Amalekites has become symbolic of those human foes that block the fulfillment of God's purposes in every generation. Each vision conceived by the Holy Spirit will be met by a host of Amalekites. They may be well meaning, they may even be our friends and coworkers, but if they are working to subvert or block the fulfillment of God's vision, they must be resisted. These people are not necessarily evil, but their actions will result in evil.

John 3:19 says, "This is the verdict: Light has come into the world, but men loved darkness instead of light because their deeds were evil."

The tragic reality is that a vision from God, because it brings into the world the light of Jesus Christ, will be met by bitter opposition from both human and supernatural realms. The visionary must be warned that vision fulfillment will not be a quiet walk in the park, but a boisterous and risky run through a combat zone.

PRACTICAL STEPS FOR FULFILLING VISION

With these sober warnings let us proceed to some of the other practical steps for fulfilling vision.

Vision Compels Obedience; Obedience Feeds Vision

As we pray for the fulfillment of vision, we need to pray with the expectation that at some point the Lord will call us to obedience. But obedience to what? Life is full of possibilities and opportunities, but which ones are from God? God gives some opportunities as first steps in achieving a vision, but other opportunities are simply time-wasting dead ends. How do we know which is which? Most of the time, doorways into God's extraordinary work are camouflaged behind ordinary circumstances so they are not always obvious.

It is vision, in combination with the Holy Spirit, that helps us see with God's eyes so we can spot these opportunities. For example in 1991 at a Prayer Mountain I (Brad) received a powerful vision of sharing with the Holy Spirit in evangelizing China. The vision had several parts to it, among which I saw myself in a seminary teaching on the work of the Holy Spirit. In the vision I had seen the Spirit fall on the students in the classroom. I had heard the Spirit say, "Get ready, you are going to China!" When I asked "How and when?" The Spirit simply answered, "Pray! Pray until you see the fulfillment."

This vision burned in me, but as I prayed and waited for several years, nothing happened. I had no contacts, no handles at all with which to work. It was like getting the inspiration of a statue to be carved in stone, standing ready with the tools, but having no stone with which to work. In waiting for the fulfillment of vision one does not wait passively; rather, it is an active preparatory waiting. So I prayed actively and kept up with my Chinese. I shared the vision of working in China wherever I was led to. A number of Chinese friends promised to pray for the vision. My eyes were keen and my will resolved to seize any opportunity, however small, that seemed to be a step toward doing evangelism in China.

Then in 1993 I went to Taiwan on a mission trip. I know Taiwan sounds like China, but because of the relationship between Mainland China and Taiwan, I might just as well have gone to the moon. Nonetheless, this was an amazing two-week trip in which we experienced many wonderful expressions of God's grace and power. One evening after a prayer meeting, the representatives of a Christian Businessmen's Mission

Group came up to me and said how excited they were about the teaching I had been giving on the Holy Spirit. What they said next started to ring the China vision bells: "We think this needs to be given in Mainland China at the seminary. Would you be willing to go with us on the trip that we have already planned?"

The invitation was less than ideal. It promised to be an expensive trip. To avoid jeopardizing the contacts in Mainland China we were to go as tourists and stay in expensive tourist hotels. There was danger too. Having no official invitation, if caught preaching or teaching I could be deported, with doors locked to my ever going back.

As I pondered this trip of doubtful value, the Holy Spirit brought to my mind the original China vision of teaching seminary students about the Holy Spirit. I heard the Holy Spirit say, "Now! This is it!" I sensed that it was time to obey the vision. I told the men "Yes," and God miraculously provided the money, the visa, and the open doors. Six months later, I was standing in a classroom filled with seminary students eagerly asking how to be filled with the Holy Spirit so they could be empowered by God for Christian ministry.

As I answered their questions, the Holy Spirit fell on them and manifestations started to take place right in the classroom. I had already seen it in the vision several years before. God was constructing the circumstances; I was obedient to the vision. Between the two of us new possibilities were created in China for some Christian students. Prayer and the step of obedience had created those new possibilities.

The China vision still works on me and is still directing my prayers and the prayers of many others who caught the vision. It continues to create the future. This first trip opened doors, and PRRMI is now engaged in equipping Chinese leaders for church renewal and evangelism in China.

Releasing Control

Another illustration of obedience occurred in 1996. Jeanne Kraak attended the PRRMI Dunamis Project teaching event in Michigan. For her and her husband, Bill, this was a life-changing event in which they met Jesus and experienced the Holy Spirit in great freedom and power. In the midst of this, Jeanne, an accountant in a well-established firm, received a vision of how her gifts and talents could be used to advance God's kingdom by working full-time for PRRMI. The conception, birthing, and nurturing of this vision took place over an extended period of time.

Jeanne took the first step of obedience and shared the vision with me. She said, "I know this is crazy! I have a good job, my husband has an excellent job in an orthopedic medical practice, my children are happy in school, and all our family is in Michigan. The idea of moving to North Carolina to join you in this faith ministry is outrageous. But this is what I think Jesus is telling us we could do for his glory!" I was delighted, but frankly did not need anyone to help me as I already had an excellent secretary. But I started to pray about it. Over the next months we had some disastrous changes in our office, and I desperately needed help in administration. I went up the mountain and wrestled with God in prayer, begging him to raise up someone to help me.

As a wonderful temporary solution God brought Lisa Bowen to us as my executive secretary. But all the while lurking in Jeanne, and planted in my heart as well, was the outrageous vision of her and her family moving from Michigan and working in Black Mountain. When it became apparent that God was calling Lisa to move to another city to be in ministry with her husband, I went back into prayer, "God, what am I to do? I am about to lose my secretary, you called me to this work, and you know I am dyslexic. I can't spell and never know what day it is. I urgently need an administrative assistant." The vision allowed us all to see the opportunity for obedience. Jeanne had all the talents we needed for the job, so I gave her a call. "The time is right. Would you be willing to move and start work in June of 1998? That is when Lisa moves to Charlotte." Now it was Jeanne's turn to discern the leading of the Holy Spirit and to obey.

As she and her family struggled with the possibility of a life-changing move to North Carolina, the vision they had beckoned them forward into a whole new life and ministry. Yet many obstacles remained: selling their house, finding a new job for Bill, and moving the family out of the familiar. But they took the risk and said yes! It was scary and yet exhilarating because in letting go and taking this step of obedience, God's presence and provision broke into their world. To see a vision become reality requires us to release control of our circumstances. God acted, providing for their house to be sold. Bill was offered an excellent job in Asheville. The children are happy in their new school. Jeanne is now doing full-time kingdom work!

"There Is a Tide . . ."

I could give many such cases of how vision has opened eyes to see opportunities that we would otherwise have remained oblivious to. Often these opportunities have not been as clear and direct as the invitation to come to China or as obvious as Jeanne's coming to work at the PRRMI office. Still, the person with vision sees God's possibilities where ordinarily human eyes see only insurmountable obstacles or meaningless circumstances. A person driven by a vision from God is constantly and actively seeking to discern those threads of opportunity and is willing to take the risk of following them to see what God may do.

On the other hand, those who have no vision or who lack the courage to obey God's vision often prove Shakespeare's verdict:

There is a tide in the affairs of men,
Which, taken at the flood, leads on to fortune;
Omitted, all the voyage of their life
Is bound in shallows and in miseries.[4]

Jumping Off Cliffs

Vision helps us to see opportunities for obedience that already exist in our circumstances. There are other times, however, when there is no opportunity and no open doors. No one has offered to help, no one has provided money, no one is remotely saying, "Come over and help us." The vision is met by the blank wall of impossibility. It is like looking out over an abyss with no way across.

At these times, God may give the visionary the gift of faith and require that he or she take a step of obedience into thin air. As the step is taken, a miracle occurs. God creates a bridge into the fulfillment of the vision. This is often terrifying as well as exhilarating. But if the visionary does not realize that the Holy Spirit will use a step of obedience to create the opportunity when before there was none, the vision may die. To return to Shakespeare's image, obedience to the vision at the leading of the Holy Spirit actually creates the tide that may be "taken at the flood [and] lead on to fortune."

I have recently experienced this dimension of vision fulfillment in the Philip Endeavor. After this vision was conceived, it was birthed in me. I embarked on the work of intercessory prayer and asked others to join me. But nothing was happening. No one asked PRRMI to start doing evangelism. No one offered financial help and no one offered to help make the vision real. While there was plenty of need for evangelism, there were no open doors for us to implement the Philip Endeavor as we envisioned it. Between the vision and the first steps toward its actualization was a gulf of impossibility.

But as I was praying, I felt the Lord say, "I am not going to start working until you take the risk and actually begin the Philip Endeavor." This was the same type of guidance I received when told to start the Presbyterian Lay Training Center in Taiwan. Acting on this guidance I received approval from the PRRMI Board of Directors on August 2, 1998, to formally begin the Philip Endeavor. I felt extremely vulnerable. Stepping out into thin air with something conceived only in one's own soul is never easy.

The day of the meeting arrived. We had eighty PRRMI leaders from the United States and Canada. I shared the vision of the Philip Endeavor and told of the mystical encounter that I had had with Jesus Christ, confirming the call to bring people into the river of life. We then had a prayer of dedication, and I announced that the Philip Endeavor had begun. We also laid hands on Rev. Bill Dean and prayed that he would be anointed to be the future director of the evangelistic initiative.

The result was amazing. Immediately the doors of opportunity were flung wide open before us. Money started to pour in. A major capital gift of $60,000 was given. People offered to help. Pastors started to call in, wanting to know how their churches could become involved in the new evangelistic initiative we had started. God had created a bridge across the abyss of impossibility and the vision was rapidly becoming a reality.

The lesson is that vision not only helps us see opportunity, it actually creates opportunity. In this way we have the joy and adventure of creating the future with God.

SUMMARY

Normally, if a vision is truly from God, it will run into opposition, especially at the point when it is birthed into reality. The visionary must often take fearful, lonely steps if he or she is to be obedient to the vision. Continuing prayer will help the visionary to discern when criticism is justified and when it is merely opposition from those opposed to God's will. As God's vision continues to burn in the heart of the visionary, it helps him or her see the opportunities and the coworkers God is bringing in support of the vision. There are times when obedience to the vision will actually create the opportunity for its own fulfillment. Finally through prayer and obedience, the visionary will share with God in creating a new reality. Something that before existed only in the mind of God has now become an objectively real expression of the kingdom of God on this earth in our time.

QUESTIONS FOR REFLECTION, DIALOGUE, AND JOURNALING

1. Think of some vision God has given you. Which of the following options is God inviting you to try:

   • Share the vision with others.
   • Invite others to participate with you in the vision.
   • Patiently withstand opposition from vision quenchers.
   • Look for new opportunities to act on your vision.
   • Jump off the cliff and create an opportunity.
   • Seek God in the face of loneliness.

2. How can you tell when someone who criticizes your vision is on the mark—or off the wall!? Do you normally assume that critics are justified in their criticisms, or do you assume the opposite?

3. What opportunities for obedience is your vision enabling you to see?

4. Is there no opportunity to be seen? Are there no open doors? Are you being called to step out in faith and with God to create the opportunity?

Chapter Eleven

THE MOSES WORK AND THE JOSHUA WORK IN VISION FULFILLMENT

Prayer is vital for the fulfillment of vision. But so, too, is human action that works to enact the vision. The participation of God brought down by prayer is like rain falling on an unsown field; the field has to be sown and cultivated to bring forth fruit. Christians constantly err in this matter. They either emphasize works so much that they neglect prayer, or they put so much emphasis on prayer that they fail to labor for the vision. In either case, vision does not move toward fulfillment and our prayers do not shape the future.

THE AMALEKITES

We see the dynamic relationship between prayer and action in the Hebrews' battle with the vision-quenching Amalekites in Exodus 17:8–16. In this great battle are four major actors: the Amalekites, who attack the escaping Hebrews; Moses, up on the mountain praying, supported by Aaron and Hur; Joshua and his army, fighting in the valley; and God, working in intercession and in battle.

Christians have usually focused on Moses the intercessor and forgotten Joshua the warrior. We seem to think that it was Moses and God who won the battle, but that is not true. The victory required Joshua to use all the courage and military skill he and his soldiers could muster; otherwise, God would have lacked the means through which to answer the prayers of Moses.

Some will reply, "Could God not have won the battle miraculously, as when he wiped out the army of Sennacherib besieging Jerusalem?" (Isaiah 37:33–38). He certainly could have, and we will discuss miraculous answers to prayer in a later chapter. But the important thing to learn from the battle with the Amalekites is that normally God wants a balance between Moses' work of intercession and Joshua's work of engagement in the world.

This is not necessarily a balance of numbers. There were only three intercessors on the mountain, whereas there were likely thousands of soldiers doing the Joshua work. In calls to prayer there often seems to be the assumption that the more people you can get praying, the more God will answer. We believe this to be a false assumption. It is not the number of intercessors that matters, but rather, whether or not those called to the work of prayer can actually enter into the place of intercession. Moreover, the degree of unity achieved seems to matter.

James 5:16 reports that "the prayer of a righteous man is powerful and effective." The next two verses cite the example of Elijah, a man like us, who had great power as an intercessor. The balance is achieved when those called to the different roles of Moses and Joshua faithfully fulfill these different roles in obedience and God-given authority. When this balance occurs, there are great works of God, and history is shaped according to God's purposes.

In the life of the man or woman who has received vision, there will be cycles of work and prayer. The visionary must know when to pray and when to work, when to call others to the work of prayer, and when to call for action. Getting this balance right is critical to the advancement of the kingdom of God. Let us therefore look at two famous historical examples that illustrate this principle in bold relief.

Intercession for Dunkirk—Getting the Balance Right

In the spring of 1940 the Germans were sweeping across Europe. Belgium and Holland had been invaded. The situation for the British army was desperate. The German army in France had trapped 338,000 British, Belgian, and French soldiers with their backs to the sea.

In this conflict, beyond the clashing armies was a clash of opposing visions. Nazism was a vision from hell, which was arrogantly hostile to God, to truth, and to humanity, while loosely pretending to be compatible with Christianity.[1] Hitler's vision was embodied in ruthless armies, concentration camps, and the extermination of Jews. It had set out not just to conquer territory, but to annihilate all other visions of reality. The struggle was military as well as ideological and spiritual.

During the first disastrous phases of the war, Rees Howells, with a few students at the Bible College of Wales, was earnestly doing the work of intercessory prayer. Surely this lonely work of intercession was joined by a great concert of prayer offered by the soldiers on the beach, their mothers in England, and others who cried desperately to God for help. But Rees Howells seems to have gained a special place of intercession. His prayer journals are full of occasions where he sensed greater and greater authority and privileges in prayer, all gained at great personal cost. This was the Moses work.

At the exact time of the impending disaster of Dunkirk, the prayer journals of Rees Howells and his students record the following:

> On May 28, Mr. Howells again was alone with God. In the meetings, the prayer was for God to intervene at Dunkirk and save the men. As the Spirit came upon them in prayer and supplication, what one prayed at the end expressed the assurance given to all: "I feel sure something has happened."

> May 29 was the day of the evacuation of Dunkirk. Mr. Howells said, "Let us be clear in our prayer that the intercession is gained. The battle is the Holy Spirit's. See Him outside yourselves tonight; He is there on the battlefield with His drawn sword."

> May 30, 7:30 p.m. "From a worldly standpoint there is no hope of victory; but God has said it. I could not come tonight and ask Him to intervene because we have already said that He is going to intervene. Instead of bad news about our soldiers, if He is on the field of battle He can change that and make it very good news. Oh, for God to lift us up tonight! We are not to run into any panic thinking the Nazis are going to win: Germany must be delivered as well as England and France. We may have to go through far greater sufferings yet, but I am not going to doubt the final issue. We state in plainest terms: The enemy will not invade Christian England."[2]

This was the extraordinary work of intercessory prayer by the Moses team led by Rees Howells. The result was a great miracle of deliverance.

When we look back now after these years, many in Britain still recall the terror of those days. Remembering the miracle of Dunkirk, acknowledged by various leaders to be an intervention from God— the calm sea allowing the smallest boats to cross, the almost complete evacuation of English troops—and then the lead Mr. Churchill gave to the nation, how thankful we are that God had this company of hidden intercessors whose lives were on the altar day after day as they stood in the gap for the deliverance of Britain.[3]

Praise God for the intercessors, but we must not forget the army of Joshuas—the fishermen and boat owners who risked their crafts and their lives to sail across the channel to rescue the soldiers. Without them the struggles of the intercessors would have been in vain.[4] If the fishermen and boat owners had been confused and rushed to the churches for prayer, the army would likely have been destroyed and World War II may have ended differently.

Victory Over Japan

In 1943, Jimmy Doolittle led his famous bombing raid over Tokyo. The Japanese had bombed Pearl Harbor, thoroughly humiliating the United States. The U.S. Navy was decimated. But the military leadership decided to risk a daring adventure, just for the sake of boosting morale, if nothing else. They sent a squadron of planes to bomb Tokyo.

This daring venture, which was considered impossible, would catch the Japanese by surprise. Defying the impossibilities, military brass devised a way of putting B–25s on aircraft carriers and training pilots to lift them from the carrier's heaving deck. The only problem was, the B–25 could not land on a carrier, so when they had flown their mission over Tokyo, they would have to go on and hopefully land in China.

Jimmy Doolittle succeeded in this raid, and the Japanese were taken off guard by it. Unfortunately, all the bombers ran out of fuel before they reached safety, and two came down in Japanese-occupied territory, including the last of the bombers, *Bat Out of Hell*. The entire crew of five was captured by the Japanese and taken back to Japan, where they were exposed to the most gruesome of tortures for the next two years.

In June 1945, the airmen found themselves in solitary confinement in Japanese-occupied Peking. Strangely, the Japanese prison guards, who were not given to generosity or kindness, allowed the prisoners to have Bibles! Each man was in a cell with nothing but his Bible, a straw mat, and a bench to sit on. The crew clung to their Bibles as though they were the staff of life. One of this crew, Jacob DeShazer, the bombardier of *Bat Out of Hell*, began to experience an extraordinary thing. The Holy Spirit came into his cell and began to use him to intercede for his Japanese captors. This is how DeShazer, a Joshua-type warrior, entered into the Moses work:

> The poor food, lack of exercise, and almost total isolation, combined with their growing despair, led to a rapid decline in strength and health. DeShazer, ill from dysentery, counted seventy-five painful boils on his body. He became delirious and kept repeating verses he had memorized from the Bible.
>
> He was so weak he could not sit upright on the stool, yet he knew he would be punished for lying down during the day. He got on his knees, faced the cell door, and started to pray to let the guards know about the wonderful religious spirit he felt was with him. A guard banged on the door and warned him to get back on his stool, but DeShazer continued to pray. Several guards entered the cell, seemingly awed by his behavior, and they laid him gently on the straw mat. A Japanese doctor gave him some injections, and he was brought milk, eggs, good bread, and nourishing soup.
>
> One morning toward the end of that summer, DeShazer heard an inner voice commanding him to pray, without stopping, for peace. He did so, from seven o'clock that morning until two in the afternoon. Then the voice told him he did not have to pray any longer because the victory had been won. The war was over.
>
> The date was August 9, 1945, the day on which the atomic bomb was dropped on Nagasaki.[5]

It is not our intent to comment on the morality or immorality of the atomic bomb or the terrible havoc that it wrought on two Japanese cities. The point is that here, too, God raised up the Moses work, and it did not need to be a great many highly spiritual people. DeShazer, who had no reason to love the Japanese, could not stop praying for them and ended up becoming a Christian missionary to Japan. His life is an example of how the power of God overcomes the power of evil and persecution through prayer. His "sphere of activity" expanded almost overnight from the few Japanese guards of his prison cell to the entire Pacific arena. During World War II, while the Allied forces planned, strategized, and fought, DeShazer provided the badly needed Moses work. He was surely joined by a host of others known only to God who contributed to the defeat of this great evil.

Let these examples serve to guide us. Intercessory prayer is necessary work, but it is not the only work. God works through prayer by releasing his power as the Joshuas also do their appointed work. Moses and Joshua must work together.

THE MOSES AND JOSHUA WORK AT THE 1993 PRESBYTERIAN CHURCH (USA) GENERAL ASSEMBLY

Doug and I have learned this lesson again and again in our adventures of praying vision into reality. The prayer vigil at the Presbyterian Church (USA) General Assembly has been especially useful as a laboratory for learning to respect this linkage between Moses and Joshua.

Over the last twenty years we have seen a protracted battle for the heart and soul of the Presbyterian Church (USA). In 1993 there came before the General Assembly a study on human sexuality that clearly set aside biblical teaching on sexual ethics. God's intentions as revealed in Scripture were replaced by the concept of "justice love," a leftover from "situation ethics" days.

We gathered in Baltimore at the Assembly ready for battle. I was joined by a number of intercessors who came to the Assembly with a sense of urgency that this was a spiritual battle that could only be won through the work of prayer.

The Assembly was marked also by a large gathering of gay rights activists, whose goal was the passage of the report. Evangelicals gathered as well, seeking to defeat the proposal. On the floor as well as in the back rooms, church politicians battled it out, working the system with amendments and counter-amendments. Out on the streets around the convention center, the gays and their supporters held protests and rallies and displayed AIDs quilts.

Generally the intercessors focused on prayer and disengaged from the political maneuverings. The politicians were too busy doing politics to pray, but several did stop by the prayer room to ask for prayer and to thank us for this work. A number of intercessors were on the floor of the Assembly and in the committee rooms praying. Others were in the prayer room on the eighteenth floor of a hotel several blocks from the convention center. The Holy Spirit led those in the prayer room as to how to pray both directly through words of knowledge and by phone calls from those who were out on the floor of the Assembly and in committees.

Fasting and Praying

On the second day after learning that the Assembly was going badly for a number of evangelical causes, I (Brad) and several others felt led to fast. It was terrible to receive this guidance because Baltimore was famous for its seafood. I put aside my hope of enjoying the food and went on what was to be a six-day fast.

I had personally never engaged so long or intensely in the work of prayer. But it seemed that the compulsion of the Holy Spirit was upon us, and we did not want to leave the prayer room. For up to eighteen hours a day, from early morning until late at night and during several nights, all night, we labored in prayer. Much of our prayer seemed to be in the realm of vision—of seeing and praying for a biblical vision of the church. That was the positive creative birthing work! The negative work was resisting another reality that seemed to be trying to invade not only the church, but also our own souls.

Finally the day of the vote came. Only three of us were left in the prayer room: Denny Finnegan, Tom Wilcox, and myself. Everyone else had felt released to pray on the floor of the Assembly. We were praying for the commissioners to vote in a way that would give glory to Jesus Christ. We were also led to pray that the demonic strongholds that were energizing this movement to reject biblical morality would be exposed and overturned. We were given a vision of what this stronghold looked like, with names such as "deception" and "Jezebel." Denny, a Presbyterian minister with proven gifts of discernment, saw this stronghold as a castle built with blocks made from various false teachings.

As we started to take authority over this stronghold in the name of Jesus and to dismantle it piece by piece, we suddenly became aware that there was a hostile presence in the room. It grew in intensity and power. I felt a pressure in my chest as though something was trying to crush my heart. It became hard to breathe. The other two men in the room felt the presence as well. An energy field in the middle of room seemed about to congeal into visible form. We were all frightened and with greater fervor called on the name of Jesus. By this time we had gripped one another's hands and were urgently praying in tongues. Each time the Holy Spirit gave a name of an evil spirit or a false teaching we commanded it to leave the church and to be replaced by some aspect of biblically revealed truth. As we battled like this, we were aware, on the edges of consciousness, that a battle was taking place in the heavenlies.

As we persisted in prayer, the hostile presence in the room suddenly left. In a vision Denny saw the castle suddenly implode and collapse. We knew that in the realm of the spirit Jesus Christ had defeated the high-level spirits and won the victory, at least for that particular battle. We started to celebrate and give thanks. About ten minutes later, calls started to come in from those who were on the floor of the General Assembly with the good news that after an intense and emotional debate, the sexuality report had been rejected. A battle had been won. We rejoiced that the vision of a denomination alive in Jesus, rooted in the Word of God and empowered by the Holy Spirit, had taken some decisive steps forward. But the war was far from over.

Teamwork

For a number of months I was convinced that our work of prayer had brought the victory and was tempted to pride. While I had learned a lot about the principles of prayer that shapes the future, my view of the work of prayer was still too simplistic. God's work was richer and more complex than I had imagined.

This realization came home to me while having supper with Rev. Denn Denning of San Mateo, California. At the General Assembly I had spent the entire time in the prayer room and had not met any of the other people involved in the battle and had not even known that Denn was at the Assembly. That evening he told me that he had been responsible for coordinating Presbyterians for Renewal's efforts at the Assembly to defeat the sexuality report.[6] Denn shared with me a blow by blow account of the battle they had fought on the floor and in the committees. In turn, I told him of our experiences in the prayer room. Amazed, we both stopped talking, realizing that God had coordinated the work of prayer and the political work on the floor of the Assembly. We did not even know of one another's existence, so the Holy Spirit must have orchestrated it. By his design the Moses work and the Joshua work had been in balance, and God acted to bring the church back from apostasy.

In more recent years, we have tried to coordinate these two aspects of the work more closely, and we have seen more progress in reclaiming our denomination for basic biblical ethics.

OTHER BIBLICAL MODELS

The two offices are called to work together—or so the Bible shows us in most cases. As we move through the Old Testament, we can see how God raised up king and priest to function in harmony with each other: Nehemiah and Ezra during postexilic times; Joshua the high priest and the governor Zerubbabel during the rebuilding of Solomon's temple.

The latter two are pictured prophetically as two olive trees (see Zechariah 4). We believe this to be a vision of how the two offices work together to build the church, the spiritual temple of God. The apostle John in the book of Revelation picks up the symbol. In the last days, God will pour out his Spirit with great power through "two witnesses" (Revelation 11:1–6). These two witnesses are not likely to be two individuals but two offices—that of the priest and the king. The church is a "royal priesthood" (1 Peter 2:9). We are called to be "a kingdom and priests to serve our God" (Revelation 5:10).[7]

John is showing us the witness of the church in the end times, during the period of the Great Tribulation. This witness is entirely dependent on the power of the Holy Spirit in signs and wonders—"'Not by might nor by power, but by my Spirit,' says the LORD Almighty" (Zechariah 4:6). This power, however, works through two witnesses, not one—the kingly and the priestly office, combined in the church.

COMBINING THE JOSHUA AND MOSES WORK

Sometimes God calls the intercessor out of the prayer room to become a Joshua. For example, if we pray for a "hidden people" to come to Christ, we may need to pack our bags, because God may require us to put feet to our prayers. If a vision burns in you, pray down God's power and provision for its fulfillment, but know that you may be needed to get up off your knees and get your hands dirty in the work of the Lord.

Martin Luther, whom we have already held up as a great intercessor, prayed in the Reformation. He saw prayer as the "almighty queen of human destiny." His daily hours of prayer were the Moses work. But he also provided his own tireless labor of preaching, teaching, and writing as a practical embodiment of the vision grasped in prayer. His written works in English constitute fifty-six volumes.[8] This is but a fraction of his colossal

Joshua work. As Luther did both the Joshua and Moses work, God birthed the new reality of the Protestant Reformation.

JOSHUA NEEDS MOSES—MOSES NEEDS JOSHUA

Sometimes the visionary recognizes that his or her gifts and calling are primarily to one side or the other. When this is the case, the visionary must discern whom God is calling to do the other work. As we share the vision, we can intentionally look for people to do the part of this work we are not gifted for.

Richard White, our pastor at Montreat Presbyterian Church, recognizes that on Sundays, with the heavy demands on him for preaching and teaching, he cannot do the Moses work of prayer. He is too busy being a Joshua. But the vision of our church growing in Jesus Christ will not happen without the work of prayer. So he has gathered teams of intercessors who pray during the worship services and the Sunday school hour. Since Richard has been intentional about having both the Moses work and the Joshua work taking place on Sunday, God has been wonderfully blessing the worship services with his presence. Richard's preaching has been greatly empowered by the Holy Spirit, and the whole congregation has taken exciting steps toward the fulfillment of their God-given vision.

The apostle Paul, in one of his testimonies before the Roman authorities, said, "So then, King Agrippa, I was not disobedient to the vision from heaven. First to those in Damascus, then to those in Jerusalem and in all Judea, and to the Gentiles also, I preached that they should repent and turn to God and prove their repentance by their deeds" (Acts 26:19–20). Through Paul's prayers and obedience the vision from heaven was fulfilled. Paul was both Moses and Joshua—and was constantly inviting others to join him in those two roles.

So may it be when each of us comes to the end of our time on earth. May we be able to say, "I was not disobedient to the vision from heaven"!

In the next chapter we explore more fully God's role in answering prayer and fulfilling vision.

SUMMARY

While some people may be gifted in the work of prayer and others in political and practical involvement, God normally requires both types of people to be involved in the work of his kingdom. Sometimes a visionary is required to be involved both as a Joshua and as a Moses. More often, the two must learn to work together.

QUESTIONS FOR REFLECTION, DIALOGUE, AND JOURNALING

1. Where in your own experience or study of history have you found evidence that supports our observation that God needs both a Joshua and a Moses to accomplish his plans?
2. As you seek to fulfill your personal vision, do your gifts and personality suit you more for the Joshua role or the Moses role? Or to both roles? If it is to only one of these, whom is God calling to fulfill the other role?
3. Spend some time with God on the mountain and ask him for guidance for a long-term strategy for fulfilling the vision that has been birthed within you. Make sure that it includes both the prayer and action components that God likes to work with.

Chapter Twelve

How God Answers Prayer

How does God take images, words, and thoughts expressed in fervent prayer and transform them into facts and deeds? This is a mystery open to observation but often hidden from analysis. Based on Scripture and our own experience, God has many means at his disposal to convert prayer into a freshly shaped future.

MANIPULATING NATURAL FORCES

One of these ways is by manipulating natural forces. The Creator is sovereign over the processes of nature and can work through nature as he pleases.

On the other hand, Westerners have increasingly, through the centuries, developed a worldview that removes God from his creation, as though he would not or could not control nature—as though nature were running on its own course. Occasional acts of God that violate the laws of nature have been called "miracles." This understanding of miracles comes largely from a Newtonian universe that operates like a well-tuned machine. According to this model, while God may have built the machine and set it in motion, he no longer has any active involvement in it. This deistic vision of reality leaves no place for prayer and for God to work in history except through interventions that defy natural law. Our scientific worldview has ruled such interventions either rare or impossible.

This worldview, however, is not at all consistent with Scripture. Whatever our understanding of the universe, the God of the Bible can make the sun stand still if he chooses. He can stop the rain, allow Peter to walk on water, speak to people, heal the sick, or raise a dead person to life.[1]

Old Testament Lessons for Pagans

In the Old Testament, God wanted to demonstrate his power in contrast to the forces of nature and the powers of demons that pagan peoples had learned to trust. He encouraged the Israelites to pray so that his power could be demonstrated among pagans, who worshiped at the altars of demons. For example, as Joshua fought the Canaanites, God made the sun stand still for about a day (Joshua 10:9–14). The last verse echoes the eyewitness's wonder at this event: "There has never been a day like it before or since, a day when the LORD listened to a man. Surely the LORD was fighting for Israel!"

This event was not just a violation of natural law. It was a sign from God to demonstrate two lessons: God answers prayer, and God is sovereign over nature. The latter lesson was especially important, for the pagans worshiped the sun, moon, and stars. Beyond the human battles were battles with high-level ruling evil spirits that the Bible has called *archons*, who encouraged people to deify nature. These beings impersonated parts of nature and used nature as a smoke screen to cover up the God who made all things.

When God parted the Red Sea, sent down fire from heaven, sent the rain at the prayers of Elijah, bombed hostile armies with hail, and stopped the sun for a day, he was answering prayers for deliverance. He was also proving to friend and foe alike that he was truly God. By stopping the movement of the sun, he demonstrated that he is Lord of heaven and earth—a radically new concept in history.

Those who cannot accept this feature of God's sovereignty will, of course, have difficulty with these demonstrations of power. Many have doubted and openly challenged the veracity of these accounts. However, the Bible tells us that in the last days, there will continue to be such demonstrations of power, and that Satan himself will get into the act (Revelation 11:6; 13:13) with counterfeit signs and wonders.

The New Testament

The New Testament also testifies to God's power over nature. In Luke 8, Jesus was asleep in a boat when a storm arose.

The disciples went and woke him, saying, "Master, Master, we're going to drown!"

He got up and rebuked the wind and the raging waters; the storm subsided, and all was calm. "Where is your faith?" he asked his disciples.

In fear and amazement they asked one another, "Who is this? He commands even the winds and the water, and they obey him." (Luke 8:24–25)

Jesus answered the desperate prayer for help, removed the threat, and demonstrated his lordship over nature.

The most common way Jesus demonstrated his lordship over nature was through healing and raising the dead. But does Jesus still answer prayer and fulfill vision by manipulating nature?

A Personal Experience

I (Brad) have seen God's sovereign intervention in nature in my own body. When I returned to the United States from Taiwan to become Executive Director of PRRMI, God spoke a clear vision and birthed it in my heart. No sooner had the vision been given than two obstacles presented themselves.

The first was my pride. After the success I had experienced in building the Presbyterian Lay Training Center in Taiwan, I arrogantly assumed that I knew how to succeed with the work of renewal in the United States.

The second was my back: I had a herniated disk. The pain was excruciating and debilitating. In this condition (both my pride and my back), there was no way I could move forward to fulfill the vision. I was reduced to lying helplessly on the floor for a week as I awaited surgery. Being helpless broke my pride. At the culmination of my eight-day enforced prayer retreat on the floor, I cried out to God, "Father, you have birthed in me this new vision for PRRMI. There are phone calls to make, people to visit, and work to do. But here I am, lying helpless on the floor. How am I supposed to do your work?"

The Lord answered, "Learn this well: You cannot do my work in your own strength!" With this word, my pride from previous successes was swept away. I realized that I could do nothing apart from Jesus Christ. There on the floor I once again surrendered my life to him and committed myself to following him, whether I was lying in pain on the floor, reduced to sitting in a wheelchair, or walking freely on my own two legs.

God's next intervention came several days later. As I was lying on the floor praying complaining prayers, suddenly I felt heat and electricity moving through my back. I actually felt bones being moved by a power that was beyond me. In a moment, the Holy Spirit restored my back. I got up—and there was no pain! When I went in for my scheduled appointment to prepare for surgery, the doctor was astonished. God had intervened in nature to restore my back so I could get on with the work he had called me to.

We would call this type of event "miraculous" or "supernatural." But on other occasions, God's work in nature is less "miraculous"—though just as much an answer to prayer. We suspect, for example, that at the battle of Dunkirk, the calm seas, while a perfectly natural phenomenon, were supernatural in their timing. They happened at just the right time to allow the smallest crafts to cross the English Channel. God's answers to prayer do not have to be miraculous to be "proven" to a believer. It is only unbelievers who need "proofs" that go beyond the so-called "natural order of things." And, as we pointed out in *The Collapse of the Brass Heaven*, even dramatic miracles are greeted by an unbelieving world with skepticism.

THROUGH ANGELS

Another way God answers prayer is through the agency of angels: "Are not all angels ministering spirits sent to serve those who will inherit salvation?" (Hebrews 1:14). There are many instances of angelic work in Scripture. One that shows the role of angels in answering prayer is the account of Peter's being released from prison in Acts 12:1–17.

Peter and the rest of the disciples were busy being faithful to the vision they had received in Jesus. As they were preaching the Gospel, they were arrested and thrown into prison. Deliverance from prison could not be automatically assumed. Stephen had been stoned and James had already been killed with the sword. King Herod, intent on destroying the church, had arrested Peter and other Christian leaders. With the government and religious authorities making moves against them, the prospects for the early church looked dim. Still, the church was in earnest prayer for Peter.

Suddenly an angel of the Lord appeared and woke Peter up. Peter followed him out of the prison, but he thought he was dreaming the whole thing! When they had walked the length of one street, suddenly the angel left him.

In the history of the advancement of the Gospel there are many similar accounts of how God removed obstacles, provided protection, and answered prayer through the agency of angels.

A Personal Encounter With an Angel

I (Brad) have personally had a number of experiences with angels that have convinced me of the reality of these gracious servants of God. One visitation took place while Laura and I were serving as missionaries in Korea on our first Christmas away from our families. We were in our little apartment on a bitter, cold New Year's Eve. We were so cold that we had built a tent out of blankets around our little coal stove. I was busy stuffing rice paper in the cracks in the windows, and Laura was washing socks. We felt utterly alone and empty and wondered why we were there, thousands of miles away from home. I was praying one of those largely unconscious prayers, "Lord, are we in the right place?"

Then Laura stepped out of the tent to get some ice from the kitchen to melt on the stove for hot chocolate. Our water pipes were frozen solid. When she came back with the ice, she had a strange look on her face.

"What's wrong?" I asked.

"Well, I don't know how to say this, but there is an angel out there in the kitchen."

"Did you see him"?

"No! I just felt him—but something really is out there."

I went outside the tent into the kitchen. I could not see anything, but there was truly a presence there. I felt him. I came back and said, "Yes, there really is an angel there. What do we do? Should we pray, sing hymns, or what?"

Laura replied, "Well, he came while we were just washing socks, so perhaps we should just continue." As we did these simple tasks, we felt a strange warmth and grace filling our frozen little apartment and us. We both knew that the angel had been sent to minister to us and to let us know that we were not alone out there on the mission field. Our souls were ministered to at a level deeper than words and thoughts. After about an hour the angel left.

God's Use of Angels

Why does God use angels to answer prayer? Perhaps it is because angels interface with the material realm in a way that is especially needed. In accounts of angels, they often do something that requires involvement with the natural order, but do not require circumventing natural law. In the case of Peter, this meant opening doors, loosing leg irons, and leading him in a dazed state out the prison doors into the street. For us in Korea, what we needed was the quiet, sweet presence of an angelic being conveying to us God's love and encouragement. An encounter with the full, blazing holiness of God would have blown us away. God knows what we need and chooses his messengers carefully.

Through Outpourings of the Holy Spirit

Another way God answers prayer is through the release of the Holy Spirit. This is how the disciples prayed as they started to run up against obstacles in the proclamation of the Gospel:

"Now, Lord, consider their threats and enable your servants to speak your word with great boldness. Stretch out your hand to heal and perform miraculous signs and wonders through the name of your holy servant Jesus."

After they prayed, the place where they were meeting was shaken. And they were all filled with the Holy Spirit and spoke the word of God boldly. (Acts 4:29–31)

"Lord, stretch out your hand ..." is the invitation for God to work through the Holy Spirit upon us and in the world. There is no greater way for the kingdom of God to be advanced than for God's Spirit to come and move in our midst. These visitations of God bring awakening to the reality of Jesus Christ. They also equip Christians with God's gifts and power for ministry. The history of revivals is the history of God's answering the prayers of his people by sending the Holy Spirit. We will explore this dynamic in a later chapter.

This prayer for the outpouring of the Holy Spirit may be the cry of the lone visionary who has faced the impossibility of seeing dreams come to fruition. It may be the cry of a congregation faced with a crisis. "'Not by might nor by power, but by my Spirit,' says the LORD Almighty" (Zechariah 4:6). I pray this prayer for the Holy Spirit before big evangelistic occasions as well as for the small daily opportunities for witness.

A Spiritual Awakening in Hong Kong

In January 1998, at a teaching mission in Hong Kong, 350 young church leaders had gathered. Six months earlier Hong Kong had just returned to China. Many of the older pastors had left for Canada and the United States, leaving these young men and women in leadership. They had gathered for teaching on the Holy Spirit because they knew they were facing an uncertain future under Communist rule. As one pastor put it, "It is a new world, and we cannot depend on the advantages we had under the British. We cannot depend on human ways of doing evangelism. We must learn God's ways."

As we prayed together, again and again the Lord spoke a vision to these church leaders. It was an audacious vision of Hong Kong being a launching pad for the Gospel into the rest of China. God was saying that Hong Kong would be the leaven to transform the whole lifeless structure of Communist China with the Gospel. With this vision came the recognition that, with the people flooding into Hong Kong in search of jobs, this vision had to start its fulfillment right then and there through evangelism. Hong Kong had now been grafted into China!

As these visions were being voiced, everyone felt helpless to achieve them. So the whole group prayed the apostles' prayer of Acts 4: "Now, Lord, consider their threats and enable your servants to speak your word with great boldness. Stretch out your hand to heal and perform miraculous signs and wonders through the name of your holy servant Jesus." At the conclusion of this five-day mission, God answered this prayer with an outpouring of the Holy Spirit. It happened as we surrendered ourselves to Jesus Christ and committed ourselves to following him into the future. Here are the words I wrote in my prayer journal:

> As we waited, rich, full silence filled the room. There was a deep peace and stillness that was not emptiness but the awesome presence of God. Jesus was there in the room with us. Then, one by one, people started to get up and go to the back of the worship hall (as I had just instructed them to do, if they wanted to receive a baptism with the Holy Spirit). As they did, the Holy Spirit fell upon them. Some fell on the floor, some received holy laughter, some wept and some started to manifest gifts of the Holy Spirit. It was all wonderful! From the front I sat and watched and gave thanks that God had once again answered the prayers of His people for empowerment and gifts for witnessing to Jesus Christ by pouring out the Holy Spirit. The prayer ministry lasted until late into the night.

The fruit of that outpouring of the Spirit was soon evident. The very next evening we conducted an evangelistic meeting in a large school auditorium. We were astonished that though there had been no advertising, about a thousand people came from every part of Hong Kong. That night the Gospel of Jesus was shared, there was wonderful ministry, and many people accepted Jesus Christ. The vision was starting to be fulfilled! God was crafting a new future through the prayers and obedience of his people. The active agent making this happen was the Holy Spirit, who had been poured out the night before.

I have seen God pour out his Spirit like this again and again in answer to prayer. The long-term results are truly significant. People's lives change. They grow in greater intimacy with Jesus. They move into expressing the gifts of the Holy Spirit for power ministry and evangelism. Such moves of the Holy Spirit advance the kingdom of God and shape history.

By Calling People Into Obedience

In these three ways—manipulating nature, using angels, and sending the Holy Spirit—God may work to answer our prayers. We now turn to a fourth way God answers prayer—by far the most common in our experience. He uses *us* to answer prayer. It is the most common because, as noted above, God loves to involve us in his projects.

In Acts 10 we read about Cornelius, a man of prayer. God wanted to do for Cornelius what at that time was viewed as impossible: including a Gentile in the promises of Abraham. Jesus Christ was to become the way of life not just for Jews but for all peoples. To fulfill this audacious vision, God used the prayers of a God-fearing Roman centurion. He then employed both human and supernatural means to answer Cornelius's prayers.

He began by sending an angel to appear to Cornelius and announce that God had heard his prayers. The angel then instructed Cornelius to send for Peter.

At the same time, God was preparing Peter to be the answer to the prayers of Cornelius. This was no small thing, for Peter, being a devout Jew, had never accepted the hospitality of a Gentile. God had to work a profound change in Peter's worldview to get him ready to participate in God's answer. God did this through a vision telling him that he should not call unclean what God has made clean.

The Holy Spirit then commanded Peter to go with the men from Cornelius. As Peter obeyed, he found himself breaking past the cultural and religious barriers to take Christianity into the Gentile world. This story shows how God uses angels and miracles—but he also uses people to answer prayer and fulfill vision.

Personal Example of Being the "Yes" to Another Man's Prayer for Guidance

Once I had just returned home from a two-week mission trip. Exhausted, I was ready to spend time with my family. Laura had sent me off to pick up something to cook for supper and to return a couple of videos. On the way to the video store, I saw a well-dressed African-American man walking down Highway 70, carrying a large duffel bag. He was not hitchhiking, just walking along. No sooner had I seen him than there burst into my mind the words, "Stop now and offer him a ride."

I said, "Lord, please not now! I really must be home with my family. I have been so faithful serving you in Brazil. Please give me a break. Besides, I don't make it a habit to pick up people I don't know. It could be dangerous!"

The Lord said, "I know him! Just stop and offer him a ride." This conversation took place as I was driving past by him.

I said, "Lord, if he is still there when I return from the video store, I'll see about picking him up." I deposited the videos and returned on Highway 70. There he was, walking along the highway. He looked quite happy and was not hitchhiking, so I just drove right on by, yet the word persisted, "Pick him up!" As I pulled into my driveway, the unsettled feeling was so strong that I said, "Okay, Lord, what do you want me to do?" To be honest, part of my hesitation in obedience was that I am white and he was black. Amid my own thoughts came another thought from the Holy Spirit: "Go back and pick up that *man*, offer him a ride to wherever he wants to go, and now also offer him supper."

Miserably, I said, "Okay, Lord, I will obey you." I turned around and went back out to the highway, secretly hoping that he would not be there. But there he was, not far from where I had seen him last. I pulled over and said, "Would you like a ride somewhere?" The young man looked surprised and said that he would like a lift to Interstate 40. He told me he was on his way to Georgia, where he lived. On the way, the Lord reminded me, "You are not finished yet! Offer him something to eat!" Just before getting to the Interstate, I turned to him and said, "You know, I was just on my way to get something for supper. Would you like something to eat?" This time he looked not only surprised but also delighted.

"I sure would!" he said. So I took him home.

But as soon as I saw Laura, she said, "We haven't seen you for two weeks! Would you please just take him out somewhere, buy him supper, and then come back?" So I took him to a local restaurant and got him a meal to go, and then drove him to the Interstate ramp. On the way I told him that I was a minister. He was intensely interested and asked how I liked being a preacher.

As he was getting out, he turned to me and said, "Sir, you will never guess what God has just done!" He then told me that he had been up in the mountains for a prayer retreat, seeking God's guidance as to whether he was to go into the Gospel ministry. "I have been struggling with a call to preach. During my prayer time I got nothing from the Lord. So finally I said, 'Lord, I will know that you are calling me if you direct a white man to give me a ride and give me something to eat.' You have just been the answer to my prayers. When I get home, I am going to give up my job and go into the ministry. Thank you for your obedience." I was overwhelmed by the realization that I had been used by God to answer another man's prayers.

About six months later, while I was driving to Savannah, Georgia, I was scanning through the local radio stations. I lingered to listen to a black Pentecostal preacher. To my amazement he was telling how God had called him into the Gospel ministry by answering his prayer through a white man in a small southern town picking him up and offering him supper.

While not as dramatic as Peter's linking up with Cornelius, my divine appointment with this African-American brother completely reshaped his future and overcame in me the sin of racial prejudice.

God's Answering Prayer Is Like Cultivating a Garden

Why is it that, no matter how God answers a prayer, the answer often seems to take a lot of time? The answer that we propose is this: The things of God have life. Whatever has life must be planted, sprout, grow, bear leaves, flower, and finally produce fruit. All this takes time. While there are some occasions when a vision comes to fruition quickly through answered prayer, most answers come as the result of a slow process, like growing a garden.

Prayer is a multifaceted reality, so we have had to use a number of different images to explore how it works. We started with a building project, then moved to the image of conception and birth; now we introduce the image of a garden, which conveys how prayer causes the works of God to sprout and grow in our various areas of activity. The building image, while helpful for understanding our responsibility in prayer, does not grasp the dynamic living nature of prayer.

Cultivating a garden is a process of acting at the right time, then waiting for the next stage in the process, and then acting again—as a gardener must do for garden plants. First the soil must be prepared, then the seeds planted. That is the human work. Then the rain and sun bring forth the mystery of life, bursting from dormancy in the seeds. God is doing his part beyond our control. But then it is our turn again. We must root out weeds and keep away pests. Finally, after many interwoven steps, we may receive a harvest. So it is with the work of prayer.

In this process, the one part we have not yet considered is how to keep away pests. There are spiritual pests who try to invade the garden of God to destroy the visions growing there. Demonic spirits roam the earth, actively opposing the visions God has given to his servants. No book on prayer and vision would be complete without considering what to do about the pests! We turn to this topic in the next chapter.

SUMMARY

God answers prayer any way he chooses. But we have seen four ways revealed in Scripture and in personal experience: through nature, through angels, through the Holy Spirit, and through us. We are not to put our confidence in angels or any created beings, but in God alone, who has given all authority to Jesus Christ (see Hebrews 1:1–14). Generally, it is best to leave up to Jesus the means he may choose to answer prayer. Models for how prayer works must be organic because dynamic prayer that shapes the future flows from the relationship between the living God and us, who are also alive in Jesus Christ.

QUESTIONS FOR REFLECTION, DIALOGUE, AND JOURNALING

1. Is the idea of miracles or angels a hard one for you to swallow? How do you explain the demonstrations of God's power in the Bible, or the presence of angels currently being witnessed in Western culture (even on TV)?

2. Do you find it easy to wait on the Lord for answers to prayer, or have you frequently become discouraged about how long it was taking and thus stopped praying? Have you ever stopped praying and then discovered much later that God had wonderfully answered a prayer?

3. In what ways have you experienced God's answers to prayer? What have you learned about the ways of God from such experiences?

4. Have you ever been the answer to someone else's prayer? What did you learn about your role in God's work from this experience?

Chapter Thirteen

HOW SATAN OPPOSES
GOD'S VISION AT EVERY STAGE

Anyone who builds something of God into this ungodly world will confront the enemy of Christ. Satan works against God's kingdom vision in three ways:

- Through our own sin
- Through other people's sin
- By the influence of rebellious demonic powers

The intercessor will have to confront all three along the way to fulfilling the vision—if, that is, the vision is truly from God.

THE BULLETIN BOARD IN HELL

My (Doug's) mentor in prayer, Dick Simmons, taught me this principle back in 1983. He used to say, "When you give your life to prayer, your name goes on a bulletin board in hell." Many of us neophytes had a hard time believing in the bulletin board in hell. If the truth were told, many of us thought that Dick was a little off. Yet what Dick said has been borne out time and again.

My (Brad's) mentor, Archer Torrey, director of Jesus Abbey in Korea, would concur with Dick. He gives the following encouragement and warning about prayer:

I think the Lord wants me to make the point that intercession is hard work, not always exciting, but desperately important and needs doing by faithful, regular intercessors. There are many jobs I would much rather be doing, but God has given me this, and all else has to take a back seat.

God let me get a glimpse into the satanic opposition we are fighting. I suddenly realized that several of these issues I have been praying about casually are coming to a head, and there is going on right now an all-out struggle with Satan. God showed it to me in terms of several very urgent issues, and the shock gave me an irregular pulse, and I went to bed and let Jane go by herself to the weekly intensive intercession meeting. I slept a few hours and am now back at exorcising Satan and defying him in the name of Jesus over these issues.

The life of intercession is dangerous. It can be dangerous to your health, and if the enemy gets wind of it, he can send his assassins after you. Live dangerously.[1]

Doug and I would just as soon skip this chapter. But the harsh reality of spiritual opposition pointed to by our mentors compels us to face this issue head-on. As we wrote in our book *The Collapse of the Brass Heaven*, the Western worldview we have grown up with has had to give way to a worldview more consistent with Scripture.

Jesus tells us of many hindrances to God's Word that prevent it from bearing fruit in us "a hundred, sixty or thirty times what was sown" (Matthew 13:8, 23). Some people hear the Word, but Satan comes like a crow along the path to snatch it away before it can take root. In our experience, these attempts to demolish a God-given vision can happen at all three stages of vision development: conception, birth, and fulfillment.

Spiritual Battles During Conception of a Vision

Here you are, in your wilderness retreat. You have surrendered your life to God so that you can begin to hear his Word and understand it. You have come away to a quiet place so that you will not be troubled by the delight in riches and the cares of the world. But Satan may try to snatch away your God-given vision before it has even been conceived within you. He may try to put static or evil pictures in your mind, hoping to muddle

God's vision. Or he may try to plant his own evil or counterfeit visions. Jesus met Satan during his time of withdrawal in the wilderness, and so will you.

One day when the Philip Endeavor was being birthed, I (Brad) received the strong and persistent guidance to go up the mountain to pray. Prayer was not a convenient thing to do, but the guidance of the Holy Spirit was persistent: "Go pray now, or you will miss the new thing I am birthing in you!" So, putting aside all the work at the office, I picked up my dog and headed up to the end of Graybeard Road, then walked along the mountain trail to the little waterfall that had become my favorite prayer place. It was peaceful and refreshing being on the mountain.

But then the battle began! I tried to quiet my spirit and focus on God. But instead, I found the memory of an old hurt welling up in me. This had been forgiven and released to the Lord a long time ago, but there it was all over again; I could feel anger rising up in me like a distracting fog. I kept lifting the person up to the Lord, blessing that individual, and calling on Jesus Christ until the anger subsided and I was able to get back on track with the work of prayer.

I read from my Bible passages relating to the Great Commission, then went into a time of praying in the Spirit, offering up praise to Jesus Christ. I started to pray for the vision of the new evangelism program. I started to see and feel the reality of people doing evangelism in the power of the Holy Spirit. Then another attack began: lust. It started with the image of a sister in Christ who was a gifted coworker, popping in my head amid the images of evangelism. There burst into my mind the thought, "Wouldn't it be wonderful to sleep with her?" This suggestion was accompanied with images and feelings that made me know it was a flaming arrow from the evil one. (A flaming arrow, as I understand Ephesians 6:16, is a temptation from Satan that resonates with and ignites an area of personal weakness and rebellion against God's will.)

I stopped praying for the vision and talked to God about what I was experiencing. I focused my thoughts on this person and affirmed that I loved her with *Christ's* love. I gave thanks for her and then asked God's forgiveness for lustful desires that, in the context of Christ's love and my marriage, were totally out of place. I then resisted Satan, telling him to get lost. Then I continued with the work of prayer. The lustful thoughts lingered a while, then faded away.

For about an hour I was caught up in a time of communion with God, during which there was birthed in me the outline of the vision statement for the Philip Endeavor. I quickly wrote it down and started back down the mountain.

Spiritual Battles During Birthing of a Vision

Once again immersed in daily life, I (Brad) discovered that the enemy had come down from the mountain with me. As I began to share the vision statement with coworkers and prayer partners, I was confronted with old patterns of self-doubt, which the enemy began to exploit. Deep within myself I felt a whisper saying, "You idiot! What did you go and waste your time praying for? This is all impossible, this so-called Philip Endeavor. None of it will ever happen. You don't have the gifts to do this. Dependence on God? What God? God is just an evolutionary adaptation to help people cope with death."

These words came like waves breaking against the beach of my peace with God. Satan was working to erode away not only my joy in the vision, but also my faith in the existence of God. This battle with doubt took me several weeks to fight through and, despite my encounters with Jesus, it still torments me sometimes.

How to Deal With Inward Assaults

How are we to deal with these inner attacks from Satan? The first way is by direct, authoritative confrontation, *rebuking Satan in the name of Jesus*. We must reject his enticements and distractions and refuse to give them ground by lingering on them. Also, we must refuse to fear our spiritual enemy or yield to threats or arguments contrary to the Gospel.

Usually, however, the difficulty does not immediately disappear. Rather, demonic interference points to weaknesses in our own character that we have to deal with. The real problem is our own sinful selves. Resisting Satan involves us not just with spiritual warfare, but also with sanctification—our process of growing in holiness and maturity of faith. We must use Satan's diversions as invitations to deal with our flaws.

Doug and I have found that the only way to effectively resist Satan is through a radical commitment to *walking in the light*.

But if we walk in the light, as he is in the light, we have fellowship with one another, and the blood of Jesus, his Son, purifies us from all sin.

If we claim to be without sin, we deceive ourselves and the truth is not in us. If we confess our sins, he is faithful and just and will forgive us our sins and purify us from all unrighteousness. (1 John 1:7–9)

To walk in the light is to become vulnerable before God and other people. As we have struggled with this challenge, we have found Leanne Payne helpful. She writes vividly about how we must learn to practice the presence of God, especially when dealing with flaming arrows and unholy thoughts:

> This listening involves, of course, coming into the presence of God and there receiving His Word and illumination as to why we feel the way we do, why we do the things we do. It involves writing down every negative, untrue, and irrational thought and attitudinal pattern as we become aware of it. For some, this is almost a full-time task at first. . . .
>
> When we write down our diseased patterns of thought, we must always listen to Him for the healing, positive, true words and patterns that are to replace the dark, negative ones! That is how we gain the mind of God and get rid of diseased patterns of thought. We first *acknowledge* we have them; then we find what they are rooted in and why we have them. Finally, we confess and get rid of them by yielding them up to God and taking in exchange the true word He is sending.[2]

In other words, when the evil one sends confusion, fear, or temptations aimed at our weaknesses, instead of letting him turn our head away from God's vision, we talk to God about what we are experiencing. We are honest and truthful with the Lord. We refuse to close him out, and we ask him for his sword and shield to deal with these flaming arrows.

This is what I tried to do when I came under attack. If I felt unforgiveness and anger, I brought them to God. If I felt lust or doubt, I brought them to God and confessed what I was experiencing. This process invites a healthy examining of our thoughts and attitudes, and I can write them in a prayer journal as I pray to God about everything.

Confessing Sin and Temptation to a Spiritual Friend

Another important component of walking in the light is confessing our struggles with others. James 5:16 says, "Therefore confess your sins to each other and pray for each other so that you may be healed." Doug and I have found that a friend who loves Jesus and the truth is an important help in overcoming Satan's assaults. At times, the two of us have taken that role in each other's lives.

The very act of confession to another person often neutralizes the attack and enables us to deal with our areas of weakness. As long as Satan can keep us isolated and afraid to share our secret struggles, he has great power over us. But brought out into the light, the weapons of temptation and deception lose their power over us. Ignatius of Loyola observed this strategy of Satan:

> In the same way, when the enemy of our human nature tempts a just soul with his wiles and seductions, he earnestly desires that they be received secretly and kept secret. But if one manifests them to a confessor, or to some other spiritual person who understands his deceits and malicious designs, the evil one is very much vexed. For he knows that he cannot succeed in his evil undertaking, once his evident deceits have been revealed.[3]

So when I left my mountain retreat, I forced myself to seek out two Christian brothers and confessed to them my battle with unforgiveness, lust, and doubt. By God's grace, Satan's assaults were pushed back and the process of birthing vision went forward.

Attacks Against One's Family

These battles, intended to distract us from conceiving and birthing vision, are not just internal and subjective. Satan can attack us through innocent people, like family, friends, and church members. I (Doug) remember an experience I had during our second General Assembly prayer vigil for our denomination, which was full of heavy birthing and travailing prayer.

My wife and I were concerned to protect our family because we sensed that the enemy might attack our teenage girls while we were in Wichita. So we asked my parents to come and stay in our home in Richmond while we were away. During the second day of the vigil, on Sunday morning, while everyone else was off to church, my mother phoned us from Richmond. My father had collapsed in church. They had interrupted the service to take him to the hospital. Tearfully, she was asking for prayer.

I saw this as a satanic attack designed to intimidate us. When the other team members returned from church, I told them what had happened. The attack immediately galvanized the prayer team and caused us to realize that we were in a serious battle for the soul of our denomination. From that time on, many team members stopped being casual about prayer and made commitments to return to the vigil annually. But it took an attack of the enemy to help us get serious and learn how to be an army.

As a result of prayer, my father was healed. He had a weak heart and had been taking medications, which had affected his blood pressure. By the end of the week, he was feeling better than he had felt in years. Somehow, his heart was strengthened so that he was able to go off the medication that was causing the problem.

I do not say that there aren't occasional casualties in spiritual warfare. But the casualties are all under God's providence and overarching care. Let us not imagine God and Satan as rival kings on a chessboard. While Satan's attacks are real, he does not have the same status and power as Jesus, the Anointed One. Jesus uses Satan for purposes of which Satan himself is unaware. If we cling to the vision of Jesus, he will keep us moving through the attacks of the evil one, and we will not be harmed.

SPIRITUAL BATTLES AFTER A VISION BEGINS TO MOVE INTO FULFILLMENT

As a vision grows through the conceiving and birthing stages into fulfillment, the spiritual warfare takes new and, in some ways, more vicious forms. As the vision moves out of one's own heart to include others in its fulfillment, the battle moves against the growing community in whom God is birthing the vision. As the scope of the vision enlarges, so does the battlefield.

Tom White, an experienced teacher on spiritual warfare, observes the following types of attacks that Satan may direct against individuals, communities, or organizations engaged in kingdom work:

- Personal weaknesses
- Curses, hexes, and spells by those involved in the occult
- Physical illness
- Diminished devotional life
- Division or breakdown in relationships
- Resistance to important ministry opportunities
- Depression and discouragement
- Barrages of fear
- Confused thoughts and battles with doubt
- Opposition from persons amenable to demonic control[4]

In the book of Acts one can see these attacks coming against the leaders of the early church. Satan worked through governing authorities to imprison and kill church leaders (Acts 12:1–3). He also moved into the churches to create deception (5:1–12).

At this stage of the process, spiritual battles often masquerade as human conflict. In other words, the enemy uses people to destroy a God-given vision, just as he used Herod to kill the apostle James. As the apostle Paul clearly warns, "our struggle is not against flesh and blood, but against the rulers, against the authorities, against the powers of this dark world and against the spiritual forces of evil in the heavenly realms" (Ephesians 6:12).

Encounters with Evil Spirits in Brazil

These powers may have developed strongholds. (Strongholds are ideologies and social structures that are opposed to God's revealed truth that may be inhabited by evil spirits who give them energy.) These things do happen in churches and cultures. They will try to block, divert, and destroy God's plans, because they are literally fighting for their lives. While most of the time these powers express their opposition through people, sometimes they attack the visionary directly. These open attacks from high-level demons usually do not happen in the ordinary course of a Christian's life. They become more probable as one moves forward to fulfill a vision that is strategic to advancing God's kingdom.

At the Healing Dunamis Project Conference near Brasilia in May 1998, God's vision began to unfold before our eyes. The team from the United States was involved in healing prayer ministry from the moment of our arrival in Brazil. Not only were wonderful healings taking place, but also the Brazilians were sharing with us in the prayer ministry. The people were amazed as they experienced the Holy Spirit working through them in healing. In this ministry Jesus was manifesting his loving, powerful, and healing presence.

Then an attack came against Todd, my translator. One of the participants at this conference was a heavily demonized man brought by his counselor for healing. A team of men had started to pray for him and was sharing with him the forgiveness of Jesus Christ. But suddenly, this man came up to Todd and, in the hearing of others, said, "I know you! We once had homosexual sex." This word had immediate impact on Todd. Saying that he felt sick all over and would be unable to translate, he went to his room. It also affected those who overheard the comment, and they were confused and appalled.

Ernie Pina, the director of the event, called me over to discuss the situation. We were confused about what to do. It looked like the whole Dunamis Project was going to be derailed by scandal. We prayed for guidance. Then I ran down to the room and found Todd, lying on his bed overcome by nausea. I asked him, "Is there any truth in this charge? There is forgiveness and restoration in Jesus Christ. If it is not true, we must know that too!" Todd sat up and said, "No, there is no truth at all. I was a virgin when I married and have been completely faithful to my wife."

"Let's ask God what we should do," I replied.

I asked several men to join in prayer for Todd and then ran back down to the youth gathering and asked the leaders to pray for the situation. I spoke again with Ernie and told him that Todd had said there was no truth in the charge. Ernie responded, "People are really concerned and believe it may be true because of Todd's reaction of getting sick. What are we to do?" I felt the Holy Spirit nudging me with the idea that this was more than an attack against Todd, but a high-level counterattack intended to divert us from the vision of the Dunamis Project. But I had no evidence!

I ran back down to the room where Todd was. After entering I could feel the presence of an evil spirit. Two men from the American team had received clear guidance that the accusation against Todd was coming from a deceiving spirit from the nearby occult healing center that had been stirred up because the power and grace of Jesus Christ were being so clearly manifested. I told Todd that this truth needed to be brought into the light and the whole group invited to pray for the situation. He agreed, saying, "I have nothing to hide, I'll be right up." So I went running back up to the main meeting building, where about two hundred were gathered in a teaching session.

Along the way, the attack began against me. I could feel pressure in my chest and became aware of an oppressive presence hovering over me. As I stood before the group and explained what we thought was happening, Todd walked in and told the group everything that had happened. He asked the group to pray for him. As we did, I was gripped by a wave of fear. Yet I also felt the Holy Spirit challenging me: "Step into the gap! In the name of Jesus intercede for your brother and for the work that I am doing in Brazil."

I said, "Yes, Lord."

Todd seemed to be overwhelmed by the assault against him. As I rushed to lay hands on him, it was as though a window in hell opened and a blast of suffocating air enveloped me. I fought to breathe and felt pain and pressure in my chest. It felt like an invisible iron fist was gripping my heart. Images of howling, cheering, demonic faces invaded my mind. I was afraid that I was going to die. I cried out in the name of Jesus for help. I commanded the evil spirits to leave Todd and me. We were joined in this warfare prayer by a group of around ten Brazilian pastors and some members of the American team. But the assault continued to intensify.

Suddenly the Holy Spirit surged through me in a burst of holy anger. I think I felt Jesus' righteous anger at the devil for bringing pain, death, and despair into the universe. I prayed at the top of my voice in tongues, in English, and in Portuguese, commanding the spirit to be gone from Todd. This lasted for what seemed an eternity but may have only been a few minutes. Then I could feel something break in the spirit realm, and I knew the high-level spirit had been thrust back. Todd and I both stopped feeling the pressure against us, and while emotionally and spiritually exhausted, we moved into praise and thanksgiving.

Immediately a storm of confusion and criticism broke loose. People were horrified at this display of emotion. This was not decent nor in order—and certainly not Presbyterian. I was accused of frightening people and of overreacting. I felt as if the devil had succeeded after all in messing up all the good work that had been accomplished.

But then came a startling revelation. Several of the young people came running up from the river where they had been having their meeting. They were terrified but exhilarated. They reported that at about the same time that the attack had lifted from us an evil presence had swept through the meeting of about eighty high school and college-age young people. Four of them had been flung to the floor. One of the leaders, Brenda—Ernie's college-age daughter—had seen, in the eyes of the spirit, a shadowlike thing leave the main meeting building and sweep toward the group. It had passed right through her, searing her soul, flinging her to the ground, and causing waves of nausea. Other young people had had other symptoms of an evil entity blowing through them. As the attack came they had started to pray in the name of Jesus for the thing to leave, and it did. It had to leave because he who is in us is greater than the god of this world.

This testimony quieted some of the confusion and led the group to a sober realization that warfare is real, but in Jesus is the victory. That night a great outpouring of the Holy Spirit occurred especially among the young people.

Why had this happened? We concluded that the healing ministry taking place in Jesus' name represented a significant advancement of the kingdom of

God in that part of Brazil. It had shaken the demonic stronghold of occult healing that is so powerful there. This evil spirit was forced out of hiding. While the immediate attack was resisted, this event did cause controversy, fear, and misunderstanding among some of the Brazilian church leaders. This intrusion tainted the clear witness of the work of the Holy Spirit through the Dunamis Project. While the enemy was defeated, he apparently did some damage on his way out. We now have to trust that God will continue to protect and prosper his work in central Brazil.

ASSAULTS INTENDED TO COMPROMISE THE VISIONARY

As a reality check, reflect on the dismal history of ministries and churches that started off with a clear vision from God, but then ended in failure. Most of the time the work failed because Satan had been able to seduce the visionary into actions that were contrary to the vision. If Satan can compromise or destroy the visionary, he has won a great victory.

This is certainly what happened to King David when he committed adultery with Bathsheba (2 Samuel 11). This assault came at the height of David's success, implementing the vision of the kingdom of Israel. His armies had been so successful that the king could afford to stay at home. Having failed on the battlefield, Satan focused his attack against David personally, tempting him to sin. David fell. He not only committed adultery with Bathsheba but murdered her husband. While David was forgiven for his sin and he (unlike his predecessor, King Saul) was allowed to remain king, its consequences ravaged his household, bringing sorrow and division. His leadership of the nation, too, was compromised.

BUT WHY?

Why does God allow Satan to ravage ministries? Without a proper understanding of this theological issue, Christians may fear Satan. They will be leery of confronting him, his works, or his underlings. Many Christians make peace treaties with Satan: "I won't bother you if you won't bother me." Out of fear they back away from the work of intercessory prayer and retreat from the arena of vision fulfillment.

But anything that God lets Satan do to us is allowed for our benefit. Jesus said to Peter, "Satan has asked to sift you as wheat. But I have prayed for you, Simon, that your faith may not fail. And when you have turned back, strengthen your brothers" (Luke 22:31–32). Jesus did not think it would harm Peter to let Satan have a good whack at him. In fact, it would strengthen Peter and force him to deal with what was in his own heart.

Leanne Payne writes:

> It is necessary that temptation and trial compel us to face honestly what is in our hearts. This is, as Chambers says, "in order that a higher and nobler character may come out of the test." No one with a ministry worth having has escaped this testing, and the tests differ according to our weaknesses—those very things within us that need healing.[5]

Satan is our adversary, committed to our damnation and the destruction of the kingdom of God. However, he plays a strange role of being God's tester, whose temptations and attacks may refine our character and deepen our dependency on Christ. To do the work of reality-shaping prayer places us in a position of leadership in the kingdom of God. With this position of power and effectiveness come all the inherent dangers of the sinful flesh: pride, self-sufficiency, and the abuse of power. To keep us useful by keeping us on the way of holiness and obedience, God may well allow Satan to offer his service of testing us. He did it for Job and for Peter, and he will certainly do it for the one called to birth God's vision into the world.

Often the place where this intensive training for leadership takes place is in spiritual wilderness. Most of us whom God has called into spiritual leadership have been through these terrible times of confronting the sin in ourselves. Wilderness is a unique opportunity for spiritual growth, but it is also extremely risky as one may fall and be removed from ministry. If you believe you may be entering such a period of fiery refinement, you may find my book *Passage Through the Wilderness: A Journey of the Soul* helpful.

Armed with this awareness—how God uses satanic sifting—we can stand against the evil one, knowing that Jesus truly is in control and looking forward to his return, when he will put all his enemies under his feet. The Bible is clear about this: Even Satan knows that his doom is sure and that there is no hope for him.

Summary

Because Jesus has an enemy, those who serve him will also be opposed if they are doing his work, building his vision. The enemy throws opposition in our path at each stage of the vision—conception, birth, and fulfillment.

This opposition cannot harm us as long as we are willing to look at our weaknesses, bring them before the Lord, confess our sin, receive God's strengthening, and be accountable to others in the body of Christ.

QUESTIONS FOR REFLECTION, DIALOGUE, AND JOURNALING

1. Have you ever been hurt by satanic assault? What harm came of it? What good came of it? Was Jesus in control? Try to be specific about the lessons you learned from the experience.
2. Does the possibility of spiritual warfare scare you? What is the scriptural antidote to fear? How do you normally deal with fears?
3. If Satan intimidates you from completing God's vision for your life, are you willing to let God succeed in that through you?

Part Four

SHAPING REALITY IN OUR
AREAS OF ACTIVITY

Chapter Fourteen

FITTING PRAYER INTO OUR PERSONAL LIVES

We now proceed to the practicalities of building prayer into each area of our lives—our personal life, our families, our church, and our nation. The first priority, of course, is to clear space *in our personal life* for prayer. It is like setting up a workshop in which to build other things. Before we can build the other things, we have to build the workshop.

Many people have attempted to do this but have found that it is not easy. Martin Luther recognized the difficulty and attributed it to the opposition of the evil one:

> When I would speak and pray to God by myself, a hundred thousand hindrances at once intervene before I get at it. Then the devil can throw all sorts of reasons for delay in my path; he can block and hinder me on all sides; as a result, I go my way and never think of it again. Let him who has not experienced this only try it. Resolve to pray earnestly, and no doubt you will see how large an assortment of your own thoughts will rush in on you and distract you, so that you cannot begin aright.[1]

Luther recognized that, from the beginning, we have to deal with a subtle foe who wants to keep us from prayer at all costs. His favorite trick is to make us feel that we are unworthy to enter God's presence. If he cannot throw hindrances and excuses in our path, he challenges our right to approach God, using feelings of unworthiness. All the more important, says Luther, that we stand squarely on the access granted by the atoning death of Jesus (the bridge over the abyss).

"JOIN ME IN MY STRUGGLE BY PRAYING TO GOD"

The apostles viewed prayer as hard work. Consider the expressions Paul used when he urged people to stay at prayer:

"Join me in my struggle by praying to God." (Romans 15:30)
"Be alert and always keep on praying." (Ephesians 6:18)
"Devote yourselves to prayer, being watchful." (Colossians 4:2)

None of these verses implies that our prayer time will always be pleasant. It looks more as if prayer will involve work and struggle.

- Children suddenly start waking up early, demanding attention during that morning quiet time.
- The telephone rings just as you are heading out the door for a time of prayer, and the conversation seems to last forever.
- You have an explosive argument with your spouse, which puts you in a foul mood just as you are about to enter prayer.
- You have unexpected late-night conversations that make it hard to get up early for prayer.
- When you wake up, you feel inexplicably alienated from God, under a cloud of heaviness.
- You have disturbing or lustful dreams that you cannot get out of your mind. These hinder prayer.

It is not always easy to tell how much of this is a spiritual attack and how much is just "normal." (Once you begin to see that you are in a spiritual battle, you can become paranoid, seeing demons where none exist.) But the Bible says that spirits hostile to Jesus oppose us and that our way of opposing them is by prayer (Ephesians 6:12–18). Therefore, does it not stand to reason that these unfriendly spirits will find ways to keep us from prayer?

Both Brad and I have run into the problem of "opposition." Knowing that Jesus wants faithfulness, we have often looked for ways to stay faithful when everything in us was tempting us away from prayer. The following ideas, principles, and techniques have been helpful to us. We give them out of an awareness that many books on prayer offer people wonderful theology and concepts but little practical help.

1. Don't Sacrifice Sleep

When we start to do the work of prayer, we must not do it at the expense of our health. There are only twenty-four hours in the day, so we must prioritize our time to make sure we get enough sleep. To do the work of prayer effectively, what must be given up is not sleep but other activities. For example:

- *Late night television* will almost certainly be the first to go. Do we really need as much stress-releasing entertainment as we think we do?
- *Late night meetings*, including those "important" church meetings, will have to be reexamined. Are they really as important as we think?
- *Late night counseling sessions* are another bugaboo for Christians who minister to needy people. To me (Doug), it does not make sense to sacrifice prayer for counseling. Often in my ministry, I have simply prayed for troubled people and soon found them gaining the insights directly from God that I would have counseled them to try.
- *Vacations* and *weekends* are a problem for many of us. In our culture, we believe that during vacations and weekends we deserve to sleep in. Maybe so. But a person who is learning prayer may get her body into a pattern of daily prayer, perhaps late at night or early in the morning. Then vacation hits. She says to herself: "God wouldn't want me to keep doing this during my vacation, would he?" So she stops the early morning prayer, sleeps in for days at a stretch, and loses all the progress she has made to develop a godly habit. At the end of the vacation, she has to start all over developing the habit of prayer. Prayer, when maintained during vacation, can move from heavy birthing prayer to the contemplative prayer we discussed above. Let vacation be a rediscovery of the joy of listening prayer rather than a laying aside of all prayer.
- *Children* want our attention. Try telling them this: "Prayer is very important. We always put God first, and then everything else in our home will go much better." Include them in the prayer for a brief

time, making suggestions about how they can pray: "Let's think of something to thank God for," or "Let's sing 'Jesus loves me, this I know.'" After a short time, help them decide on a separate activity in another room and pray with them that God will bless them in their play.

2. Exercise

Not only does a lack of sleep hinder my (Brad's) prayer life, so does a lack of regular exercise. If I don't exercise every day and keep my body in good physical shape, I find it impossible to sit still long enough to pray. I also find it difficult to sleep. My solution has been to combine exercise and prayer. Every night after my wife and children are asleep I run about a mile up the mountain. Going up is exercise; coming down is usually an effective prayer time. When I exercise, I feel better and can concentrate on everything better, including prayer.

3. Develop a Regular Schedule

Pray at the same time each day, whether in the early morning, before bedtime, or at noon. Bodies grow accustomed to a regular schedule and develop habits. A godly habit, like early morning or late night prayer, goes a long way to encourage us to stay at prayer.

4. Get Awake; Stay Awake

Especially for those who choose an early morning prayer time, staying alert can be a challenge. Jesus says, "Be watchful." Easier said than done, at 5 A.M.! The answer is so simple it is remarkable more Christians have not thought of it: Vary your posture. No one posture is biblical; no one posture is "the right posture."

- Get up and walk around, especially when you are feeling groggy—as the watchmen on the walls of Jerusalem used to do—walking back and forth to stay alert.
- Open your eyes some of the time, especially if you are walking around!
- Kneel. This is not the exclusive prerogative of Catholics and Anglicans.
- Lift up your hands.

- Jump. Shout. Lean against a chair. Dance. Sing. Let yourself get into it. Get out of the rut of folding hands, bowing head, and being still. Being still and knowing the Lord is God (see Psalm 46:10) is okay some of the time, but it is not meant for the entire prayer time.

I (Brad) always feel a little guilty whenever I am around Doug. He is an early morning prayer person. I am a night person and, try as I might (and believe me, I have tried), I cannot pray in the morning unless it is after 8:30. I become wide-awake at about 11:00 P.M. and usually have to make myself go to bed at around 1:00 A.M. This is my most awake and creative time of the day. It is a wonderful time, with no phone calls and a quiet house. Each of us is free to select the prayer time and approach that is best for us. Experiment! See what works for you.

5. Begin With Worship

Many times prayer refuses to flow even though I (Doug) have arrived at a place of prayer with every intention of praying. I try to pray, but I feel paralyzed. I wonder, "Is this what it's like recovering from a stroke?"

I compare it to the times when I want to write. I sit down at my computer with every intention of writing, but then, with fingers poised over the keyboard, nothing happens. No words come forth. What to do?

When this heaviness or paralysis makes God seem far away, I remember the words of the brother of our Lord: "Resist the devil, and he will flee from you" (James 4:7). Often these difficulties come from satanic interference—as though a bank of clouds has come in and kept the sun of righteousness from shining into our lives. How do we resist these subtle attempts to discourage our prayers?

I recommend three ways to begin prayer, all of them ways of worship. The Bible says, "Enter his gates with thanksgiving and his courts with praise" (Psalm 100:4). Thanksgiving and praise enter into God's courts. Worship is the way we get into God's presence.

> Therefore, brothers, since we have confidence to enter the Most Holy Place by the blood of Jesus, by the new and living way opened for us through the curtain, that is, his body, and since we have a great priest over the house of God, let us draw near to God with a sincere heart in full assurance of faith. (Hebrews 10:19–22)

Through Jesus, therefore, let us continually offer to God a sacrifice of praise—the fruit of lips that confess his name. (Hebrews 13:15)

Sometimes praise feels like a sacrifice. We don't feel like doing it. But it moves us into God's presence, and then prayer becomes easier. Worship corrects whatever wrong attitudes we may bring with us into the holy place. Worship confronts our coldness of heart and whatever deception the devil is using against our emotions. By worship we can "resist the devil." I therefore always start my time of prayer with one or more of these options:

- Singing hymns and praise songs out of our church's hymnbook and songbook
- Telling God of my love and appreciation, expressing love as an act of will, not feeling
- Invoking God to bring me into his presence: "My spirit longs for you" (Isaiah 26:9); "to you, O LORD, I lift up my soul" (Psalm 25:1); "I would rather be a doorkeeper in the house of my God than dwell in the tents of the wicked" (Psalm 84:10).

6. Develop Your Own Structure of Prayer

I (Brad) have found that a structure or plan helps me to build my prayers in an orderly fashion. As led by the Holy Spirit, we may use these basic ingredients or building blocks both in private prayer and (even more important) in corporate prayer.

BUILDING BLOCKS FOR PRAYER

1. *Adoration and praise:* We adore God for who he is; we praise him for what he is doing.
   Revelation 4:11; Psalm 22:3; 147:1
2. *Confession and forgiveness:* Sin brings separation between God and us.
   Isaiah 6:1–5; 1 John 1:9
3. *Meditation:* To think deeply and continuously, reflect, ponder, or muse:
   a. on the law of God (Psalm 1:1–2)

> b. on the precepts and ways of God (Psalm 119:15)
> c. on God and who he is (Psalm 63)
> d. on what God has done and is doing (Psalm 77:11–12; 143:5)
> 4. *Listening:* Entering silently into God's presence, where he may speak.
>   Psalm 37:7; Ezekiel 2:1–2; Habakkuk 2:20
> 5. *Petition:* We come to our heavenly Father and make our requests known.
>   Philippians 4:6
> 6. *Intercession:* We join Jesus in standing in the gap for those in need.
>   John 14:12–13
> 7. *Praise and thanksgiving:* Always conclude by returning to give praise to Jesus.[2]

7. Expand Your Prayer Style

Starting with this map, let the Holy Spirit creatively elaborate on your expressions of prayer. Get beyond murmuring and whispering your prayers with head quietly bowed, eyes glued to the knees. John Welch, the son-in-law of John Knox, whose intercessory prayers were instrumental in birthing the Presbyterian Church in Scotland, "used to allow his affections full expression, and prayed not only with an audible, but sometimes a loud voice."[3] As the Spirit nudges you, try some of the following:

- Shout to the Lord (Psalm 47:1; 132:9).
- Sing new praise songs and old hymns (Matthew 13:52).
- Chant Scriptures (Psalm 119:54ff.).
- Command dark angels with authority (Luke 10:19).
- Preach to the principalities and powers in the heavenly realms (Ephesians 3:10).
- Quote Scriptures aloud (Ephesians 6:17).
- Address "one another with psalms, hymns and spiritual songs" (we define "spiritual songs" as singing in tongues—what Augustine called "jubilation") (Ephesians 5:19; cf. 1 Corinthians 14:14).

8. Create a Place for Prayer

Jesus told us to find a prayer closet where we could pray just between God and us (Matthew 6:6, KJV). A closet is a place that is separated from distractions. Two hundred years ago, a "closet" was not a place for hanging clothes, but a small room, usually designed for one person alone. Distractions are another bugaboo for a person who wishes to grow in prayer. Some people find that their bathroom and their car are de facto prayer closets. Others have found that a particular place in their yard or garden is their prayer place.

But I (Doug) want to make a case for an *altar*—that is, a focal point in your home used exclusively for prayer. I will have more to say about this in chapter 15. But for now, let me point out that we have rooms for all other important activities in our lives. If we are serious about making prayer a priority, why not have a small room, or even a corner of a room, designed for prayer?

9. Find a Prayer Partner

Most of us find it hard to pray alone, day after day, week after week. An excellent solution to this problem is to find a prayer partner. When I (Doug) was called into prayer, my wife was called simultaneously, so that we learned how to stay at prayer together. Together we have battled the temptations and difficulties of praying. When I am feeling unmotivated, she kicks me out of bed and vice versa.

Those whose spouse has not been called into intensive prayer can find someone who does have the calling. For example, I had an elder in my church who, when I started to talk about prayer, wanted to come and pray with us. He would show up many days at 5 A.M. When we felt like sleeping in, we knew that we could not, because Harry would ring our doorbell, and we had to get up. These prayer times were important for all three of us.

My wife, one day a week, has a prayer appointment with a woman in our church. They agree to phone each other at a certain time every Sunday morning.

Over the years I have driven to places in our city where early morning prayer was happening. We kept each other accountable for city-wide prayer.

Prayer partnerships do not always flow smoothly at first, but they are worth the investment of learning. As in a marriage, we have to get past the first incompatibilities, learn how to agree in prayer, learn to gently confront problems in our prayer time, debrief constructively and creatively every once in a while, and grow together in prayer until we can pray in one accord.

As in a marriage, those who enter into a prayer partnership, expecting it to flow blissfully from one spiritual high to the next, are likely to be disappointed. It is better if we enter into this type of relationship with our eyes open:

- Don't harbor secret grudges or questions about prayers that your partner prays. Always give your partner the benefit of the doubt.
- Take time to debrief after prayer sessions, especially if your partnership is new. "How did you feel about our prayer time? How was the Holy Spirit leading? Did I do anything that was incomprehensible to you? What did you mean when you prayed _____?"
- When you cannot make your prayer appointment, call your partner in advance. If you are unable to do that, make sure you apologize afterward. Never take your partnership for granted.

10. Develop a Prayer Journal

A prayer journal is like a journal for a long trip. It converts a series of disconnected events into a journey that has continuity. It helps us keep track of where we have been so we can see where we are headed. I use my prayer journal for the following purposes:

- To record insights, lessons, picture-parables, dreams, and Scripture verses by which God has spoken into my life. This includes lessons learned both inside and outside the prayer time. If our prayer time is healthy, it will not be separated from the rest of our day. It will feed into the day and be fed from it.
- To reflect on opposition from the enemy—attacks, struggles, dreams, temptations—the ups and downs of spiritual warfare. This personal debriefing helps me to take note of where I stand on the battlefield. It helps me to keep my wits about me. For example, several times I have received e-mail messages from intercessor friends in other parts of the country detailing satanic assignments (demonic schemes, discerned in prayer) against family members or myself. These have been remarkably accurate; I record them word for word in my prayer journal so I don't lose them.

- To list long-term prayer concerns that I want to pray for over a season of time. Not every prayer concern is intended to be everlasting, but some are nearly so. They are burdens that the Lord gives us to carry over the long haul—for example, a burden for a particular unreached people group.
- To record answers to prayer, so I can remember God's faithfulness and be encouraged.

11. Jot Down Distracting Thoughts

As I pray, my mind is often filled with thoughts that have nothing to do with prayer. They are like flies buzzing around my head. Often these are reminders of things I have to do later that day. I used to allow these buzzing thoughts to distract me from prayer. Then I learned to jot them down on a separate pad of paper (not my prayer journal). This habit swats the distractions so they no longer buzz around.

Sometimes these reminders do seem to come from God; they are something God wants me to take care of that day. But whether they are from God or not, jotting them down frees me to pray.

Summary

It is easy to discuss prayer and to read books about it. But the actual practice of prayer is difficult. To help maintain consistency in prayer, we have recommended in this chapter eleven helpful suggestions. While perhaps not all of them will work for you, we believe that they are worth trying.

Questions for Reflection, Dialogue, and Journaling

1. Which of the difficulties we have mentioned perpetually plague your prayer times, and what can you do to solve the problem?
2. Which of the above recommendations seem especially "pregnant" or appropriate for you right now?

Chapter Fifteen

SHAPING HOUSEHOLDS WITH PRAYER

In 1983, my wife and I (Doug) began to pray together every day, early in the morning, at home. It was as though God was saying, "Make your home a house of prayer."

This calling, first given to us fifteen years ago, was renewed in 1994 when we moved into our present house. Late one afternoon, as I was installing screens, a storm came up, and a bolt of lightning struck nearby, somewhere on our property. The next day, as I was driving into our long gravel driveway, I noticed a fresh charred gash on the tree at the end of the driveway, right where I had planned to place a sign: "The McMurrys." God had just placed a sign of his own there, or so it seemed to me. I asked the Lord about this, and the phrase "Revelation 8:5" came into my head. I looked the passage up, and this is what I read:

> The smoke of the incense, together with the prayers of the saints, went up before God from the angel's hand. Then the angel took the censer, filled it with fire from the altar, and hurled it on the earth; and there came peals of thunder, rumblings, flashes of lightning and an earthquake. (Revelation 8:4–5)

Lightning and thunder are images of divine power flowing from the prayers of the saints. The idea that God was specifically designating *our home* as a place of prayer dawned on me. As I studied the matter in the

Scriptures, I began to realize that God has always wanted people to build godly homes full of prayer. More recently I have seen well-meaning intercessors praying for the nation but allowing their spiritual enemy to wreak havoc in their own homes.

JACOB BUILDS AN ALTAR

The patriarch Jacob had a personal encounter with God at a place called Luz (Genesis 28:10–22). Years later, God spoke to him to establish his household at that same place and to build an altar there. The result?

> So Jacob said to his household and to all who were with him, "Get rid of the foreign gods you have with you, and purify yourselves and change your clothes. Then come, let us go up to Bethel, where I will build an altar to God, who answered me in the day of my distress and who has been with me wherever I have gone." So they gave Jacob all the foreign gods they had and the rings in their ears, and Jacob buried them under the oak at Shechem. Then they set out, and the terror of God fell upon the towns all around them so that no one pursued them.
>
> Jacob and all the people with him came to Luz (that is, Bethel) in the land of Canaan. There he built an altar, and he called the place El Bethel. . . . (Genesis 35:2–7)

God was making a covenant not just with Jacob, but with Jacob's household. God seems to care about households, and he wanted to bless Jacob's family as an extension of his covenant with the patriarch. Jacob was being offered God's blessing and protection for every member of his household. Even before they had completed the steps commanded by God, they were already experiencing the protection of the "terror" of God, as they walked among their enemies to Luz.

This "terror" brought a spiritual power encounter against demonic powers and the peoples who worshiped at their altars, who suddenly became aware that a greater, higher power was moving with Jacob through territories they had possessed for generations. Wow! What an assurance and blessing that must have been!

This story shows two steps that I have found basic to the process of building a Christian household: putting away our household gods, and building an altar in our home.

FIRST STEP: PUTTING AWAY HOUSEHOLD GODS

The "foreign" gods that Jacob's wife, children, and servants were commanded to put away were probably the gods Rachel brought with her from her father's house (Genesis 31:19). Actually, she stole them from her father. Archaeological discoveries at Nuzi shed light on why Rachel stole these gods. They gave the one who owned them the right to inherit the ancestral property. Rachel had stolen these "gods" as property insurance.

God told her to trust in his care by burying the household gods. Burying these idols represented a clean break with the past—her ties with whatever demonic bondage was preserved through these devoted objects, her natural craftiness inherited from her father, and her confidence in her ability to live by her own wits. There was a cost to giving these up: It required her to trust in God's care.

We too have household gods, though they take different forms from the gargoyle-like idols of Jacob's day. I (Doug) remember the day when we noticed in our daughters' CD collections some New Age symbols on one of the jackets. We brought this to the attention of our girls, who had been getting more and more enamored with certain secular musical groups. After first objecting to our objections, they began to see that their musical tastes were actually drawing them away from Christ. Then they went through their collection of CDs and culled out those that might be objectionable to the Lord, and we had a CD-breaking ceremony in our living room.

From that day, Lisa and Elizabeth began to gain a new love for worship songs. At the time of this writing, worship songs constitute at least 95 percent of their musical interest. More than that, their decision has had a deep and lasting effect on their spirits, and both are seeking ways to devote themselves to God for the rest of their lives. Significantly, both have become women of prayer.

A household god is anything that has power to pull us away from God or divide our loyalties—a porn stash in the basement, "demon" rum, the TV set that fascinates us with seventy channels of entertainment, satanic music, occult books, and so on. Those who wish to go on to Step 2—significant prayer—must first pay attention to Step 1. Ask God: "Are there any household gods in my home or in my life?"

SECOND STEP: BUILDING AN "ALTAR"

God told Jacob to go to Luz and *live* there. The altar he built there was for his place of dwelling, his home.

Could God seriously want us to make our home a house of prayer by building an altar there? Our children see us watching TV, enjoying our hobbies, eating, sleeping, and doing the chores. Do they see us in prayer? Do they see that our relationship with God is the center of our lives when we are at home? It is at home, not at church, that we live out our real belief system.

The Bible puts great emphasis on households. For most Christians, the household is a sphere of activity—perhaps the most significant one, and certainly one that most Christians must deal with. God cares about our households. Look at the elaborate way he took the Israelites out of Egypt. He had them take a branch of hyssop, dip it in the blood of a lamb, and place the blood on the sides and tops of the doorframes of their houses. Why? If God wanted to save his people, why did he not just save them?

I believe God was planting a redemptive analogy[1] among the Israelites, to help their descendants understand Jesus, the Lamb of God, and his ministry to them. His death was given as a protection over their households. The blood of the Passover lamb pointed to a spiritual reality: the protection of the blood of the Lamb of God, who takes away the sin of the world. Just as the "terror" of God protected Jacob from his spiritual enemies and just as God protected the Israelites from the angel of death, so Jesus protects our households today, as we place our faith in him. God planned for the blood of Jesus to protect *our households*. He did not have the Israelites put the blood of the lamb on their foreheads, but on their doorposts. Maybe it was this awareness of God's care for households that caused the apostle Paul to baptize believers *together with their whole household* (Acts 16:15, 31–34).

I remember one occasion when our son was very young and we were just beginning the early morning prayer. Phil told us about some bullies who were threatening him at school. We prayed for him at the end of our morning prayer time and as he departed for school that day.

When he came home that afternoon, he was *so* excited. He shouted, "Mom, Mom, guess what happened! Those boys came up to bother me again. One kid started to punch me in the stomach, but his hand hit something invisible just in front of my stomach, he got scared and ran away." Those boys never troubled our son again. We believe that was God's protection in direct answer to prayer for this "area of activity," our family.

Martin Luther was among the first to teach on the importance of households at the close of the medieval period. He saw households, not monasteries, as the main place where the discipling of a new generation should take place. He wrote:

> In the management of the household father and mother are the instruments through which the house and household affairs are governed. But they themselves should also acknowledge that by their own power, diligence, or effort they could never bring up their children properly and successfully.
>
> ... But you could find many who do not acknowledge this higher power and wisdom in governing. If any obstacles are put in their way, they suppose that they will set things right more properly if they apply greater severity in their punishments, so that their subjects are held in check by the fear of the punishments and are driven to obey even against their will. Surely there is need of discipline—and rather stern discipline at that—especially in the matter of these morals of ours; but it is completely certain that you will never achieve anything without prayer.[2]

DESPAIR OR PRAYER

My wife and I (Doug) learned much about the power of prayer to shape our home through our struggles with Marna. In 1972, when we lived in Oregon, we adopted a baby Korean girl. From the moment Marna arrived, we knew she had been through serious trauma. Abandoned on a doorstep by her mother, brought by a night watchman to a police station, then delivered to an adoption agency and placed in foster care homes where she did not get proper care, Marna had been through hell. The skin on her back was scaly, and there was a bald spot on the back of her head, both signs of serious neglect. When she came to us at five-and-a-half months old, this nine-pound China doll stiff-armed us. She had already learned that adults could not be trusted!

In my pastoral counseling, I had seen the damage done by early childhood trauma and its effects on personality and relationships. When Marna became a teenager, she displayed all the effects of unresolved early childhood trauma. She resisted love because she had not resolved the trust issue, which, according to psychologist Erik Erikson, is the first challenge of life that people face as babies.[3]

We grieved for her, did as much inner healing as we could, and saw a few results (she stopped having the nightmares that had dogged her in her sleep). Yet her lack of trust and her inability to form secure love relationships were still a problem, and the darkness from early childhood trauma also created problems in our household.

After we moved to Virginia, my sister in Minnesota invited Marna to live with them during her high school years. Marna left our household to live with my sister and her husband, who had been an adopted child. After a year or two, my sister became concerned about Marna's behavior and sought therapy from a professional who specialized in adoptive problems. The therapist's conclusion: Marna would never be able to develop normal relationships. As if to confirm this conclusion, one year, when Marna was to be with us for Christmas, she did not show up. Science was telling us what we already knew, and the verdict of the therapist, repeated to us over the phone, crushed our hopes. But we believed in the power of prayer. Science had done all it could. But what did God say?

This situation was the acid test for our household prayer. We faced only two choices: despair or prayer. During our prayer times, God had given us a simple word for Marna: "In my time, I make all things beautiful." For seven years we had only this one word, and it guided our prayers every day, though we had no evidence God was doing anything. But it was as though Marna's spirit needed to be birthed, and prayer was the blood flowing into this spiritual womb in which a new Marna was being shaped.

One day, we happened to mention to Marna on the phone that we were taking our family vacation in the Great Smokies. Marna, surprisingly and uncharacteristically, said she wanted to come camp with us! This was the first sign that God was answering our prayer. That summer, she drove all the way to Tennessee from Minnesota, alone, in a ramshackle car of doubtful reliability (with bald tires showing steel and a door that didn't open) to be with us. We enjoyed wonderful healing in our relationship, and, apparently, God healed Marna's childhood trauma. During the following year, we were able to talk about the past and forgive and be forgiven, and God healed all the hurts in our relationship. We are a family again.

We still pray for Marna every day, because we believe that God still has many blessings for her that she has not yet experienced. Now that

God has restored her to us, we can pray more confidently than ever that God will "make all things beautiful" for her.

The beautiful thing about prayer is that it is nonmanipulative. We don't have to nag our children to go to church or to read the Bible or to become Christians. God's ways are gentle. Prayer, though powerful, respects the integrity of the people we pray for. God invites us to lift our children before his throne of grace each day, whether individually or as a couple. It seems to be an important way for us to cooperate with him, to fulfill his promises to the children of believers.

WHAT IS AN "ALTAR"?

Go into a Buddhist's home. You will find an actual altar there. The Japanese call this their Butsu-dan. It contains a Buddha icon, a picture of an ancestor, candles, cups, and so on. The altar proclaims to everyone who enters the home that this family is Buddhist.

We Westerners have succeeded in tearing down our altars to "foreign gods." But we have not been accustomed to building anything in their place. An "altar" is not necessarily a piece of furniture. (When did you ever go to your local furniture store and ask for their selection of family altars?) A household altar is a focal point, a place free from distractions where you keep your Bible, prayer journal, devotional book, notes about prayer concerns, *Global Prayer Digest,* and so on. On the walls, you may have posted some artwork, a picture of Jesus, a cross, or some Scriptures God has quickened for you. But what makes the place an altar is the prayer and worship that go on there, not the furniture or the artwork.

Of course, more important than the altar itself is the question of how to develop prayer. Many husbands and wives imagine that they will slip easily into a habit of daily prayer. It sounds easy. Most people seem to think it will be easy. Yet the old adage, "The couple that prays together stays together" (which I [Doug] learned in tenth grade in a public school) is easier said than done. I have not talked to a single couple who have found it easy. I recommend it because it is rewarding, not because it is easy. The couple who can successfully achieve a daily habit of praying together have accomplished something rare and significant.[4]

PRAYING TOGETHER

Carla and I (Doug) have been able to succeed in long-term daily prayer only after stumbling and falling many times. I would like to share in the next few pages some of the practical lessons we have learned, which may be helpful for other couples who would like to aspire to bow to God together at a family altar.

1. Approach Prayer As Equals

Discuss the prayer time together, making sure both partners feel respected and are equally free to shape the family altar. When one partner feels like a lesser contributor, household prayer rarely lasts. If the husband believes that he is inferior to his wife because "she's the spiritual one," or the wife believes that she is the inferior one because "the husband is the head and he makes all the decisions," then spouses are not coming to God as "co-heirs" (see Romans 8:17; 1 Peter 3:7, RSV).

Whatever we may theorize of the relations between husband and wife, whenever the Bible pictures a husband and wife in a healthy prayer relationship, it pictures them as equals. For example, Peter tells husbands to treat their wives as "heirs with you of the gracious gift of life, so that nothing will hinder your prayers" (1 Peter 3:7). Peter (himself a married man) is saying that, while husbands may think their wives are inferior because they are physically weaker, God does not look at them that way at all. In God's sight the two are co-heirs—and the Greek word he uses strongly denotes equality in God's sight. Any sense that one partner is inferior to the other will hinder prayer.

Likewise, the apostle Paul wrote that when a couple decide to abstain from sexual relations for a season in order to devote themselves to prayer, they should do so "by agreement" (1 Corinthians 7:5, RSV), or "mutual consent" (NIV). In other words, neither is to lay down the law ("I am going to fast for three days, so …"), unilaterally proclaim a fast ("God told me to …"), or treat the partner as though that person did not have a relationship with God too. On the contrary, they are to "outdo one another in showing honor" (Romans 12:10, RSV), as all Christians do with each other. This is part of the basic love command that applies in marriage, as everywhere else.

Prayer tests the fabric of a marriage and challenges two people to respect each other's relationship with God. A daily prayer time forces both spouses to deal with issues that have cropped up in their relationship— secret resentments, a lifetime of dishonoring, spiritual manipulation, codependency, ungodly habits, and secret sin (such as adultery in the thought life). Prayer forces us to deal with holiness and love, as we already said in our chapter on vision. Marital prayer is the same: It forces us to deal with marital holiness and marital love.

2. Debrief Often About Your Prayer

After the prayer time, Carla and I sometimes talk about how our prayer went or how we believe it should be changed. This debriefing time is probably the most important single ingredient that has enabled us to keep marital prayer going day after day for fifteen years.

If we have no way of talking about how the prayer is going, we have no forum for addressing misunderstandings, grievances, or frustrations. Nor do we have a way to let the Holy Spirit lead us into fresh changes. Without a debriefing time, we are likely to develop ruts. Expecting prayer to fall into place is about as realistic as expecting a marriage to fall into place, or expecting sex to be golden and glorious every time, even though we never talk about it. Great idea, in theory.

Typical problems that often need to be talked through might include:

- Someone prays preachy prayers or lectures the other spouse.
- Prayers go on too long, so that no agreement can take place.
- Scattered prayer reflects a lack of focus or direction.

These issues have been addressed in chapter 3. The point here is that couples must address them, speaking the truth in a loving way and working through them gently.

3. Recognize Differences in Temperament

Men and women see the world differently, and sometimes our differences in temperament and perspective can hinder prayer. When one partner is highly rational and the other intuitive, or when one partner sees prayer as cultivating a relationship while the other sees it as spiritual warfare, then their prayer time may get off to a doubtful start.

To solve this problem, try to see how God has given each of you a different gift and wants to use your partner's gift to complement your own. Your partner can teach you about an area of prayer to which you are insensitive. For example, though some men don't like to admit it, God sometimes guides their wives in prayer through Spirit-guided intuitions. Conversely, an intuitive person may get frustrated with a highly rational partner, until it becomes clear that God can use an articulate rational mind to guide prayer. Try to see how your partner can become more balanced by being connected to the opposite tendency in yourself, and vice versa.

We can be co-heirs, learning to respect each other's strong suit. We can keep each other balanced by determining in our hearts to stick together until we have worked out our differences in style, perspective, and temperament. Speak the truth in love, listen to each other, and then keep going. Don't let temporary setbacks destroy household prayer. Let your home be a *Beth-el*, a house of God.

WHAT IF YOUR HOME IS THE BATTLEGROUND? A PERSONAL STORY

In some homes, couples cannot pray together. One or the other partner feels trapped in a marriage with an unbeliever or is profoundly frustrated, unloved, and desperate. Following is a testimony from a sister in the Lord whose home is a battleground. She speaks from personal experience.

———

As I reflect on the way God has led me to pray for my home, the following Scripture stands out in my mind.

> Therefore, since we have been justified through faith, we have peace with God through our Lord Jesus Christ, through whom we have gained access by faith into this grace in which we now stand. And we rejoice in the hope of the glory of God. Not only so, but we also rejoice in our sufferings, because we know that suffering produces perseverance; perseverance, character; and character, hope. And hope does not disappoint us, because God has poured out his love into our hearts by the Holy Spirit, whom he has given us. (Romans 5:1–5)

This passage encourages me and gives me direction for household prayer.

Standing in God's Grace

When I was feeling alienated from my husband, I realized I was standing in God's grace. And not only I, but my household as well. I observed that in hard times God can come very close. He gave me dreams, visions, words of encouragement, teaching, and discernment for prayer. I also found he raised up intercessors for prayer support. Often people came to me whom I hardly knew and told me that God had asked them to pray for our household. What an encouragement! I felt covered by God at a time when all other covering had been stripped away. I constantly visualized each family member standing in God's grace and prayed from that position.

Another aspect of standing in grace is to "choose life" (Deuteronomy 30:19). During this period, when there was great tension and hostility in my home, I had a dream that my family was on the Titanic. The captain directed my children and me to the lifeboat. I hesitated and turned to see that my spouse had remained behind. I started to turn back, but the captain told me I had to board with my children. I felt my heart tear and I cried out in my sleep as I stepped into the boat without my spouse.

A friend's response to the dream was, "Praise God for the lifeboat." I believe that this lifeboat represented God's grace supplied for my household, and that I needed to obey by "choosing life" for my children and myself. This was my prerogative as a Christian, and I was not to let my husband's failure to do this deter me. When in conversation or prayer with others I agreed with that which was life-giving and hope-instilling. The rest—words of discouragement or unbelief—I just let roll off of me; I refused to let them land.

By the way, I believe that this dream revealed the present condition, but not the future, of my spouse. The overall promises of the Lord concerning my spouse were pointing to hope and life. I hung on to those promises with all the faith I had—they were my life raft. I prayed every day that God would honor his word by bringing my spouse to salvation.

At that time, I came to God in prayer as a way of choosing life. I praised God, I envisioned his face shining on me, and I asked him to breathe his life and light on all areas of my being, exposing those areas where I had chosen death. I then prayed that my household would also experience this life. I especially had to repent of attitudes or behaviors that had ministered death to them (judgments, criticism, pride, stubbornness, etc.). I prayed that God would reveal ways that I could be life-giving to them. I found this exercise helpful in combating depression and despair.

Rejoice

Romans 1:21 states that part of what initiates our downhill slide from God is an ungrateful heart. I took this lesson to heart and learned to practice thankfulness. I was surprised to find how thankfulness could soften my heart. Many times I found myself lost in the wonder of God's love.

I began my prayer time with worship and continued prayer in an atmosphere of praise. Scripture says God inhabits the praises of his people. If you want God to inhabit your home, be in an attitude of praise. Praise music is helpful, but if your heart isn't full of praise, your household will rightly see hypocrisy. I would constantly list those qualities that I admired and appreciated in the members of my household and took advantage of opportunities to express that admiration and appreciation.

Hope Does Not Disappoint Us

"'For I know the plans I have for you,' declares the LORD, 'plans to prosper you and not to harm you, plans to give you hope and a future'" (Jeremiah 29:11). God gave many promises concerning the future of my household. I had to remind myself of these promises and take hold of them in prayer. God told me to walk the boundaries of our land and claim it for him. I took a large bowl of water and prayed that it would be the blood of Jesus covering us. I then walked all over our property and house, praying and sprinkling the blood of Jesus on everything—walkways, windows, doors, stairs, furniture, basement, everything I could think of. I stood in the promise that this household belonged to Jesus.

What has been the effect of my struggle to be faithful in prayer? Has my husband changed? Yes! He has become a Christian, and while he often stumbles, he is sincerely walking with Jesus. Have I changed? Yes! Through prayer I have found a patience and a love that are certainly not my own. The atmosphere of our home has changed as well. It is much more peaceful. My love, faith, and the work of prayer, while far from perfect, has provided a safe place for our children. They are happy and are growing emotionally and spiritually. Is my marriage still a battleground? I admit it: Some days it is still very hard.

LIGHTHOUSES OF PRAYER

Recently, Ed Silvoso of Harvest Evangelism and author of the book *That None Should Perish* has been encouraging Christians to designate their homes as "lighthouses of prayer" for their neighborhoods and cities. Just before we heard of this, my wife and I (Doug) began to sense that God was calling us to do this. That is, we were to see our home as a prayer center for the neighborhood. We began this summer to go out from our home every day, at the end of our prayer time, praying for all of our neighbors by name—all twenty-nine households. This prayer journey that begins and ends at our house has yielded many divine appointments, and we look for discipling opportunities and Bread Groups to result from it (see page 82).

What an encouragement it is to know that, as God has led us to make our home a house of prayer, Christian leaders around the country are seeing the same vision and calling many thousands of people to do the same.

If our homes are to be houses of prayer, so too is the church called to be a house of prayer. In the next chapter we will expand the challenge as well as the battle to shaping the church through prayer. We will also move forward to explore how to make the church a context of prayer that will shape the world.

SUMMARY

Often we see church buildings as places of prayer, but not our homes. The New Testament church gathered in homes, and households were far more important in New Testament Christianity than most of us realize today. We recommend two steps in building a place of prayer in our homes: that we allow God to show us "idols" we serve in our homes and, having cleared those idols away, we establish an "altar" or place of prayer in our homes.

To make marital prayer (as couples) work, we recommend that a husband and wife approach prayer as equals and that they debrief often about their prayer time to clear away misunderstandings and explore new ideas. But not everyone has a home and marriage that fit the ideal. For some the home is the battleground. Some suggestions are made by a person who has faithfully lived her life of prayer in such a context. She offers hope that prayer can be part of the process of actually changing the situation. Homes of prayer may play a role in God's larger work in neighborhoods and nations.

QUESTIONS FOR REFLECTION, DIALOGUE, AND JOURNALING

1. Do you need to clear away any household gods in order to devote your household to prayer?
2. What hindrances keep you from consistent prayer in your household? Discuss these with your spouse or prayer partner. Work toward resolution.
3. If it is not possible to pray with your spouse, what alternatives do you have to develop prayer in your household?

Chapter Sixteen

SHAPING CHURCHES BY PRAYER

Many of the greatest Christian leaders of the past have noticed a curious phenomenon: When Christians pray separately, their prayers are not as effective as when they pray together. If "one man [could] chase a thousand," then "two [could] put ten thousand to flight."[1] The increase in power and results is exponential.

We see this potential in Acts 1, when the disciples came together and prayed in one accord in Jerusalem. What was the result? God created the first great wave of Christian evangelistic outreach.

"COMMON" PRAYER

Martin Luther, the great German Reformer, noticed that gathering Christians together increased their prayer power. For Luther, "common prayer" was prayer that Christians prayed "in common" with other Christians in church. The following quote has so affected my own life and ministry that I (Doug) have posted it on my study wall:

> O if any congregation were to pray in this way, so that a common, earnest, heartfelt cry of the whole people were to rise up to God, what immeasurable virtue and help would result from such a prayer! What more terrible thing could happen to all evil spirits? What greater work could be done on earth whereby so many

pious souls would be preserved and so many sinners would be converted?

For indeed, the Christian church has no greater power or work against everything that may oppose it than such common prayer. The evil spirit knows this well, and therefore he does all that he can to prevent such prayer. This is why he lets us build handsome churches, endow many colleges, make anthems, read and sing, celebrate many masses, and multiply ceremonies beyond all measure. This brings him no sorrow. On the contrary, he helps us to do it, so that we will regard such ways the best and think that in doing them we have done our whole duty. But when this common, effectual, and fruitful prayer suffers meanwhile, and remains unnoticed because of such hypocrisy, then he has gotten what he is after. For when prayer is subordinated, nobody takes anything from him and nobody resists him. But if he noticed that we wished to practice this prayer, even if it was under a straw roof or in a pigsty, he would not tolerate it for an instant. He would fear such a pigsty far more than all the high, great, and lovely churches, towers, and bells that ever were, if such prayer were not in them. What matters is not the places and buildings where we assemble, but this unconquerable prayer alone, and our really praying it together and offering it to God.[2]

If what Jesus said is true—that "the gates of hell shall not prevail against [the church]" (Matthew 16:18, KJV)—it is true only insofar as the church uses the weapons Christ has given us. Christ did not specifically call us into a political arena, or into a therapeutic arena, or into accumulating buildings and wealth, though all these ingredients may have their place. He called us *into prayer*.

Jesus addressed his words about the gates of hell not to individual Christians, but to the church. He wants Christians to pray *as the church*. He wants to form us into an army, subdivided into cohorts who are learning to pray in one accord. The effective army is the army that learns to communicate well, to trust its leaders, to reconnaissance regularly—in short, to function *together in one accord*. The evil one, Luther noted, does everything he can to prevent this from happening, because he wants to keep his gates intact.

The first part of this chapter will deal with the practical issue of how a local congregation might develop "common prayer" that will conquer

Satan and shape God's future. We will then look at a case study of a congregation that has been profoundly shaped through the work of prayer.

A WORK IN PROCESS

Montreat Presbyterian Church is the place where my family and I (Brad) worship. A traditional evangelical Presbyterian church, it maintains a deep interest in overseas missions. Under the pastoral leadership of Rev. Calvin Thielman for thirty-three years and now under the leadership of Rev. Richard White, the church has been a praying church.

Over the last several years, we have watched this congregation grow in dynamic prayer. Observing and participating in this process has enabled me to see some principles that may be useful for any church wishing to grow in prayer.

A Praying Pastor

The pastor profoundly affects the atmosphere of a congregation. P. T. Forsyth said, "The preacher whose chief power is not in studious prayer is, to that extent, a man who does not know his business. Prayer is the minister's business." Our pastor, Richard White, takes prayer seriously. He knows that to do the work of ministry he must both be in prayer and have other people praying for him.

If the pastoral leadership takes prayer seriously, that will set the stage for the church to become a praying church. But if the pastor does not take prayer seriously, it will be much harder for the congregation to move into the powerful "common prayer" that Martin Luther described.

If you are a layperson, pray for your pastor to become a man or woman of prayer. Offer to pray for them and, if appropriate, with them. If you are a pastor, ask God to teach you how to pray. Most likely he will drive you into the wilderness, where you will learn to despair of your own abilities and come to know the necessity of prayer.

Vision Comes From Prayer and Drives the Church to Prayer

Several years ago our pastor and elders started praying for a clear vision for the church. At the leading of the Holy Spirit they spent a weekend at a mountain retreat center praying for fresh vision. There a vision was conceived and birthed in the leadership of the church. This took the form of a written vision statement that was brought before the congregation. This was, in part, "a people called by God to declare the praises of Jesus Christ through the power of the Holy Spirit...."[3]

After the vision was shared with the congregation, the church determined to move forward to fulfill the vision. With this came the strong recognition that in our own strength it would be impossible. The vision conceived in prayer now called us to do some birthing prayer in the midst of the congregation. Pastor Richard expressed it well one day: "You know we have an excellent vision statement, but it is not going to get off the paper it is printed on unless there is a great deal of prayer. I know I can't make it happen. Only God can."

To cultivate a praying church, it is necessary to have received a vision from God, which will drive the leadership and eventually the congregation to prayer. A visionless church will often be a prayerless church—and a prayerless church does not receive a vision from God.

The challenge that faces many congregations is how to break through a cycle of prayerlessness. A catalytic event may take place that drives the church to prayer—such as a called prayer event or a natural disaster. At other times, a single intercessor or prayer group may catch a vision of the necessity of prayer—and then start to pray.

Learning to Follow the Holy Spirit

For a church to grow in the work of prayer it must be willing to be led by the Holy Spirit. Without the Holy Spirit, prayer becomes simply a matter of rehearsing our own needs and agendas. This is why church prayer meetings often become so boring that people quit attending them. But with the Holy Spirit, prayer becomes an adventure of exploring new frontiers of cooperating with God.

In his *Lectures on Revival*, Charles Finney insisted on this point. Following the leading of the Spirit, more than anything else, was what made prayer meetings exciting and productive:

> Great pains should be taken both by the leader and others, to watch narrowly the motions of the Spirit of God. Let them not pray without the Spirit, but follow his leadings. Be sure not to quench the Spirit for the sake of praying according to the regular custom....
>
> An ill-conducted prayer meeting often does more hurt than good. In many churches, the general manner of conducting

prayer meetings is such that Christians have not the least idea of the design or the power of such meetings.[4]

Many congregations do not know how to be led by the Holy Spirit. They have never seen it modeled for them and are terrified of letting go of control. Here again the pastor is usually either the one who ignites participation with the Holy Spirit or quenches it.

Our pastor has been a spark plug. This goes back to his own deep hunger to grow in intimacy with Jesus Christ and in usefulness to his kingdom. About a year ago at a Dunamis Project retreat, he prayed that he would be filled with the Holy Spirit, to be more empowered to pastor the church. As the group prayed for him, he received no outward signs but simply received the Spirit in faith. Later Richard noted the following change:

> Ever since the group prayed for me at Dunamis, my preaching has changed. Preparation time has become more of a fellowship with God, and I have a sense of expectation when I step into the pulpit. I can't wait to preach, to see what God is going to do. I know it's the Holy Spirit who does his work through me to proclaim the glory of Christ.

I observed a new power and freshness in Richard's preaching. I noted something else as well. He was better able to discern what the Holy Spirit wanted to do and let the Holy Spirit lead. During Sunday worship Richard realized that the Holy Spirit was giving invitations to the congregation to actually experience what was being preached. Our services would often end in an altar call or an invitation to pray or in some way to act on the word that had been preached.

One Sunday I was invited to bring a report to the congregation about the issues facing an upcoming General Assembly. I was to speak five minutes and then offer a prayer for the Assembly. This was the traditional way of prayer in our church. Prayer was always done by the up-front leadership, not by the people in the pews. As I spoke, I felt the Holy Spirit saying to me, "You are not to pray afterwards."

Richard soon confirmed this word: "I don't think you are supposed to pray. God has something different in mind!" Then he turned to the congregation and invited anyone feeling the Holy Spirit's leading to stand up and pray for the Presbyterian Church (USA). This represented a risky releasing of control to the Holy Spirit. Person after person stood and offered heartfelt prayers to God, asking him to send repentance and revival to our denomination. These individual prayers received softly spoken "amens" and other signs of agreement from the rest of the congregation. This was the "common prayer" that Martin Luther urged the church to engage in. It had not been in our bulletin but had been inspired and directed by the Holy Spirit. The pastor's role had been to take a risk, giving people permission to obey the leading of the Spirit.

The People Respond to the Call to Intercession

Sometimes the Holy Spirit directly invites people to intercede for a leader. One Thursday morning as I was driving to my office, I felt the Lord say, "Pray for Richard. He is struggling to write his Sunday sermon." Ever since that morning, the call has been upon me to pray for him. Others in the congregation have received the same leading of the Holy Spirit to intercede for Richard and his family.

At other times the pastor will receive the guidance to ask others to pray for him. The apostle Paul did this. His letters usually conclude with requests for prayer for his protection and empowerment to proclaim the Gospel of Jesus Christ.

One Sunday Portia, Richard's wife, was extremely frustrated with her junior high Sunday school class. The students not only showed no interest in God but were also resistant and disruptive. This crisis eventually birthed a prayer group of three to ten people during the Sunday school hour that intercedes for the teachers and students. Part of the success of this meeting is that the pastor is there praying with the intercessors.

In observing the way the Holy Spirit was leading the church more and more into the work of prayer Richard reported:

> I felt that this prayer covered our Sunday school hour, but what about the worship service? I then had the idea of randomly inserting twenty prayer guides into the morning worship bulletin. In these we instructed the people to stay where they were and simply pray for the congregation through each part of the worship service. Included in this prayer guide were instructions for praying for revival and for the church's vision. Church members found this to be a new way to participate in the work of prayer during worship and were quite excited.

A little later the Lord provided further guidance that prayer teams were also to be in a back room during the service itself, and then to be available to pray for people after or during the worship service.

This work of prayer led by the Holy Spirit has been a real strength for a number of us, most of all me as the pastor. It has required trusting the Holy Spirit and the people. To do that I found I have had to give up the role of controlling everything and become a nurturer of the people's engagement with the Holy Spirit. These efforts, however, were preparation for the Holy Spirit's invitation to keep going deeper in our cooperation with him in the work of prayer.

An Invitation to Go Deeper Into Prayer

The prayer at Montreat has contributed to an atmosphere of expectancy that God will work. One Sunday he did—in an unexpected way. Richard had been preaching through the book of Acts. He had preached on how the early church was a church of prayer and how their prayers had shaped history. Many of us in the congregation felt the Holy Spirit powerfully present. Richard concluded the service with this invitation: "Do you have a hunger to know the power of God? Do you have a hunger to pray like they did in Acts and then see God at work? I do! I yearn for this level of engagement with God with all my heart. If you want to grow in prayer, then come back to church tonight at 5 o'clock and let's see how the Holy Spirit leads us." One could feel the excitement! At 5:00 P.M., even though it was a lovely early summer evening, about thirty people showed up, eager to embark on an adventure of prayer.

Why one more meeting? Richard explains:

As the group gathered, I was looking out over the people. More had come than I had expected. I was thinking, "Lord, what are we supposed to do now? What is your purpose in calling us together?" As we started to wait on the Lord in prayer, Portia received a word from the Lord: "In the same way, the Spirit helps us in our weakness. We do not know what we ought to pray for, but the Spirit himself intercedes for us with groans that words cannot express" (Romans 8:26). As she read these words I sensed that God had spoken to us to give us the purpose of the prayer meeting. We were to let the Holy Spirit pray through us according to his agenda and not ours. The purpose of this meeting was to learn to "pray in the Spirit."

How Do We Pray As Led by the Holy Spirit?

Then began the struggle! Just how does a group of Christians listen together to the Holy Spirit and then pray according to his direction? Most of us had no idea how to do this. We found ourselves quickly falling into our habitual patterns of prayer and not listening to each other or to the Spirit. The excitement wore off in a few weeks, and we had to learn some difficult lessons in self-discipline to avoid some of the bad habits mentioned in chapter 2. Thus far we have found a few things helpful in fulfilling the Romans 8:26 way of praying as led by the Holy Spirit.

1. We found that we needed some recognized structure to guide us through the process of prayer. So we started using the flow of "praise, thanksgiving, confession, silent listening to the Spirit, petition, intercession, and then return to praise." Having this framework helped people know what to say and when. This has not been rigidly enforced; sometimes the Holy Spirit would lead us only to pray prayers of petition, at other times prayers of intercession. The Holy Spirit is free to lead us into departures any time.

2. We found that the leaders needed to teach and model prayer led by the Holy Spirit. Richard would teach on this way of praying, share some experiences, and model it out. He was honest in letting us all know that he was a student in the school of prayer, but he often took the risk of trying to be led by the Spirit. He helped the rest of the group begin to listen and to risk by doing it himself.

3. We learned to pay attention to how the Holy Spirit was leading the whole group. This required us to pay attention to each other's prayers. We had to learn to recognize the Holy Spirit when he was speaking either in the depths of our hearts or in someone else. This required more teaching on the rules for discernment. It has also required debriefing afterwards on what happened at the prayer meeting. Then everyone would analyze the flow of the meeting and honestly ask one another whether we were on track with the Holy Spirit. As Richard puts it:

I found that my role as pastor was not necessarily to have all the answers, but rather to facilitate the process of discernment. I have had to learn to listen and to realize that the Holy Spirit may be speaking to the least member of the group rather than to me. At times this has been a real blow to my pride. I find that I can facilitate corporate discernment by asking such questions as, "What is Jesus speaking to your heart? What burden do you sense? Does anyone have guidance about the direction the Holy Spirit may be leading?"

Even as I (Brad) was writing this chapter, our church had a prayer time in which we experienced Spirit-led prayer, prayer that we believe is shaping the future. That evening, I personally came with a burden. It was a sense of evil related to the 1998 terrorist attacks against United States embassies in Kenya and Tanzania. I had stayed up late, compelled to pray God's light and power into the darkness of the Islamic fanatics who had declared Holy War against the United States. I did not know whether this was my personal prayer burden or whether it was for the whole group.

When we started to pray, the prayer was mostly popcorn style—prayer petitions jumping in unrelated directions. It seemed like people had to unload their own burdens to the Lord before they could really listen to what the Holy Spirit wanted us to do. Finally about midway into the meeting, someone started to pray for the African and American families who lost loved ones in the terrorist attacks. When they did, I felt the Spirit say, "Now share what I have been calling you to do." So I took the risk and told the group that I felt we were called to pray against some impending evil. Others confirmed this, so we were able to come into agreement as a group for an extended season of intercession.

But then one person, right in the middle of this growing intensity, started to pray for a church member. It felt completely out of the flow of what the Holy Spirit was doing. The group sensed that the person was out of order and brought the flow back to where the Holy Spirit wanted it. (Sometimes this requires intervention by the prayer leader or pastor.) By the end of the evening, we all knew that we had been used by God to shape the future in prayer in some way. We left the meeting exhilarated, even though we didn't know exactly how God answered our prayer.

The Results of Prayer at Montreat Presbyterian Church

The result of these prayer efforts has been a decisive change in the church's atmosphere. We experience God's presence and reality more fully. There is the expectation that God will speak and act in our midst. The preaching has been biblical, Christ-centered, and right to our hearts, and the worship has deepened. A practical expression of God's working in our midst is that the church grew by thirty percent last year. Another indication that something exciting is happening is that several hundred more people have been attending Sunday worship than are on our membership roles. We have had to move to two Sunday services because we are outgrowing our sanctuary. The greatest result of this prayer is not the numbers, but that Jesus Christ is being actually experienced as the Lord of the church.

How Prayer Shaped a Church

"Common prayer" has also deeply affected my own congregation. I (Doug) was called to Richmond, Virginia, fourteen years ago to be an Apollos and to water a church that another man had planted (see 1 Corinthians 3:5–8). This distinct calling from the Lord in 1985 pulled me from a relatively thriving church in Oregon to a small, troubled church at the other end of the country.

Its founding pastor had started this church five years before. For several years, Christ Presbyterian Church had met in the gymnasium of an elementary school. There it grew and prospered. Then our presbytery invited them to move into an abandoned church facility in a different part of town, which they could rent until they were able to purchase it.

This seemed like a good plan. Yet from the moment they moved into this facility, they began to have problems. The spirit of joy and peace that had characterized this "charismatic" Presbyterian church flew out the window. There were arguments, then controversies, and then a terrible split. Shortly thereafter, the pastor left, and most of the people were scattered to other churches, leaving behind a small cadre of wounded stalwarts—the ones who now invited me to be their pastor.

When I arrived, I noticed an inexplicable heaviness that hovered over us whenever we came together for worship. This heaviness was so thick it caused me to want to run away, just as many others were doing. From the first day I set foot in that building, I didn't feel good about the place. It seemed dark and unfriendly. I thought the building needed brighter lightbulbs.

Immediately, I learned several things about that property. First, several other pastors had tried to build a church there for over twenty-six years, but none had succeeded. The church that had originally occupied the property disbanded and gave the property back to the presbytery, mostly unpaid for. The presbytery, of course, was hoping that we would pay for it. Yet, there were those who were convinced that a church could never succeed there. Moreover, I also learned that a Masonic Lodge was located adjacent to the church.

A Desperate Struggle

Fresh from a prayer battle against the Rajneeshpuram cult, I was excited about the power of prayer to win victories for Jesus. However, few others in the congregation wanted to pray much. They were all tired and discouraged over the struggles of the last three years and did not want to struggle anymore, either in prayer or in any other way.

I soon felt as they did. As the months dragged on, I often dreamed about leaving that church to go somewhere else where I would not have to struggle. For three years, we lost members. Since we had started out with only forty, every loss was a major catastrophe, especially when the big givers left.

The spiritual struggle I faced in Richmond made the prayer battle against the Rajneeshies look tame by comparison. (Incidentally, several other pastors who have since come to Richmond from other pastorates around the world have said similar things. Here they have run into hardships and heaviness of spirit the like of which they never had to fight anywhere else.) For three years, nothing I did for this little church seemed to stop the hemorrhage of people who wanted to leave. At heart, I understood that I was simply to keep on praying and that I should labor in poor soil for a while, trusting God for the outcome.

Seedlings Poke Up Above Ground

After three years, God sovereignly began to lead young people to this congregation. Many were from the campuses of Richmond universities, though we were not located near any of these campuses. Many of these were young ladies, who expressed one day the desire to have more young men come to the church. I said, "Why don't you pray for some young men?" and they did.

Soon, some young men began to visit the church. Within a year or two, we began to have weddings—six or seven a year, beginning in 1991.

These young people formed families, got jobs, had children, and attracted more young families to the church. In time, our congregation was in a pattern of stable growth. However, students are notoriously poor, so we were still in financial crisis.

Early in 1991, I was teaching at a PRRMI Dunamis Conference at Lake George, New York. A pastor who knew nothing about my church prophesied that God was going to remove our financial struggles. The next Sunday a woman visited our church from our neighborhood. She said that she had never been to a church before, but that God had called her to become a committed Christian and had told her that she needed to tithe her income. Therefore, she came to our church because she was looking for a place where she could give her tithe. This is the only time I can remember when anyone came to my church looking for a place to tithe. God used her to confirm the prophecy I had just received in New York.

That month our income doubled from the previous month, not just because of this woman, but because God was fulfilling his promise. From that day to this, our church has had enough for the work of ministry, even to the point of sending teams onto the mission field almost annually. I tell this story to demonstrate how prayer to invite God to shape our areas of activity works.

Whose Land Is This?

Once a solid growth pattern had been established, I began to talk with the presbytery about purchasing the property from them. You would have thought that the presbytery would be more than happy to have a Presbyterian church take over a failed and vacant church facility that was of no use to them. But inexplicably, mysteriously, I began to have opposition from people I had never met, people who avoided me, working behind the scenes to prevent the property from being sold to our congregation.

Not only was this opposition inexplicable to me, it was also inexplicable to many others in the presbytery, who came to me in private and apologized for what seemed to them uncaring behavior. I knew that our church had made mistakes in its relationship with our presbytery, but almost the entire church was now made up of different people. My explanations, however, fell on deaf ears.

After two years of battling, the presbytery representative who had been trying to secure this property for us came to me with tears in his eyes and said, "These people just don't want you. Maybe you should leave our denomination and join some other one."

The problem with his suggestion, however, was that God had called us to labor in this Presbyterian church and to remain within the denomination. In fact, it was just at this time that he was leading us to begin the denominational prayer efforts at the General Assembly; leaving the denomination simply could not have been a part of that strategy. Sensing that the enemy was trying to get us to leave the denomination, we refused.

We tried to keep speaking the truth in love as best we could, even visiting our Presbyterian opponents in their offices to hash things out and to try to understand where they were coming from. My wife and I continued in prayer, and in prayer sought to overcome our personal resentments against those who opposed us. Bitterness can be a terrible poison to our prayer life and to any vision from God, so we kept trying to practice the basic pattern of "faith working through love."

The Next Prayer Battle

Those who had opposed us finally relinquished the property to us after three years of struggle. However, the opposition of certain presbyters was only a part of a total pattern we saw more clearly during the next phase of the takeover of this property.

We had been renting the church manse to a family as an extra source of income for the church. But by 1996, the church had grown to the point that we needed the manse for office and classroom space. We therefore asked the renters to vacate and began to make plans to remodel the manse.

From the moment we began to actually remodel the place, however, the people who had agreed to do the work began to have inexplicable problems. A carpenter wanted to contribute his time, but then his boss required him to work long hours, so he could not do the work on the manse. Another carpenter in my church took his place—and was promptly fired by his employer, for whom he had worked for decades. His wife immediately ran into problems with her job, too, so that both were suddenly unemployed at the same time. Other volunteers got sick. The list of harassments grew longer and longer and are too numerous to list here. But it became obvious that we were being opposed "not [by] flesh and blood, but [by] the rulers . . . the powers of this dark world and . . . the spiritual forces of evil" (Ephesians 6:12). You would think that remodeling a house would be a simple matter, but for us it was like walking against a driving rain in a hurricane.

After several months of struggle, we completed the remodeling work, much of it done by myself. But when I moved my office into the remodeled facilities, nothing worked properly. Especially frustrating was the heating system.

At last, I became so frustrated by the failure of all our efforts to claim this property for the Lord's use that my wife and I decided to have our morning prayer time in these newly remodeled offices. We picked up our songbooks and Bibles and had our entire two-hour prayer time over there rather than in our home. We cried out to God at the top of our lungs, with all the energy of frustration that had been building up over months of hard work. It was as Martin Luther once described about God in his inimitable German way:

> He does not give what the saints seek on the surface of their hearts and with that foam of words, but He is an almighty and exceedingly rich Bestower who gives in accordance with the depth of that sighing. Therefore He lets prayer be directed, grow, and be increased: and He does not hear immediately. For if He were to answer at the first outcry or petition, prayer would not increase, but would become cold. Therefore He defers help. As a result, prayer grows from day to day and becomes more efficacious. The sobbing of the heart also becomes deeper and more ardent until it comes to the point of despair, as it were. Then prayer becomes most ardent and passionate. . . . [5]

Light Dawns

As we did this, the light dawned on why we had had so many problems in this church from Day One. We were fighting a territorial spirit, somehow connected with Freemasonry. This spirit had maintained its dominion over this entire region and did not want to give up its hold to a bunch of Christians. Apparently this spirit had blinded us to its actual presence. Diverse struggles began to fit together into a pattern:

- A history of failed attempts to build churches at the same location
- The sudden difficulties the church encountered as soon as it moved to this property
- The heaviness we had to fight off every time we came to worship
- Unloving relationships that provoked increasing spite and bitterness between church members and the presbytery

- The clear opposition toward our remodeling project
- The frustration in getting things to work properly on the new section of property

Any one of these difficulties could have been explained naturally, but combined into a pattern, we saw that we were fighting unseen principalities and powers. How do you fight what you cannot see? *By prayer.*

We stormed the gates of hell, because we suddenly saw that we had entered a city that had been occupied by evil spirits, and the promise of Jesus was that the gates of hell could not prevail against the church. We bound the hindering spirits in Jesus' name. We specifically addressed the spirits associated with Freemasonry and the worship of the so-called "god" Ja-ba-la.

It was as though a great breakthrough was happening in our spirits. We felt lighter, as though God were near. He gave us ideas about how we could get the heating system to work—and soon we had it working. It was not so much that the system was haunted by gremlins as that a cloud of confusion seemed to have hindered us from seeing what we needed to do. Now, both confusion and heaviness lifted away from us. Those prayers, which we prayed in January of 1997, created a spiritual breakthrough for the manse and, to some degree, for the church.

The victory of that prayer also led to an increase of common prayer throughout our church. Within a year, for example, our early Sunday prayer team that gathered to pray for our Sunday ministries had tripled in size. The result of this increase of common prayer, in turn, has had a dramatic impact on our Sunday worship services. The presence and joy of God more consistently monopolize our services, lifting us out of darkness and into his marvelous light. We are now at the point of aggressively moving against Freemasonry in prayer walks. We would like to see the place closed down and occupied for Christian ministry, as the Rajneeshpuram property has been.

What we have seen in this experience is that prayer confronts spiritual powers that are blocking the fulfillment of God's vision and are keeping churches from prospering. Nothing else has power to make much difference when it is a spiritual problem that afflicts a church. We believe that many churches are afflicted with spiritual problems that merely mask as conflicts, factions, fear, or immorality among leaders. Until they address these problems in prayer, they will not see a release.

From these two practical examples, Montreat Presbyterian and Christ Presbyterian, we can see how churches may do the work of reality-shaping prayer. God has called all churches to be "a house of prayer for all nations." As we respond to this calling, God will expand our "area of activity" to include not only our local congregation, but also the citywide church in our region and our denomination, if we belong to one. Further, he will take us into missions.

It is surely this prayer challenge that Martin Luther was referring to when he wrote:

> In both the spiritual and the temporal realms the very greatest works in the world—even though they are not recognized and acknowledged as such—are continuously performed by Christians. Among these works are the destruction of the devil's realm, the deliverance of souls, the conversion of hearts, victory, the preservation of peace in the land and nation, help, protection, and salvation in all sorts of distress and emergencies. All this, Christ says, is to come to pass through the Christians, because they believe in Him and derive everything from Him as their Head.... Therefore it may all be called the Christians' works and wonders, which they perform until the last Day.[6]

SUMMARY

Many churches have lost the concept that God brings them together primarily to be a "royal priesthood"—to pray. There is a unique calling that Jesus gives to congregations that he gives to no one else—to learn how to pray together. If this is to happen, the pastor must see the vision and pray it into his or her congregation. The congregation must learn how to discern the leadings of the Holy Spirit, and the pastor must be willing to give up control to the Holy Spirit. Often, churches do not experience freedom from chronic problems until they learn to do this.

QUESTIONS FOR REFLECTION, DIALOGUE, AND JOURNALING

1. Is God building prayer anywhere among Christians in your community? How can you get your church to participate, to catch the fire?
2. In what specific ways is the Holy Spirit calling you to share with him in the work of prayer?

3. If you belong to a denomination or a cluster of churches, is God calling you to include them in your prayers?
4. In your congregation what do you discern are the specific things blocking the conception, birthing, and fulfillment of God's vision?
5. Do you believe that God has given to the Christian church the kind of authority in prayer that Martin Luther described in the selections we quoted? How would this affect your personal vision as a Christian?

Chapter Seventeen

SHAPING SOCIETIES THROUGH PRAYER

s we have explored our cooperation with God in prayer, we have seen how prayer opens us up to ever-widening spheres of activity. This movement into God's heart usually begins with us, then expands to our family, our church, our community, our nation, and finally the world. Our heart becomes God's heart, which embraces the whole of creation.

More and more Christians today are praying for revival of societies and people groups around the world. For example, Intercessors For America publishes a monthly newsletter to sustain the urgency of prayer for the United States.[1] *The Global Prayer Digest*, published under the auspices of the United States Center for World Mission, nurtures the urgent calling to pray for people groups still unreached with the Gospel.[2] In conjunction with that, many Christians are praying for worldwide revival.

My prayer mentor, Dick Simmons, opened up to me (Doug) a pattern of history that had somehow eluded me. Cycles of revival happen every fifty years or so. The term *revival* as used here is not to be confused with the ordinary way that we use that word—to refer to special preaching missions that run several nights in a row. True revival is a vast, mysterious, and overwhelming visitation of God, who mercifully lifts us out of widespread self-destruction into his life. These visitations are partial fulfillments of God's vision for the end of the age:

And he made known to us the mystery of his will according to his good pleasure, which he purposed in Christ, to be put into effect when the times will have reached their fulfillment—to bring all things in heaven and on earth together under one head, even Christ. (Ephesians 1:9–10)

Hidden History

These mysterious and overwhelming visitations of God began to fascinate me fifteen years ago, and I have been collecting first-hand accounts of revivals ever since. They are a part of our history that most historians, even church historians, have hidden away, as though they were embarrassed by them. Human sin and demonic deception seem to conspire to keep under wraps these extraordinary acts of God that glorify Jesus Christ.

Let me recount a firsthand story from my collection, this one, from Charles Finney. Finney has been accused of fostering a false idea of revival, which has been labeled "revivalism"—a sort of human contrivance or counterfeit version of true heaven-sent revival. Judge for yourself if this was contrived:

> That evening . . . we undertook to hold a prayer and conference meeting in a large school house. But the meeting was hardly begun before the feeling deepened so much that, to prevent an undesirable outburst of overwhelming feeling, I proposed to Mr. Gillett that we should dismiss the meeting, and request the people to go in silence, and Christians to spend the evening in secret prayer, or in family prayer, as might seem right to them. Sinners were exhorted not to sleep until they gave their hearts to God. After this the work became so general that I preached every night, I think, for about twenty nights in succession, and twice on the Sabbath. Every day, . . . we held a prayer meeting and a meeting for inquiry, and preaching in the evening. There was a solemnity covering the whole place, an awe that made everybody feel that God was there.
>
> Ministers came in from neighboring towns, and expressed great astonishment at what they saw and heard, as well they might. Conversions multiplied so rapidly. . . . We were every night surprized by the numbers & class of the persons that came forward. . . .

The state of things in the village and in the neighborhood round about was such that no one could come into the village without feeling awe-stricken, and the solemn impression that God was there in a peculiar and wonderful manner. As an illustration of this I will relate an incident. The sheriff of the county resided in Utica. . . . He afterwards told me that he had heard of the state of things at Rome; and he, together with others, had a good deal of laughing . . . about what they had heard. . . .

But one day it was necessary for him to go to Rome. . . . He said as soon as he crossed the old canal an awful impression came over him, an awe so deep that he could not shake it off. He felt as if God pervaded the whole atmosphere. . . . He stopped at Mr. Flint's hotel. . . . He went into the house, and found the gentleman there with whom he had business. He said that they were manifestly all so much impressed they could hardly attend to business. He said that several times in the course of the short time he was there, he had to arise from the table abruptly and go to the window and look out, and try to divert his attention, to keep from weeping. He observed, he said, that everybody else appeared to feel just as he did. Such an awe, such a solemnity, such a state of things he had never had any conception of before. He hastened through with his business and returned to Utica; but, as he said, never to speak lightly of the work at Rome again. A few weeks later at Utica he was . . . converted. . . .

As the work proceeded it gathered in nearly the whole population. Nearly every one of the lawyers, merchants, and physicians, and nearly all the principal men,—and indeed nearly all the adult population of the village were brought in, and especially those who had belonged to Mr. Gillett's congregation. He said to me before I left, "So far as my congregation is concerned, the Millennium is come already."[3]

Why have some people accused Finney of promoting "revivalism"? I believe that it may be because Finney emphasized human complicity in bringing about revival. Always stressing human responsibility, he saw the necessity of prayer and repentance. Read Finney's *Lectures on Revival*, and you will get the impression that revival will happen whenever people fulfill the conditions required by God.

I believe that Finney's teaching was a corrective badly needed during his generation, where Calvinism had evolved into hyper-Calvinism. People were spouting double predestination, the fatalistic and extreme belief that "God's gonna do whatever God's gonna do." Finney needed to counteract this irresponsible fatalism, and so he called people into prayer and repentance, without which he knew that there would be no revival.

We agree. Our intention in writing this book is to call us to do our part of praying and obeying God's vision of the future.

YEARS OF JUBILEE

Dick Simmons teaches that these revival seasons are perennial. They cycle through every fifty years or so. Could it be that this pattern reflects the grace and mercy in God's heart as he described it even in the Law of Moses? Could these seasons of revival be a reflection of the "Year of Jubilee" described in Leviticus 25:8–55?

The Israelites were told that they should proclaim, every fifty years, a Year of Jubilee. This would be a year of mercy, when the whole nation would get a fresh start in life. If a Hebrew man lost all his money and was sold into slavery, he was to automatically gain release during the Year of Jubilee. All debts were to be canceled in that year. In that year, too, inherited land lost by fraud, foolishness, or foul weather was returned to the original owner. Land was never to pass permanently out of the possession of the family to whom God had given it. Children were not forced to pay for the mistakes of their parents.

As far as I know, this instruction never made it into Israelite/Jewish culture and society. Even the Pharisees, who claimed that they wanted to follow every single provision of the Law of Moses, never followed this one. They liked only the laws that would "tie up heavy loads and put them on men's shoulders" (Matthew 23:4). But this one was meant to take the burdens off.

The Year of Jubilee reflects God's heart regardless of human obedience or disobedience. To those who believe that the laws of the Bible are just borrowed from other cultures, no other culture ever had laws like this. It can only have come from God's heart. Could it be that, even though people have never actually followed this provision of the law, God has decided to fulfill it anyway?

Under the new covenant, God does not lay down laws. Rather, he invites us to participate with him in a work of grace—by praying for revival, a "new covenant Year of Jubilee." As J. Edwin Orr has said, "When God wants to send revival, he always sets people to praying."

We will examine these fifty-year cycles of revival and then see how God called people to pray them into being.

CYCLES OF REVIVAL

Dick Simmons taught that these cycles of revival contain four ingredients. We will look at his paradigm—his model for interpreting history.

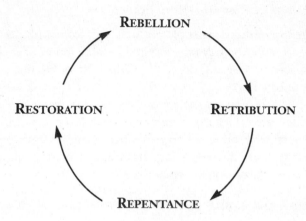

REBELLION

RESTORATION   RETRIBUTION

REPENTANCE

Rebellion

Beginning from the top, the first stage in the fifty-year cycle is *rebellion*. People develop a worldview that excludes God. Filled with self-confidence, they see the sin of other generations and cultures but not their own. The stupidities of parents and grandparents are roundly condemned. The learned become enamored of science or of nature religion—what William James called "healthy-mindedness." All this is based on self-confidence. The one quality that most eludes people at this stage is brokenness.

Retribution

The second stage brings forth the fruits of rebellion. Dick labeled this stage *retribution*. This ugly-sounding word is perhaps not as foreboding as it seems. *The New Webster's Dictionary* defines it simply as "just and suitable return, especially for evil deeds." People do not want to believe that evil deeds will have consequences. But the Word of God says that whatever we sow, that is what we will also reap—a just and suitable return. We live in an "if-then" world. Every sin has its unforeseen consequences, and those consequences are summed up in this word *retribution*.

Life goes incredibly wrong. The cheap substitutes for God that people have chosen are like poker hands. They want a new deal and hope the next hand will be better. When it does not turn out that way, people become cynical as to whether poker is a bad deal all the way around. The game, it seems, is fixed—and it stinks.

The Beginnings of Revival—Repentance

When great numbers of people are weighed down with desperation because they are suffering from the just and suitable return of their deeds, they wake up and cry out to God: "O God, be merciful to me, a sinner." (A prayer! A prayer!)

God responds by granting widespread *repentance*, leading to what the Bible calls "life" (*zoe*). This is a state of existence full of love, joy, peace, righteousness, and fruitfulness. Large numbers of people turning back to God, embracing Jesus the true King, and filling Christian churches to overflowing mark the season of repentance.

Restoration

The fourth period, *restoration*, shows the peaceful fruit of righteousness, as whole societies discover God's pattern and learn to live it out. Rather than remaining in denial or blaming their problems on God, they buckle down and learn God's ways. The church fulfills its true calling by discipling this new generation of believers in "the pattern of sound teaching." This generation, having experienced God's grace in Jesus Christ, devotes itself to spreading the word about Jesus to fulfill the Great Commission: "Go . . . make disciples . . . baptize" (Matthew 28:19). Large numbers of Christians move out into the mission field, filled with the news that God is good. They want others to experience the same grace and goodness of God that they have known. Most of the denominations that survive to this day were birthed in seasons of revival, which were birthed, in turn, by prayer.

Then Down Again!

But the cycle keeps turning. A new generation replaces the revival generation. They take for granted the blessings of revival but lack the joy that is hidden inside brokenness. They do not see the value of God's grace because, in their unbroken condition, they see only Christian platitudes, which do not stir their hearts. If they are Christians, they tend to be mere churchgoers, for whom Christianity is nothing but a religion. They have "the form of religion" without its power.

A third generation emerges, who see the hypocrisy in their parents and grow impatient with them. They create new dreams and visions, based on science and/or New Age religion, which seem more intelligent to them. And so the cycle continues. In the last three hundred years, for example, we have seen various seasons of revival, as shown on the chart.

Date	Event	Description
1740–44	The Great Awakening	Throughout U.S. and England, including Wesley, Whitefield, Edwards, the Tennents
1799–1800	Second Great Awakening	Clapham Sect in England, Kentucky Revival, and massive revival throughout U.S.
1858	Prayer Revival	Cities in the U.S., Scotland
1905–7	Worldwide Revival	U.S., India, Korea, China, Europe, Azusa Street, and birth of Pentecostal denominations; time of R. A. Torrey, Jonathan Goforth
1948	The Latter Rain Movement	Canada, Argentina, the Hebrides Islands

Is this just an endless cycle of falling away and restoration? No! These successive waves of the Holy Spirit result in the deepening and expanding of the kingdom of God. They will culminate at the end of the age in the return of Jesus Christ and the transformation of this world into a new reality, revealed in the book of Revelation.

Jonathan Edwards, the great Reformed theologian, grasped this grand vision and saw its connection with the waves of revival that God was sending as jubilee moments in history. Richard Lovelace observes,

> Edwards conceived of the Christian movement as a kind of army of spiritual liberation moving out to free the world from an occupying force of demons that had already been defeated in principle at the cross. . . .
>
> According to Edwards' postmillennial optimism, Christianity is destined to sweep outwards in a series of such pulsations until the whole earth is full of the knowledge and the glory of God, as the waters cover the sea.[4]

TEN CONSISTENT PATTERNS IN REVIVAL

Looking over these seasons, we can see patterns or ingredients that the Holy Spirit brings back again and again. Seasons of revival usually contain the following ingredients:

- Awareness of our need for faith in Christ, as opposed to mere altruism or good intentions
- A strong respect for the Bible as the unique revelation of God's heart and will for us
- The necessity of prayer as the first step in birthing all other Christian ministry
- Profound conviction of sin, leading to daily concern about whether our lives please God
- A distaste for mere formalism, externalism, and religious show, because they do not give God what God is after
- A renewed passion to complete the Great Commission, so that every people group will know of Christ and have a disciple-making church
- A reliance on the Holy Spirit rather than on human contrivances alone
- Manifestations of God's power in signs and wonders
- Often, attacks and opposition of Satan, including satanic counterfeits, cults, false prophets, and the like, as Satan tries to discredit the revival

- People cleaning up society according to God's Word. This aspect does not happen purely through political reform. The Holy Spirit brings changes of heart one person at a time. He changes so many hearts that the political tone of a nation is deeply affected. Example: the abolition movement was fueled by the great prayer revival of 1858, from concern over the Golden Rule, which did not fit the institution of slavery.[5]

Each season of revival has had its own unique characteristics as God moves to emphasize one or another gift he wants to give to the church. For example, with the Reformation it was justification by faith, not works. With the Scottish Reformation, it was biblical government and respect for human conscience. With the Quakers, it was the inner work of the Holy Spirit. With the Puritans, it was personal godliness. With the Great Awakening and the Second Great Awakening, it was conviction of sin. During the Revival of 1858, it was prayer. During the Azusa Street Revival, it was the manifestations of the Holy Spirit and an extraordinary (but short-lived) outbreak of racial reconciliation.

THE ROLE OF PRAYER IN REVIVAL

If revivals are God's way of advancing his kingdom worldwide and if we are called to serve as coworkers with him, then part of the work of prayer will be to prepare for these transforming events. We share with Finney the conviction that God has called us to the work of prayer. Without this work God's sovereign plans may be thwarted for a season and an immense blessing may be missed. A case can be made that this is why the Revival of 1949 never touched the United States. American Christians were too absorbed in the post-war political achievements, science, and building buildings to the glory of God. Few were praying with the intense sort of prayer as is described in this book.

As J. Edwin Orr has so carefully demonstrated during a lifetime of teaching and writing, at the beginning of each great advancement of the kingdom of God, the hidden work of prayer prepared the way and shaped the future. Note the following examples.

Who Prayed in the "Great Awakening"?

We recounted in chapter 2 the story of Count Nikolaus von Zinzendorf and the dynamic prayer ministry of his colony called Herrnhut. We saw how the colony's twenty-four-hour prayer watch not only changed the face of that community but also had far-reaching effects throughout the Western world.

To this day, the Moravians look back to "that golden summer of 1727" as the birthing of the Moravian church. This significant prayer movement eventually led to the beginnings of modern evangelical missions—as young men left Herrnhut for the West Indies to bring the Gospel to black slaves, for whom God had given them his extraordinary love. (Many of them died within a few years of arriving in the West Indies.) This was one of the ways the Christian faith entered into the African-American community during the early slave days. Moravian prayer was shaping the future.

More relevant to our study, the Moravians witnessed to John Wesley and were thus used of God to bring spiritual awakening to the leaders of the Great Awakening.

The accounts we have of "The Love Feast in Fetter Lane," London, New Year's Day, 1739, give us an insight into the beginnings of another great movement that originated in that same period. Included in a meeting of seven Oxford Methodists—John and Charles Wesley, George Whitefield, Wesley Hall, Benjamin Ingham, Charles Kinchin, and Richard Hutchins, all ordained clergymen of the Church of England—were about sixty Moravians. Of that meeting Wesley writes:

> About three in the morning, as we were continuing instant in prayer, the power of God came mightily upon us, insomuch that many cried for exceeding joy, and many fell to the ground. As soon as we were recovered a little from that awe and amazement at the presence of His Majesty, we broke out with one voice— "We praise Thee, O God; we acknowledge Thee to be the Lord!"[6]

Who Prayed in the "Second Great Awakening"?

It is often difficult to trace the connection between prayer and revival. Intercessors are often self-effacing and hidden from view. However, J. Edwin Orr has pried into the hidden things of the late eighteenth century to unearth this connection:

> Dr. A. T. Pierson once said, "There has never been a spiritual awakening in any country or locality that did not begin in united

prayer." Let me recount what God has done through concerted, united, and sustained prayer.

... There was a Scottish Presbyterian minister in Edinburgh named John Erskine, who published a Memorial (he called it) pleading with the people of Scotland and elsewhere to unite in prayer for the revival of religion. He sent one copy of this little book to Jonathan Edwards in New England. (Edwards had been a leader of the Great Awakening in America, and was now a veteran with fond memories of "the old days" fifty years before.) The great theologian was so moved he wrote a response which grew longer than a letter, so that finally he published it as a book, entitled: "A Humble Attempt to Promote Explicit Agreement and Visible Union of All God's People in Extraordinary Prayer for the Revival of Religion and the Advancement of Christ's Kingdom on Earth, Pursuant to Scripture Promises and Prophecies Concerning the Last Time." That was the title of the book, not the book itself.[7]

Widespread prayer began to happen, both in Britain and in America. Typical of this prayer was the prayer union that Rev. James M'Gready organized in Logan County, Kentucky. Logan County was so lawless that it had earned the nickname "Rogues' Harbor." All attempts to bring people to account for crimes (murder, thievery, and rape—the obvious things) had come to nothing. The few Christians of Logan County had become desperate. So when James M'Gready called for prayer, they came from their Baptist, Methodist, and Presbyterian enclaves to pray together for a visitation of God.

One day, M'Gready scheduled a communion service for his praying friends. Unexpectedly, hundreds of people began to show up in wagons, mysteriously drawn to the place by God's power. Preaching went forth from a hastily erected pulpit (there were too many people to fit inside the Presbyterian chapel). There were many astonishing manifestations of the Holy Spirit. For example, the unconverted were struck violently to the ground, and believers were caught up into God's glory. Many people were converted to Christ. They cleaned up their lives and were formed into churches on the spot. Who would have thought that Kentucky could be civilized?

Many examples could be given to confirm the direct relationship with the work of prayer and the awesome visitations of God that we call "revivals." The important thing is that this work of prayer is our responsibility; it is the primary way that we may have a part in shaping the future in accord with God's vision.

THE TIME IS RIPE

Many Christians today see the moral and spiritual decline all around us. We have become every bit as uncivilized as Kentucky was in 1799. Who can civilize us?

Nearly a hundred years have elapsed since the prayer movements that birthed the great worldwide revival of 1905, which included the Welsh Revival, the Korean Revival, the Azusa Street Revival, the Indian Revival in the Khasia Hills,[8] the Chinese Revival of Jonathan Goforth, and so on. God is now inviting large numbers of Christians again to intercede for revival. He is calling us to shape the future.

David Bryant, who has led hundreds of citywide concerts of prayer, recently summarized what God is doing in our country today:

> Is it possible that God could kindle the fires of spiritual revival in our nation at this critical point in our history? In my travels around the country in recent months, I've witnessed an unprecedented grass-roots prayer movement that I'm convinced will prove to be the precursor of a sweeping moral and spiritual rebirth in America. Something extraordinary is taking place. It may be the most hopeful sign of our times.[9]

We agree. We believe that we are at the edge of the greatest move of the Holy Spirit yet to take place throughout the world. The book *The Rising Revival* describes the extraordinary revival in Argentina during the last seventeen years.[10] The leaders of that revival are challenging American churches to open their eyes to what God wants to do here and in other countries.

On college campuses and in churches here and there are little springs of revival welling up in the United States and Canada. God is visiting many people with his power and awesome presence—but only as Christians pray. God shows us how these rivulets will one day converge into a mighty river to flood the whole earth with the knowledge of God:

> Then the angel showed me the river of the water of life, as clear as crystal, flowing from the throne of God and of the Lamb

down the middle of the great street of the city. On each side of the river stood the tree of life, bearing twelve crops of fruit, yielding its fruit every month. And the leaves of the tree are for the healing of the nations. No longer will there be any curse. The throne of God and of the Lamb will be in the city, and his servants will serve him. They will see his face, and his name will be on their foreheads. There will be no more night. They will not need the light of a lamp or the light of the sun, for the Lord God will give them light. And they will reign for ever and ever. (Revelation 22:1–5)

Each of us can have a part in bringing this new creation into being. By the work of prayer, this river of life will flow through our own hearts to transform our families, our churches, and our societies. It will overflow the dikes of Islam that stand against it and fill the empty spaces of Buddhism and Hinduism. The wasteland of Western culture will become green again, and all the nations will be brought into the kingdom of God.

This is the vision, the big picture, and every Christian has a calling to help shape this wonderful future, building canals for the river of life and the walls, gates, and buildings of the New Jerusalem. The call to us is to do the work of prayer. In the power and direction of the Holy Spirit—pray! With the single-minded purpose of exalting Jesus Christ—pray! Fired with a vision of the kingdom of God—pray!

SUMMARY

God's kingdom is not only concerned for the propagation of churches. He wants to transform the entire world. He wants to bring justice, love, and moral integrity. He has proven that he can visit whole cities, countries, and people groups, to transform them through the power of the Holy Spirit in visitations of God.

Seasons of revival have been happening in various places worldwide every fifty years or so. They are always brought about by intensive, dynamic prayer by Christians. God is leading many thousands of Christians throughout the world to pray for just such a season of revival now, which could lead to the transformation of whole societies. Through Jesus Christ, empowered by the Holy Spirit, each Christian is called to share in advancing the kingdom of God. This is how our prayers will shape the future.

QUESTIONS FOR REFLECTION, DIALOGUE, AND JOURNALING

1. How do you feel about joining together with other Christians to pray for the reshaping of our society, as God gives a vision for revival to many of us simultaneously? Is it easy to pray with Christians of other traditions?

2. Ponder the stories of the great moves of God and let these historical events awaken in you a soul-deep hunger for God to act in the same way in your own church, community, and nation. Let these past awakenings call you to the work of praying for God's visitation in revival.

3. Do you see evidence of spiritual awakening in your part of the world? Do you share David Bryant's sense of hope, and how does that hope motivate you to increase your prayer commitments?

Notes

Chapter One

1. Archer Torrey, in *The Dunamis Project: The Power of Prayer*, by Zeb Bradford Long, Douglas McMurry, and David Partington (Black Mountain, N.C.: Presbyterian and Reformed Renewal Ministries International, 1998), p. 122.
2. Christine Babcock, "Young Life Officially Secures Huge Ranch in Central Oregon," *Christian News Northwest* (March 1998).

Chapter Two

1. From Luther's "Treatise on Good Works," in *What Luther Says*, ed. Ewald M. Plass (St. Louis: Concordia, 1959), 2:1084.
2. "Letter to Philip Melanchthon," dated April 8, 1540.
3. *What Luther Says*, 2:1088.
4. Luther's comments on John 16:23 in his *Commentary on John*, ed. Jaroslav Pelikan, vol. 24, *Luther's Works*, (St. Louis: Concordia, 1960), p. 383.
5. E. G. Carré, *Praying Hyde* (Asheville, N.C.: Revival Literature, n.d.), p. 25.
6. J. Edwin Orr, *Evangelical Awakenings In India* (New Delhi: Masichi Sahitya Sanstha, 1970), p. 62.
7. Ibid., pp. 67–68.
8. John Howie, *Scots Worthies* (New York: Robert Carter, 1854), p. 295.
9. E. M. Bounds, *A Treasury of Prayer* (Minneapolis: Bethany, 1961), p. 100.
10. For these insights about "areas of activity" I am indebted to the D.Min. thesis of Tom Willcox on "High Level Spiritual Warfare."

Chapter Three

1. Jonathan Goforth, *By My Spirit*, Classic Books for Today, No. 51 (Newton, Kans.: Herald of His Coming, 1993), p. 8.
2. Martin Luther, comments on Genesis 19:18–20, *Commentary on Genesis*, ed. Jaroslav Pelikan, vol. 3, *Luther's Works* (St. Louis: Concordia, 1960), p. 289.

3. Quoted in Ken Gire, *Between Heaven and Earth* (San Francisco: HarperCollins, 1997), p. 40. Gire is quoting from E. M. Bounds, *A Treasury of Prayer* (Minneapolis: Bethany, 1961), pp. 64–65.
4. Gire, *Between Heaven and Earth*, p. 8: quoting Bounds, *A Treasury of Prayer*, pp. 98–99.
5. Charles G. Finney, *Lectures on Revivals of Religion* (New York: Fleming H. Revell, 1888), p. 117.
6. Ibid., p. 122.
7. Gire, *Between Heaven and Earth*, p. 30.

Chapter Four

1. Paul Yonggi Cho, *The Fourth Dimension: The Key to Putting Your Faith to Work for a Successful Life* (Plainfield, N.J.: Logos International, 1979), p. 36. Cho now goes by the name David Yonggi Cho.
2. Ibid., p. 40.
3. Samaveda, Thandiyamaha-Brahmanam: quoted by Paravasthu S. N. Rao, *Proof Exhibitor* (self-published in India, n.d.), p. 17. This personal testimony from a Brahmin priest acquainted with the Vedas in the original Sanskrit tells the story of his conversion to Christ when he discovered Vedic prophecy that could only point to Jesus.
4. Bilguis Sheikh, *I Dared to Call Him Father* (Grand Rapids: Baker, 1980), pp. 48–49.

Chapter Five

1. John Calvin, *Institutes of the Christian Religion* (Philadelphia: Westminster Press, 1960), 3.20.3 (p. 853).
2. Ibid., 3.20.2 (p. 851).
3. Martin Luther, in his exegesis of Genesis 19:18–20; see his *Commentary on Genesis*, ed. Jaroslav Pelikan, vol. 3, *Luther's Works* (St. Louis: Concordia, 1960), p. 288.

Chapter Six

1. Zeb Bradford Long and Douglas McMurry, *Receiving the Power: Preparing the Way for the Holy Spirit* (Grand Rapids: Chosen, 1996). We have also carefully taught on the gift of tongues and the other gifts of the Holy Spirit in the PRRMI *Dunamis Project* teaching events. This is a context for both sound biblical teaching and practical experience of the work of the Holy Spirit.

2. Martin Luther, in his comments on Genesis 44:18, in his *Commentary on Genesis*, ed. Jaroslav Pelikan, vol. 7, *Luther's Works*, (St. Louis: Concordia, 1960), p. 370.
3. Richard Foster and James Bryan Smith, *Devotional Classics* (San Francisco: HarperCollins, 1993), p. 239. Foster and Smith are introducing some of the letters of Isaac Penington.
4. An ecumenical conference held in Minneapolis, Minnesota, in November of 1993, which tried to reintroduce Gnostic and neopagan ideas into the Christian churches by "reimagining" God in unbiblical ways.

Chapter Seven

1. Richard Foster, *Richmond Times Dispatch* (July 4, 1998), p. B8.
2. Jonathan Goforth, *By My Spirit*, Classic Books for Today, No. 51 (Newton, Kans.: Herald of His Coming, 1993), p. 2, emphasis added.
3. Ibid., p. 5.
4. Ibid., p. 6.

Chapter Eight

1. François Fénelon, excerpts from his "Christian Perfection," *Devotional Classics*, ed. Richard J. Foster and James Bryan Smith (San Francisco: HarperCollins, 1990), pp. 47–48.
2. Evelyn Underhill, *Mysticism* (New York: E. P. Dutton, 1961), p. 173.
3. Arnold Toynbee, *A Study of History: Abridgment of Vols. 1–6*, ed. D. C. Somerville (New York: Oxford Univ. Press, 1947), p. 217.
4. Ibid., pp. 212–13. (Toynbee is actually quoting the French philosopher Henri Bergson.)
5. Other similar occasions were Mark 6:45–46; 9:2; 14:32–33.
6. I (Brad) have more fully elaborated this aspect of gaining vision in my book *Passage Through the Wilderness: A Journey of the Soul* (Grand Rapids: Baker, 1996).
7. Catherine de Hueck Doherty, *Poustinia: Christian Spirituality of the East for Western Man* (Notre Dame: Ave Maria, 1974), pp. 30–31.
8. David Partington and Brad Long originally wrote the following section on *lectio divina* for the PRRMI Dunamis Project, *The Power of the Prayer* (Black Mountain, N.C.: Presbyterian and Reformed Renewal Ministries International, rev. 1998), pp. 62–80.
9. Foster and Smith, *Devotional Classics*, pp. 2–3.

10. Thomas Keating, *Open Mind and Open Heart: The Contemplative Dimension of the Gospel* (Lockport, Mass.: Element, 1992), p. 138.

11. A Benedictine monk (1858–1923) from Ireland who lived in France for most of his life and was known as a gifted spiritual director and writer.

12. Thelma Hall, *Too Deep for Words: Rediscovering* Lectio Divina (New York: Paulist, 1988), p. 44.

13. Tilden Edwards, *Living in the Presence: Disciplines for the Spiritual Heart* (San Francisco: Harper & Row, 1987), p. 94.

14. MacRina Wiederkehr, *A Tree Full of Angels: Seeing the Holy in the Ordinary* (New York: HarperCollins, 1990), p. 52.

15. *The Dark Night*, in *The Collected Works of St. John of the Cross*, trans. Kieran Kavanaugh and Otilio Rodriguez (Washington, D.C.: ICS Publications Institute of Carmelite Studies, 1991), 1.10.6 (p. 382). Commentary is on the verse "Fired with love's urgent longings."

16. William H. Shannon, *Thomas Merton's Dark Path: The Inner Experience of a Contemplative* (New York: Penguin, 1981), p. 26.

17. C. S. Lewis, *The Last Battle* (New York: Macmillan, 1956), p. 158.

Chapter Nine

1. Oswald Chambers, *My Utmost for His Highest: Selections for the Year* (New York: Dodd, Mead, 1935), p. 123.

2. Ibid.

3. *Presbyterian Global Prayer Digest* 17/7 (July 1998), p. 23.

Chapter Ten

1. By "Spirit-filled," I mean both the Spirit working in people to change character and also the Spirit coming upon them for power and gifts.

2. See Romans 15:31; Ephesians 6:19–20; Colossians 4:3–4; 1 Thessalonians 5:25; 2 Thessalonians 3:1–3; perhaps Hebrews 13:18–19. In all these places Paul specifically asks for prayer that the vision may be blessed and not hindered.

3. There are many passages that clearly show Paul working with a team of coworkers to fulfill the vision (e.g., Acts 15:40; Colossians 4:10; Philemon 24). In Acts 16 after the vision of the man from Macedonia, there is the "we" and "us" language that strongly suggests a company traveling with Paul.

4. *Julius Caesar*, Act IV, Scene 3, Line 217.

Chapter Eleven

1. Hitler had devised a cross designed to convince Christians that their faith was compatible to his occult philosophy. In it the huge black swastika or hermetic cross had a small white Christian cross at its center. The visual effect was that the huge black cross completely swallowed the small white one.
2. Norman Grubb, *Rees Howells, Intercessor* (Fort Washington, Pa.: Christian Literature Crusade, 1952), p. 239.
3. Ibid., pp. 239–40.
4. Klaus Fischer, *Nazi Germany: A New History* (New York: Continuum, 1995), pp. 456–57.
5. Duane Schultz, *The Doolittle Raid* (New York: St. Martin, 1988), p. 339.
6. Presbyterians for Renewal is an evangelical special organization that works within the Presbyterian Church (USA), like our organization, for spiritual renewal.
7. A more complete picture is given in Jesus Christ, who perfectly fulfills the threefold offices of prophet, priest, and king and empowers the church through the Holy Spirit to continue these three offices.
8. *Luther's Works*, ed. Hilton C. Oswald (St. Louis: Concordia, n.d.), 56 vols.

Chapter Twelve

1. We have addressed these worldview issues in our book, *The Collapse of the Brass Heaven: Rebuilding Our Worldview to Embrace the Power of God* (Grand Rapids: Baker, 1994).

Chapter Thirteen

1. Brad Long, in a personal interview with Archer Torrey, December 1992.
2. Leanne Payne, *Restoring the Christian Soul* (Grand Rapids: Baker, 1991), p. 28.
3. Louis J. Puhl, *The Spiritual Exercises of St. Ignatius* (Chicago: Loyola University Press, 1951), pp. 145–46.
4. Brad Long, Ken Shay, and Tom White, *Spiritual Warfare and Kingdom Advancement: PRRMI Dunamis Project Manual* (Black Mountain, N.C.: Presbyterian & Reformed Renewal Ministries International, 1993), p. 118.
5. Payne, *Restoring the Christian Soul*, p. 20.

Chapter Fourteen

1. Martin Luther, *What Luther Says*, ed. Ewald M. Plass (St. Louis: Concordia, 1959), 2:1083 (from Luther's exposition of John 16:23).
2. Zeb Bradford Long, Douglas McMurry, David Partington, *The Power of Prayer*, The PRRMI Dunamis Project (Black Mountain, N.C.: Presbyterian & Reformed Renewal Ministries International, 1998), p. 82.
3. John Howie, *Scots Worthies* (New York: Carter, 1854), p. 295.

Chapter Fifteen

1. Don Richardson coined this term as it applies to missions. A redemptive analogy is a concept that God plants in a culture to help people in that culture understand the redemptive sacrifice of Jesus. See his book *Peace Child* (Ventura, Calif.: Regal Books, 1975).
2. Martin Luther, in his comments on Genesis 27:11–14 in *Commentary on Genesis*, ed. Jaroslav Pelikan, vol. 5, *Luther's Works*, (St. Louis: Concordia, 1960), p. 124.
3. Erik H. Erikson, *Childhood and Society* (Harmondsworth, England: Pelican, 1969), p. 239.
4. We should also remember, by contrast, that Augustine was converted through the prayers of his mother alone. It should not be assumed that both partners must be involved together for prayer to be effective.

Chapter Sixteen

1. The quote is from Deuteronomy 32:30, but Leviticus 26:8–9 expresses the principle more relevantly as a promise to God's people.
2. Martin Luther, "Treatise on Good Works," ed. Jaroslav Pelikan, vol. 44, *Luther's Works* (St. Louis: Concordia, 1960), p. 66.
3. In crafting the vision statement, first the elders chose 1 Peter 2:9–10 as a statement of their identity as the church of Jesus Christ. The rest of the vision reads as follows: "In response to His gracious invitation, we covenant together to be a people called by God to declare the praises of Jesus Christ through the power of the Holy Spirit: in worship and *prayer*, individual and corporate; in works of compassion, evangelism and discipleship; in leading our children into the covenant of grace by loving and

faithful witness; in renewing the Church and its institutions; in sending the Church into the world as salt and light; in challenging everyone to wholehearted obedience to God and His Word; in humility seeking reconciliation and community, in the love of Christ, within the Montreat Valley and beyond.

4. Charles G. Finney, *Lectures On Revivals of Religion* (New York: Fleming H. Revell, 1888), pp. 28, 31.

5. Martin Luther, comments on Genesis 30:22–24 in *Commentary on Genesis*, ed. Jaroslav Pelikan, vol. 5, *Luther's Works* (St. Louis: Concordia, 1960), pp. 359–60.

6. Martin Luther, comments on John 14:12, in *Commentary on John*, vol. 24, *Luther's Works*, p. 82.

Chapter Seventeen

1. *Intercessors For America Newsletter* can be ordered from IFA, Box 4477, Leesburg, VA 20177, or call (703) 777–0003.

2. Contact the U.S. Center for World Mission, 1605 Elizabeth St., Pasadena, CA 91104, or call (626) 398–2249.

3. Charles G. Finney, *The Memoirs of Charles Finney*, ed. Garth M. Rosell and Richard A. G. Dupuis (Grand Rapids: Zondervan, 1989), pp. 161–62, 166–67, 164. Used by permission.

4. Richard Lovelace, "The Occult Revival in Historical Perspective," *Demon Possession*, ed. Warwick Mongomery (Minneapolis: Bethany, 1976), p. 87.

5. Harriet Beecher Stowe's book *Uncle Tom's Cabin* played a central role in the abolition movement.

6. Jonathan Goforth, *By My Spirit* (Newton, Kansas: Herald of His Coming, 1993 reprint), p. 1.

7. J. Edwin Orr, "The Role of Prayer in Spiritual Awakening," (script of a Campus Crusade film), pp. 1–2.

8. A noteworthy revival began among the Khasi people in the state of Assam in northeast India beginning about 1904, one of several revival movements that arose in various parts of India during the early twentieth century.

9. David Bryant, "The Most Hopeful Sign of Our Times: A Growing Prayer Movement Points America Toward Spiritual Renewal," *National & International Religion Special Report*, p. 1.

10. *The Rising Revival: Firsthand Accounts of the Incredible Argentine Revival and How It Can Spread Throughout the World*, ed. C. Peter Wagner and Pablo Deiros (Ventura, Calif.: Regal Books, 1998).

For more information about the ministries of Brad Long and Doug McMurry, please contact:

**Presbyterian and Reformed Renewal
Ministries International (PRRMI)**

115 Richardson Boulevard
P.O. Box 429
Black Mountain, NC 28711-0429
Telephone: 828-669-7373
Fax: 828-669-4880
E-mail: prrmi@prrmi.org
Web page: http://www.prrmi.org

PRRMI is a growing worldwide fellowship of Christians from the Presbyterian and Reformed churches who are committed to spiritual renewal and to doing the work of Jesus Christ in the gifts and power of the Holy Spirit.

Fresh Wind, Fresh Fire

What Happens When God's
Spirit Invades the Hearts
of His People

by Jim Cymbala
with Dean Merrill

In 1972, The Brooklyn Tabernacle's
spark was almost out.

Then the Holy Spirit lit a fire that
couldn't be quenched.

Pastor Jim Cymbala shares the lessons he learned when the Spirit ignited his heart to pray and began to move through the people in amazing ways. This unforgettable story will set a fire burning in your own heart to experience God's mercy, power, and love through prayer as though for the first time.

"This is an important book for all whose Christianity has become still and sterile. *Fresh Wind, Fresh Fire* signals that God is at work in our day and that he wishes to be at work in our lives."

—Dr. Joseph M. Stowell

"This book will drive you to your knees. Be prepared to be provoked but also greatly challenged. You can be sure that reading this book will change you forever."

—David Wilkerson

Hardcover 0-310-21188-3
Audio 0-310-21199-9

Whole Prayer

Speaking and Listening to God

by Walter Wangerin Jr.

Prayer is meant to be a holy conversation about everyday needs, sorrows, and joys that shape our lives. But too often our efforts fall short of our hopes. We feel listless, frustrated, or thirsty, as though caught in a desert storm. We long for the refreshing presence of God to clear the air and slake our thirst.

Perhaps we have not yet learned what it means to really pray, to talk with God rather than to him. Walter Wangerin, award-winning author of *The Book of God*, points out that whole prayer is a circle closed and complete. We pour out our hearts and minds to God, who listens as we do. Then we listen intently for his voice when he speaks. Walter Wangerin knows the simplicity of prayer, and helps us see it, understand it, and use it to enrich our lives.

Hardcover 0-310-20197-7

Discovering How to Pray

by Hope MacDonald

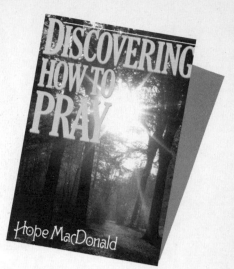

If you think there's nothing new that can be written on prayer—think again! In this practical and inspiring book, Hope MacDonald gives refreshing new insights into a perennial problem of Christians—how, when, where, and why we should pray.

The author distinguishes two kinds of prayer—"arrow" prayer (the kind we shoot up at God all day long) and the prayer of worship and intercession. Although arrow prayers are an important part of Christian life, says MacDonald, we cannot live on them unless they are "grounded upon the foundation of our prayers of worship and intercession."

MacDonald outlines nine steps that can lead you to a meaningful life of prayer and worship:

- Making time to pray
- Finding a quiet place
- Worshiping and meditating
- Confession
- Time of thanksgiving
- Saying a prayer of protection
- Inner listening
- The prayer of faith
- Picturing the prayer as answered

Softcover 0-310-28361-2

We want to hear from you. Please send your comments about this book to us in care of the address below. Thank you.

ZondervanPublishingHouse
Grand Rapids, Michigan 49530
http://www.zondervan.com